FORMAL SPECIFICATION AND VERIFICATION OF DIGITAL SYSTEMS

FORMAL SPECIFICATION AND VERIFICATION OF DIGITAL SYSTEMS

George Milne

School of Computer and Information Science
University of South Australia

McGRAW-HILL BOOK COMPANY

London · New York · St Louis · San Francisco · Auckland
Bogotá · Caracas · Lisbon · Madrid · Mexico · Milan · Montreal
New Delhi · Panama · Paris · San Juan · São Paulo · Singapore
Sydney · Tokyo · Toronto

Published by
McGRAW-HILL Book Company Europe
Shoppenhangers Road, Maidenhead, Berkshire, SL6 2QL, England
Telephone 0628 23432
Fax 0628 770224

British Library Cataloguing in Publication Data
Milne, George J.
Formal Specification and Verification of
Digital Systems
I. Title
621.392

ISBN 0-07-707811-X

Library of Congress Cataloging-in-Publication Data
Milne, George J.
Formal specification and verification of digital systems / George Milne.
p. cm.
Includes bibliographical references (p.) and index.
ISBN 0-07-707811-X
1. Digital integrated circuits--Design and construction--Data processing. 2. Integrated circuits--Verification. 3. Hardware description languages. I. Title.
TK7874.65.M55 1994
621.39′2--dc20 93-29419
CIP

12345CUP97654

Typeset by Keyword Publishing Services
and printed and bound in Great Britain at the University Press, Cambridge

To
Sharon, Fergus and Kirsty

CONTENTS

PREFACE

This book provides an introduction to the subject of formal hardware verification. It is intended to serve both as a class text for computer science and electrical engineering students and as a guide to the subject for software and hardware engineers. The book concerns itself with the task of rigorously validating the correctness of digital hardware systems. A design may be considered correct when its implementation functions in a prescribed way, this prescription being captured by a specification of all or part of its intended behaviour.

In the hardware design community, simulation is the state-of-the-art technique for validating the correctness of a completed design. The necessity to produce error-free integrated circuits follows from the cost and inconvenience which ensue if errors are found to be present in a completed design. With the emergence of highly-critical systems controlled by integrated circuits, this means that a high degree of confidence in the correctness of designs before manufacture is required. This can be achieved by exhaustive simulation, which is costly in terms of CPU time, but exhaustive simulation using all test cases can very rarely be achieved in practice. These problems with simulation have prompted investigation of the feasibility of automatic approaches to design validation, based on mathematical theories such as logic to establish design correctness. These formal verification techniques are now emerging as a realistic alternative to simulation; what was once just in the realm of the academic researcher is now beginning to take a hold in industry. Major electronics companies have begun the active development and successful use of their own hardware verification tools. Increased activity in the academic community, the establishment of formal hardware verification as a research discipline in its own right, and its use in industry will, I am sure, continue even more rapidly in the future.

A necessary prerequisite for formal hardware verification is the ability to create a rigorous, formal specification of the intended behaviour of a design. We must also be able to describe rigorously possible design implementations, and particular behavioural properties required by an implementation. The book therefore concerns itself with aspects of hardware specification and description as well as hardware verification.

OVERVIEW OF THE BOOK

Two complementary approaches to hardware verification are developed in detail in the book. They are based on the use of higher-order logic, and a particular process calculus, respectively. These two contrasting mathematical theories, one assertional and the other operational in nature, provide the basis for performing mathematical proofs to establish design correctness. These two formalisms have their own hardware description languages associated with them, HOL and XCircal, and these are used to create models of the hardware under analysis. Both formalisms have been mechanized, and the HOL and Circal systems make these formal verification techniques accessible to users in the circuit design community.

All of the HOL and Circal examples given in the book may be used with the appropriate system. This permits the reader to learn about formal verification by actually writing specifications and conducting proofs. The ability to use the HOL and Circal systems to formulate and prove properties of the examples in the text takes the place of more traditional paper and pencil exercises. Details of how to obtain these systems are given in the Appendix.

The material is divided into three parts. The first concerns itself with the role of hardware specification, and specification languages, in the formal verification process. The traditional validation technique, that of simulation, is discussed and is contrasted with what we term *formal hardware verification*. The second part describes the use of higher-order logic in the specification and verification of hardware. Finally, the third part presents a particular process calculus as an appropriate formalism for rigorous design analysis. In the second and third parts of the book the fundamental concepts of higher-order logic and process calculi are introduced, and techniques for using these concepts to describe and verify hardware are presented by use of an extensive set of examples.

CONTENTS OF THE CHAPTERS

Chapter 1 introduces the central idea of using a model to reason about the behaviour of a physical system. The necessity of rigorously specifying both the behaviour and the structure of a hardware system is discussed. I have tried to isolate the necessary underlying concepts which must be met by any hardware specification and verification formalism, and I also discuss the limitations of traditional models such as Boolean algebra.

Chapter 2 focuses on the task of describing hardware structure. A number of hardware design and description languages, including the VHDL language, are used to illustrate some of the key features of structural description.

Chapter 3 discusses the necessity of behavioural description and the role that behaviour has in the hardware design process. Various primitive notions which behavioural description languages must possess are identified, and the VHDL language is again used to illustrate how behaviour is represented in a commercial description and simulation language.

Chapter 4 introduces the concept of formal verification as an alternative to test-case simulation, and the two approaches to correctness validation are compared. The possibility of performing validation during, rather than after, the design cycle is discussed.

Chapters 5 and 6 constitute the second main part of the text. Chapter 5 deals with the use of a particular variant of higher-order logic, called HOL, for describing both the structure and behaviour of hardware. Chapter 6 then illustrates how to verify the correctness of digital hardware using the HOL theory. A significant worked example is given, and the chapter concludes with a discussion of the HOL proof assistant system.

Chapters 7, 8 and 9 form the third and final part of the book. They concern themselves with the Circal process calculus. Chapter 7 discusses the Circal theory, and the XCircal description language which is developed from it, and hardware modelling techniques are presented by the extensive use of example. In Chapter 8 we describe what is meant by correctness verification in Circal and illustrate this by formulating a number of example proofs. Finally, Chapter 9 presents an introduction to the Circal system, a fully automatic hardware proof environment.

PREREQUISITES

I have written the book with the intention that it can be used by both computer scientists and electrical or electronic engineers. The distinct backgrounds of the two groups of readers poses some problems, including that of terminology, which I have tried to rectify. A reader will need to have some prior knowledge of digital hardware as well as a basic understanding of algebra and logic. However, I have tried to present necessary mathematical concepts in as understandable a way as possible. Readers with a practical computer science or electronics background should hopefully be able to follow all of the mathematical theory that is used.

Much of the material has been used to teach final year undergraduate and graduate students. Some of it has also been taught at summer schools to a mixture of graduate researchers and industrial participants. The book views two complementary approaches to hardware verification: many other approaches, some distinct and some related, may be taken, and these are referenced where possible. The material is intended to serve as a stand-alone introduction to the subject of hardware verification, but I would recommend that readers obtain copies of the HOL and Circal systems because 'hands on' experience will greatly help the assimilation of the ideas discussed.

ACKNOWLEDGEMENTS

A number of people have contributed material to this book, both directly and indirectly, and I am very grateful to them all. In particular I must mention Jeff Joyce for his contribution of Chapter 6, on hardware verification using higher-order logic, and George McCaskill for his contribution of Chapter 7, on hardware description using Circal. Examples produced by Andrew Bailey, Bruce Davie, Wenbo Mao and Jim McIntosh are used in the book, and John Van Tassel commented on the HOL and VHDL sections. Finally, I would like to thank Marie Stewart who has done an exceptional job in typing much of the manuscript and Christopher Rough for producing many of the figures.

George Milne

CHAPTER

ONE

SPECIFICATION, VERIFICATION AND DESIGN

Designing integrated circuits that perform as intended when they are put into operation is an exceptionally difficult task. Designing *any* complex system, whether hardware, software or a hybrid of the two, is hard; designing such a system which will work correctly is even harder.

The ever-increasing complexity of devices renders many present-day design and analysis techniques unusable, or at least usable only in a rather limited way. The scaling necessary to deal with the complexities that technological advances have made available is frequently not possible using traditional design and validation techniques. However, new techniques are constantly being developed in which the 'size' of the system under consideration is not the crucial issue that it has been in the past, and these techniques are becoming well enough understood for some basic principles to have emerged. It is these basic principles that are presented here.

Two distinct tasks face the designer of a VLSI circuit; carrying out the design process itself, and then ensuring that the system will work correctly when put into operation. Design and analysis are usually treated as two separate phases of the overall process. After a circuit is designed it is frequently exercised before fabrication by simulating its real behaviour and redesigning where and when necessary. After fabrication the circuit is tested using patterns of data to determine whether the fabrication process has been carried out successfully. Design errors should have been eliminated before fabrication; if they are discovered later, a costly redesign and refabrication is necessary. Establishing the correctness of a design before fabrication is thus a crucial aspect of the design process. Design correctness, and how we may establish it, is the main theme of this text.

In this introductory chapter we discuss the role of specification in the design process. We will indicate the necessary properties required of any specification formalism, and isolate the significant features of digital systems which require specification. Central to any formalism or language for specification and design is the ability to describe both behaviour and structure; behaviour since we must be able to describe the functionality of a digital system, and structure since we also have to describe certain physical aspects, including how the hardware is constructed. The need for behavioural and structural specification and how it can be achieved will be developed in this and the following two chapters.

In this chapter we also discuss the concept of a model of hardware behaviour. The specification and description of digital hardware is usually given in terms of a model created in an appropriate modelling formalism. Necessary properties of such a formalism which allow accurate and succinct specification and description will be presented. In Chapter 2 the specification of hardware structure is discussed in detail, while in Chapter 3 behavioural specification is comprehensively treated. In both of these chapters features common to both structural and behavioural specification are isolated, and particular languages and formalisms used for specification are introduced to illustrate them.

1.1 SPECIFICATION AND DESCRIPTION

The ability to *specify* and *describe* hardware is fundamental to the process of designing correct digital systems. Much of the design process entails describing hardware modules at varying levels of detail. The notion of descriptive level and its realization within a descriptive language are concepts which are central to the design of complex systems in silicon. This follows from the need to adopt a structured design philosophy where distinct design issues are isolated and performed by separate design steps. In addition, the result of performing a given *design step* has to be validated before subsequent design steps are embarked upon. This is achieved by establishing that the adjacent design representations are consistent, using various validation and analysis techniques.

Figure 1.1 illustrates some distinct levels of description currently used in circuit design. As we move towards a lower level of description, the description of a component becomes more detailed and its information content increases. As we move to higher levels, a description contains less information and becomes more abstract, hence the term *level of abstraction*.

The traditional levels of description in Fig. 1.1 refer only to distinct points in a spectrum of descriptive detail. Descriptive frameworks at different levels of abstraction are generally unrelated, such as the use of Boolean logic to describe hardware at the gate level and switching theory for the description of transistors, so preventing a natural transition between abstraction levels. There is no inherent reason why this should be so, and in subsequent chapters we present in detail two descriptive frameworks which can both be used to describe hardware ranging from complete microprocessors down to the transistor level.

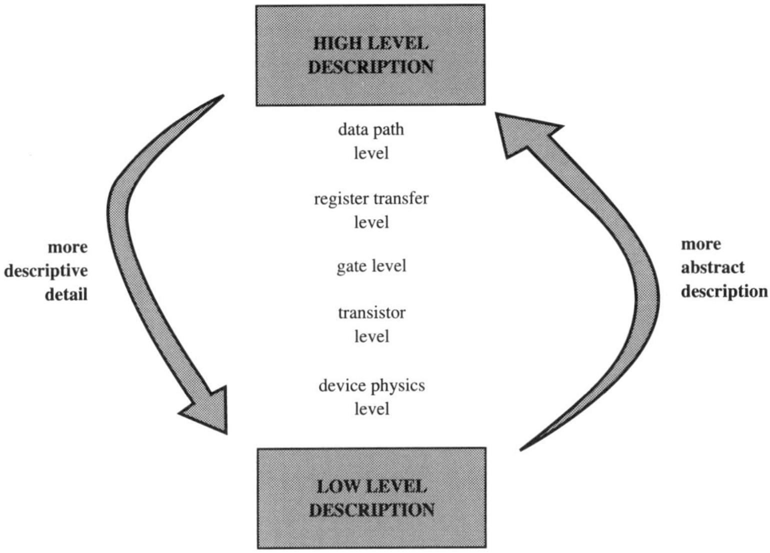

Figure 1.1 Levels of description.

We will assume that hardware design in general, and VLSI design in particular, entails generating larger and more detailed descriptions from somewhat simpler ones. Design can be categorized as *top-down*, *bottom-up* or a hybrid of the two. Whichever approach is adopted, the final result is the same; a design of immense descriptive complexity. Looking at Fig. 1.2 we can see four levels of cell or module description where each hardware component is pictured as a box. These boxes may correspond to any type of hardware, from a piece of random logic through to a complete computer constructed out of some number of individual integrated circuit chips on a board.

Top-down design involves taking a specification and implementing it at a lower level of abstraction in terms of a number of component modules, at that lower level. For example, in Fig. 1.2 module A is specified at abstraction level 5. It may then be implemented in terms of three components, one of which is called B. The transition between the two abstraction levels is known as a *design step*. This process repeats itself until a primitive set of building-block components is reached: p-type and n-type transistors, power and ground lines, and connecting wires and buses, if we are designing in CMOS. In bottom-up design we start with the primitive components and work up the abstraction spectrum, constructing ever larger and more complex descriptions as the size of the design is built up. To introduce some of the terms and concepts which will be used and developed throughout this book, we present in Fig. 1.3 the picture of a single top-down design step between two adjacent levels of design abstraction.

The diagram in Fig. 1.3 refers to both *structure* and *behaviour*. Structure

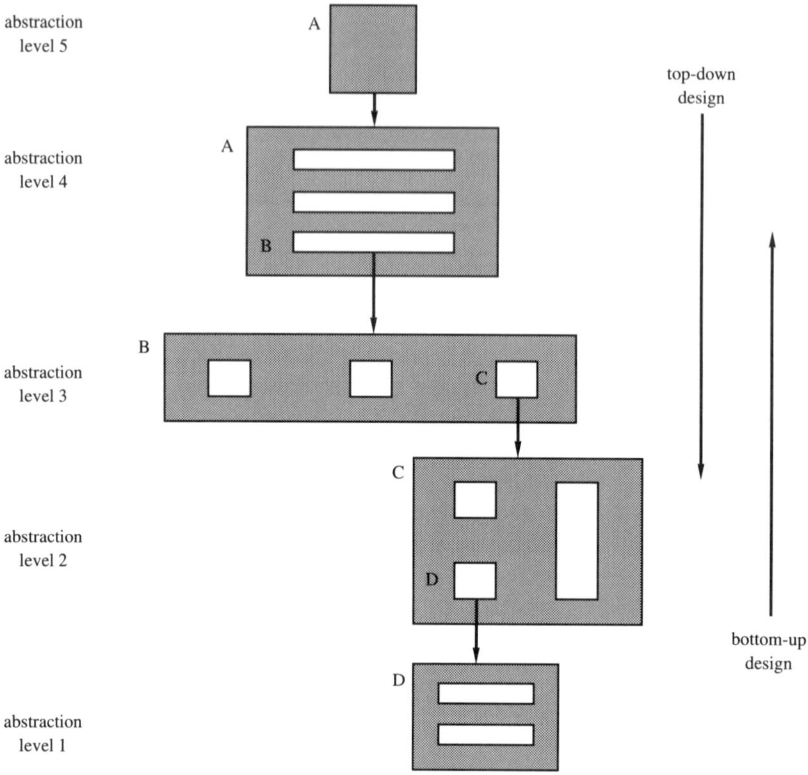

Figure 1.2 Generating detailed descriptions.

because we conceive of a design in terms of the structure of the interconnected components from which it is built, and behaviour because we are concerned with designing a piece of active hardware which performs some function, and as such has a behaviour. From the figure we can see that there are three component tasks which make up a complete design step between two descriptive levels. These are design partitioning, specification and description and validation.

- *Design partitioning* involves making design decisions so that a component represented at one level of design abstraction is implemented in terms of 'smaller' components at the next lower level. By smaller we mean physically smaller in the sense that a larger module is constructed out of a number of smaller modules. When this is performed repeatedly we have a hierarchical form of design. Figure 1.2 represents the hierarchical structure of a design.
- *Specification* and *description* are related tasks which take structural components and assign a behaviour to them. For example, a structural cell called INVERTER may have the logical negation function associated with it, with

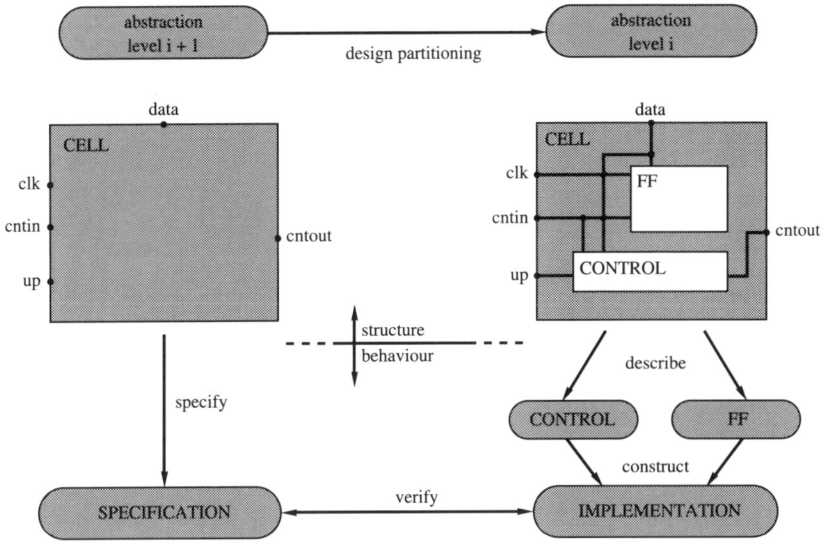

Figure 1.3 Example of top-down design.

negation being the behaviour of an inverter gate. Construction is part of the descriptive process where behavioural descriptions of larger modules are built out of the description of the components. This *constructive* approach to describing complex hardware is fundamental as it partitions up the description process into manageable sub-tasks.

- *Validation* is the procedure where the behaviour of two design representations at adjacent levels of abstraction are related, hence the need for behavioural description.

Obviously we require that the behaviour at the lower level of abstraction, the implementation, matches that at the higher level, the specification. Simulation techniques could be used to ensure this, by simulating on both descriptions and comparing the outcomes. The limitation of simulation, as described in Chapter 4, leads to the use of alternative techniques for establishing that the given design step is in fact a correct implementation of the specification. Techniques for formally *verifying* that the specification is faithfully implemented by a given design step are presented in Chapter 5 and subsequent chapters.

While Fig. 1.3 represents a single design step in a top-down design methodology, Fig. 1.4 represents a single design step when design is conducted bottom-up. In this case, rather than having a design partitioning task taking us from the higher to the lower level of description, we have instead a design construction or synthesis step, synthesizing components taken from the lower level into a component at the higher level. Significantly, we still need to produce a specification at the higher level and we must also perform the verification task relating the constructed behaviour to this specification.

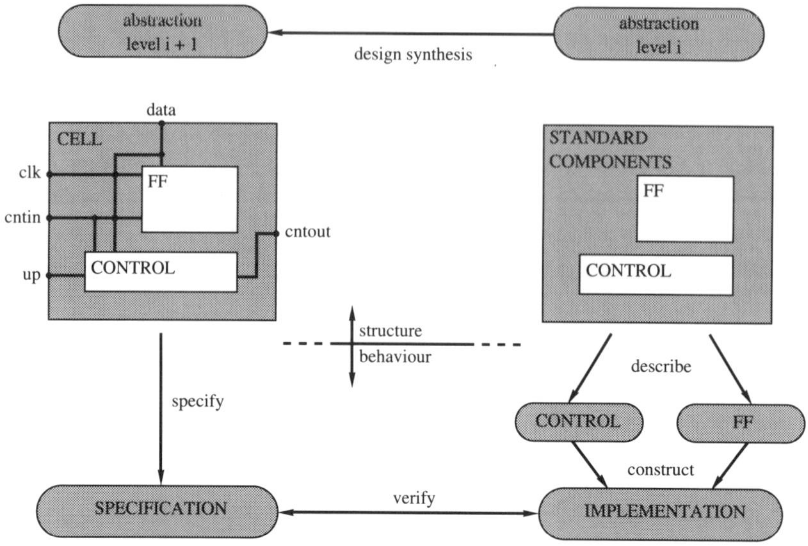

Figure 1.4 Example of bottom-up design.

1.2 THE NEED FOR SPECIFICATION

Present-day design systems follow many distinct approaches to the specification of design requirements. This results in a variety of descriptive techniques such as schematics, timing diagrams and description languages. This effort is due, in the first instance, to the need to communicate the designer's intentions as to how a design is to be constructed, what its structure should be, and how it should function. Furthermore, there are two additional uses of specification which are crucial to the design and production of integrated circuit hardware; as a medium to be used in the validation phase of the design process, and as an interface to drive circuit design software. We can then see the significance of specification in fulfilling the following three distinct roles:

- a medium for the communication of design requirements
- a necessary prerequisite for design validation
- an interface to design tools.

Traditionally a number of distinct and unrelated approaches are used to achieve these requirements. Geometrical diagrams and graph theory have been used to specify structure, Boolean algebra and programming languages have been used to specify behaviour, and timing diagrams involving waveforms have been used to specify timing information. In all of these types of specification the natural language (English, in this case) is used extensively to aid the specification task. This approach suffers from some obvious difficulties. Many different specification frameworks will be used for each design, and this leads to the expenditure of much effort in specification production. The disjoint nature of the distinct specifications cause consistency problems when moving from one representation framework to another. Furthermore, a common problem is that design requirements may be specified incompletely or ambiguously, so creating problems for the hardware designer. Increasingly there has been a move towards streamlining the specification task by using specialist specification languages. These languages aim to provide designers and users of VLSI hardware with a single medium for description and specification, a single interface to design tools, and a unique way of accurately communicating information concerning designs. These languages are known as *hardware description languages* or HDLs, and owing to their central role in the design process may also be considered as hardware *design* languages. ISPS (Barbacci and Siewiorek, 1982) Verilog (Gateway, 1989), ELLA (Morison *et al.*, 1985), and VHDL (IEEE, 1988) are well-known hardware description languages.

1.3 FORMAL AND INFORMAL SPECIFICATION

Computer systems are currently among the most complex manufactured systems. Central to our ability to create them, alter them, maintain them and use them successfully is our ability to communicate various descriptions of them. Whether we are concerned with a single VLSI circuit or a network of computers each containing a complex of individual integrated circuits, our ability to design, understand and use them requires an ability to communicate information relating to their behaviour. This varied information will require to be communicated between the individuals who make up a design team, between vendors and customers, and between the designer and the available design tools. Written language is the natural medium, though not the only one, in which to communicate, and our ability to perform design and analysis tasks is made possible by this use of descriptive language.

Prior to the realization that descriptive languages had a pivotal role to play in the design process, the most widely used descriptive technique was pictorial representation. Logic diagrams can successfully be used to describe structure, that is components and how they interconnect, and waveforms can be used to describe some aspects of behaviour such as functionality and timing information, but they can only ever give partial and incomplete descriptions because of the inherent limitations of their descriptive ability. For example, consider how impossible it would be to use a diagram to accurately describe the behaviour of a complete microprocessor.

In this book we present the case for the use of languages as the main approach to design and description, although much of the design task still involves diagrammatic description. There are good and bad reasons for this. The good one is that pictures and diagrams give us a natural way of conceiving and understanding certain aspects of the design tasks; the bad one is inertia and the past investment in currently used but technically outdated design systems. We will mention briefly in later chapters how the necessarily powerful use of diagrams can still be retained and integrated into description languages, particularly as an interface to them.

The earliest use of a form of language to describe hardware behaviour was that of Shannon (1938), where the language of Boolean algebra was used to describe the action of relay circuits. The syntax of Boolean algebra was used for description and the rules of the algebra used for validation. We will discuss Boolean algebra as a descriptive language in Sec. 2.3.

There are a number of areas where the influence of design and description language is significant. The following list embraces much of what may be considered as the design process itself, and the advent of such languages has had a significant impact by introducing new approaches to the design of ever more complex hardware.

Description languges provide:

- *documentation* for communication among designers and users
- an *interface* in which to communicate with design tools
- a *framework* for the invention and implementation of design tools
- an aid to the *discovery* of new design methodologies
- the ability to *manage* design data.

1.4 SPECIFICATION LANGUAGE REQUIREMENTS

In the light of the perceived uses of a hardware description language and the role of specification in the design process, we can isolate a number of required *features*:

- The ability to represent structure: this is necessary for the design partitioning phases of the design process.
- The ability to represent sequential and simultaneous behaviour, both functional and timing. This information is required to guide design decisions and is required in the validation phase.
- To support hierarchical description: required to manage the inherent complexity of designs.
- To represent design behaviour at distinct levels of representational abstraction: this supports the creation of different design methodologies.
- To be able to mix descriptions at distinct levels of abstractions: this aids description since different design components may be more naturally described at distinct levels of abstraction.
- To describe behaviour naturally across the spectrum from abstract system specification down to gate level description using a single language. This feature simplifies the design process.

- To support directly simulation and verification techniques by the presence of an underlying formal system giving a semantics, or meaning, to the language syntax.

These required features will be illustrated and justified throughout the book. No present-day description language contains all of them. VHDL (IEEE, 1988) which is presented in the next chapter, comes close but does not support formal verification techniques, nor does it have the flexibility to describe behaviour naturally at all (mixed) levels of abstraction. In later chapters we describe two distinct formal systems and their associated description languages which permit both formal hardware specification and verification.

1.5 VALIDATING HARDWARE CORRECTNESS

As mentioned earlier, two distinct tasks face any hardware designer; performing the creative step of generating the design itself, and then ensuring that the design will work *correctly* when put into operation. The process of validating design correctness must be performed before manufacture, because the discovery of design errors after fabrication require a costly redesign and refabrication exercise to eliminate them. Contrast this with the analogous situation in software design, where the presence of an error in a computer program can be quickly rectified by a local, self-contained repair effort without the complete rebuilding of the whole software complex.

Establishing the correctness of a design before fabrication is a central aspect of the design process. The validation step illustrated in Fig. 1.3 requires the prior description of the implementation in a framework in which its behaviour can be accurately and succinctly expressed. For a design described using a traditional hardware description language, validation is usually achieved by exercising the design to mimic its real behaviour using a *simulation* program. All simulators have the common feature in that they use a *model* of the hardware component being validated. Similarly the use of proof techniques for validation, which we call *formal verification*, also requires the presence of a model. This model is created within a *formal system* and provides a designer with a descriptive framework and also the analytical techniques required to perform verification. The use of both validation techniques, simulation and verification, is introduced in Chapter 4, but the need for a model with which to describe hardware behaviour is discussed in the next section.

1.6 MODELLING HARDWARE

A necessary prerequisite to performing design analysis before fabrication is the availability of a model constructed in a formal system or *formalism* which is used to represent hardware behaviour. The use of models to represent physical objects and phenomena is common to many branches of science and engineering. Physicists model subatomic behaviour using the differential calculus, biochemists use three-dimensional models of interlinked atoms to represent complex molecules, and engineers use both physical and mathematical models of structures such as bridges.

This last example can be used to illustrate the two different types of model. One is purely physical, such as a balsa-wood scale model, and provides us with a three-dimensional representation of the structure of the actual object under consideration. But a bridge also has a dynamic quality, or behaviour. This may not seem obvious at first, but consider what happens to a bridge if it is overloaded with traffic in a strong wind. It may well move: if the movement is severe enough, it may even collapse. These dynamic properties are hard to model physically in the scale model, and mathematical representations are normally used. This example also indicates why we use a model to discover how a bridge behaves under external stimuli: it would obviously be impractical, if not impossible (and highly dangerous), to build the bridge itself and then subject it to all possible stresses and strains.

The two distinct types of models, structural and behavioural, may further be contrasted in that the latter is primarily intended as a framework in which to analyse the behaviour of a structure before construction, while the former lacks this analytical role. This behavioural representation will then be subjected to stimuli and used to *simulate* the actual physical behaviour. The resulting data will be of crucial importance in determining whether the proposed design is good or bad.

The civil engineering analogy fits in closely with integrated circuit design. Like bridge-building, the fabrication of an integrated circuit is an expensive process. The need for modelling a specific design both structurally and behaviourally, and for using these representations to perform analysis, is therefore fairly clear. As with designing bridges, a VLSI designer will need to discover and understand the limitations of the design by exercising a *representation* of the physical object in the model. The need to design circuits within certain time and area bounds sets a limit on any conservative design philosophy involving 'overengineering'. Just as a bridge can have some extra struts added if there is some doubt as to its strength, whether they are absolutely necessary or not, so an integrated circuit can also be overdesigned. It is the lack of an accurate and tractable modelling formalism that has resulted in the adoption of conservative design styles, in particular the sequential solution to inherently concurrent problems met in synchronous hardware by the use of a 'sequentializing' system clock. Powerful hardware modelling formalisms are therefore of real importance for VLSI design and analysis.

Many issues are open for debate, because the area of VLSI modelling and analysis is one of active research interest. Here are some of the issues which should be considered before embarking on analysing a design using a behavioural model:

- What formal system should we use?
- How do we represent a specific design as a model within the formalism?
- How do we analyse or validate our model of the design?

We need to use a formalism which accurately captures physical properties in a natural and concise way, and once the model is available it must be used carefully if a faithful description of a digital system is to be achieved. Finally, analysis using the model must be as accurate as possible.

The description and analysis of digital hardware using a model is useful only if the model truly represents the real circuit and is used properly, and if the validation techniques are formally sound. If just one of these conditions does not hold then the results of the analysis are probably worthless.

There are many modelling formalisms in existence capturing various features of circuit behaviour such as functional behaviour and logic, timing and electrical properties. These formalisms capture different behavioural aspects of the structure under investigation representing the 'real world' in greater or less detail. This level of representation is frequently termed the *level of abstraction*, with different abstractions of the 'real world' being used to give a tractable and hopefully accurate approximation of the physical behaviour in the modelling framework. In this book we also use the concept of an abstraction operator, which *hides out* structural information in a design representation.

Note that in the literature, and indeed in this book, the term 'model' may be used in an ambiguous way; the actual formalism in which a circuit is represented is sometimes called a model, and the description of a specific hardware module in the formalism is also called a model. For instance we may talk about the model of a flip-flop in a formalism such as Boolean algebra, or we may talk about the Boolean algebra model!

1.7 BOOLEAN ALGEBRA AS A CIRCUIT MODEL

Boolean algebra is a mathematical formalism which permits hardware to be described and formally analysed by mathematical reasoning. It allows the logical behaviour of simple components to be described by Boolean expressions, and permits these expressions to be manipulated using the algebraic laws to establish formally properties of the circuit under investigation.

The following example illustrates how a simple device may be described and analysed using the simple description framework provided by Boolean algebra.

A proof is used to establish the behaviour of the simple combinational logic circuit given in Fig. 1.5 using our understanding of the behaviour of INVERTER and NOR gates together with the algebraic laws. This simple proof establishes that the logical value of output c is a function of the inputs a and b such that c = a$\vee$b. We can then infer from this analysis by proof that if a circuit is constructed out of two component gates as in Fig. 1.5 then we have created a circuit which implements logical OR.

The proof is generated as follows:

1. `c=NOT(NOR(a,b))`	from the circuit by convention
2. `NOR(a,b) = ¬ (a ∨ b)`	by definition of **NOR**
3. `NOT(NOR(a,b)) = ¬(¬(a∨b))`	by definition of **NOT**
4. `c = a∨b`	by 3 using law: `¬(¬ x) = x`

This example illustrates a number of features that are required if a formalism is to be used for description and analysis.

A *descriptive language*, or syntax, is used to describe the circuit under examination. Line 1 shows how a simple functional language of logic component primitives can be used to describe any piece of combinational logic. The interconnection of the component parts such as the **NOR** and INVERTER gates is implicitly expressed by describing the gates as Boolean functions which evaluate to their output values.

A semantics gives meaning to the descriptive syntax. Boolean logic is the underlying model used to express the semantics of the language, with line 3 denoting the behaviour of the NOT component in terms of the logical operator '¬'.

Mathematical properties of the model, in this case the Boolean laws such as that applied in line 4, are used to complete the proof that the truth value of output c is the disjunction of inputs a and b. As the intended behaviour of the circuit could have been specified directly as c = a$\vee$ b, the proof demonstrates that the circuit described pictorially in Fig. 1.5 implements logical OR as required.

Boolean algebra, while frequently used to describe and reason about combinational logic circuits, is not suitable as a descriptive formalism for much of digital hardware for a number of reasons. It models continuous behaviour using two discrete values; this has proved to be restrictive for modelling VLSI circuits at the transistor level, and multivalued logics have been developed to allow more accurate discrete approximations of the continuous behaviour to be made (Bryant, 1986; Hayes 1982). In Boolean algebra charge storage cannot be modelled, and this prevents memory components from being described and analysed.

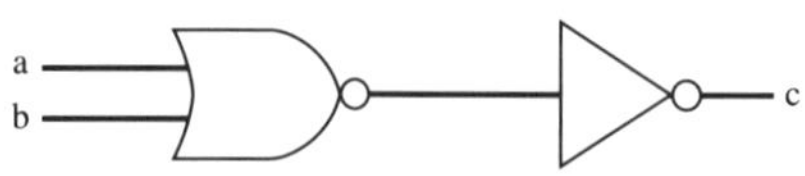

Figure 1.5 Description of Boolean algebra.

In addition, timing attributes of the circuit also require validation. As can be seen from the above example, no mention is made of timing other than some implicit assumption that there is no delay across the components; this is much too severe an approximation of the physical behaviour of logic gates. Finally, data types other than Booleans such as integers, microcode words and vectors, which are the natural way to model at certain levels of abstraction, cannot be represented concisely.

While Boolean algebra does give us the ability to perform rigorous proof, it suffers from an inability to explicitly represent circuit structure, and from an inability to represent certain aspects of behaviour. While combinational logic can be naturally represented, timing and charge storage cannot and this results in the failure of Boolean algebra as a satisfactory hardware description model. This situation has caused the development of more sophisticated formalisms with which to describe, simulate, and formally verify circuit behaviour.

1.8 DESCRIBING STRUCTURE AND BEHAVIOUR

Two distinct features require representation within a modelling formalism: structure and behaviour.

Structural description concerns itself with denoting the interconnection of components to construct a complex system. VLSI structures are exceedingly complex, so a rigorous technique for representing structure which mirrors any natural hierarchy in a design will be required.

Behavioural description is fundamental to a modelling formalism, since it is the behaviour of the structure under investigation which we require to analyse and validate. A good design will have a natural hierarchical structure, so its behavioural description can be constructed in a manner which reflects this structure, thus greatly aiding the descriptive task.

A *description language* is used to represent both structural and behavioural information. Traditionally, *hardware description languages* are used to describe a circuit requiring analysis by simulation, but other logical frameworks such as Boolean algebra and higher-order logic may also be used to describe digital behaviour and give access to more formal validation techniques. As shown above with the Boolean algebra formalism, such systems consist of a language in which to syntactically express behaviour and structure and manipulative laws which give a *semantics* to the language *syntax*. These laws permit direct access to mathematical techniques for behaviour validation which in principle allow design correctness to be established without recourse to exhaustive simulation.

Figure 1.6 illustrates some of the desirable features of a formal system to be used for digital hardware specification and validation. Current formalisms generally only contain certain features: for instance, Boolean algebra fails to represent structure and the timing and charge storage properties of a circuit. However, the process algebra and higher-order logic formalisms presented in later chapters do satisfy all of these requirements.

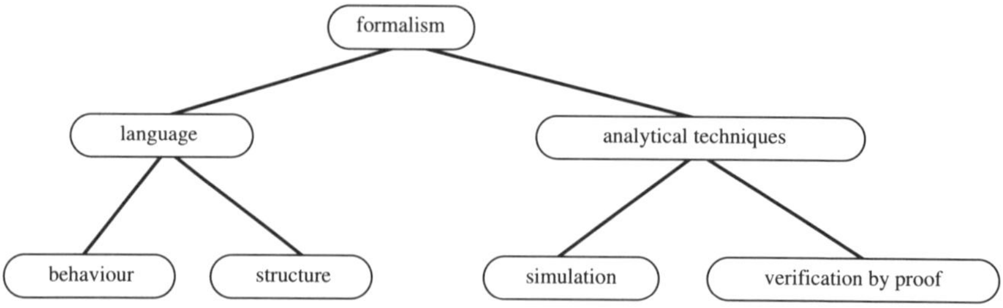

Figure 1.6 Formal system for digital hardware specification.

1.9 A MODELLING EXAMPLE: A PASS TRANSISTOR

Consider a transistor which is designed to function as an ideal switch. Its structure may be represented pictorially as in Fig. 1.7, and its behaviour described either as a logic formula or in terms of an English language sentence.

The behaviour of a transistor may be described as:

```
(g=1) ⇒ a=b
```

In Fig. 1.7 the natural structure of an MOS (metal-oxide semiconductor) pass transistor is exhibited diagrammatically. It has two connections, which we call `a` and `b` for future reference and a gate connection `g` which is used to control the flow of information (electrons) between `a` and `b`. Other than the three ports and their relative ordering the only other property captured by the diagram is the *type* of object being pictured. In this example we know it is a transmission gate or pass transistor because the conventional symbol for a transistor indicating the gate, source, and drain is used in one case and the letter `T` in the other. These are used to distinguish this gate from other types of gates such as NOR and NAND.

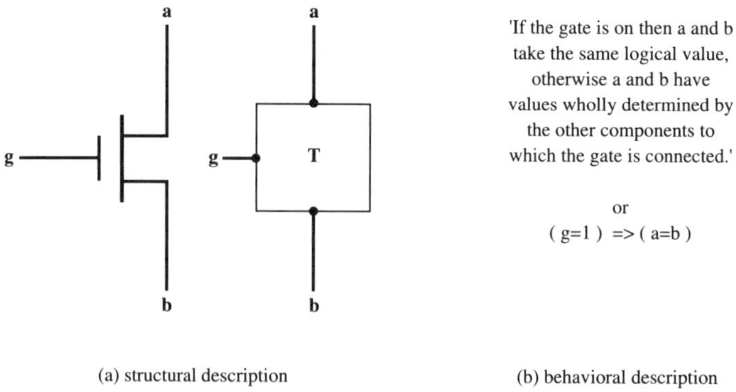

Figure 1.7 Transistor structure. (a) Structural description. (b) Behavioural description.

The behaviour of a pass transistor is often taken to be that of a switch. If this is the case, then we can express the behaviour in many ways. The example uses a logic proposition which reads 'if `g` is equal to 1 then `a` and `b` have the same value', while a more general English language statement may also be used. The advantage of using a logic formalism rather than English is that it is unambiguous and permits logical manipulation, which may then allow device analysis, as with the Boolean algebra example given above.

This transistor example illustrates how structure and behaviour may be represented using distinct frameworks. The structure is represented pictorially, while the behaviour is represented either as a logic proposition or using English text. While many descriptive frameworks do not naturally allow the representation of *both* structure and behaviour, some of the recent descriptive languages such as VHDL (IEEE, 1988) do permit this and these will be discussed later.

1.10 LIMITATIONS OF SIMPLE MODELS

As with Boolean algebra, the example above illustrates the limitation of these simple models to describe accurately the behaviour of frequently occurring components such as pass transistors and other logic gates. While their behaviour may easily be represented by logic propositions, this *level of representation* is of limited use because of the approximate representations produced.

Describing inherently continuous circuit behaviour in a discrete model naturally relies on approximation to make the description notationally and analytically tractable. However, if the approximation is severe then little confidence can be attached to the result of the analysis of this (by now potentially inaccurate) description. In Fig. 1.7 the physical behaviour of the pass transistor is approximated by a much simpler representation than the one that really exists. The behaviour of a transistor is inherently continuous, in other words its behaviour is actually analogue, but it is usually considered to consist only of changes to the discrete values 0 and 1. These values in turn may represent different voltage levels such as 0 V and +5 V. Other approximations, rather closer to reality, are made by device physicists who model a transistor using the differential calculus. For some purposes representing a pass transistor as a simple switch will be adequate, but this model has built-in limitations on its applicability and more accurate approximations may be required. For instance, a more detailed representation of a transistor might concern itself with rise and fall times, voltage ratios, bidirectionality of information transfer, or a three-valued logic. Switch-level modelling formalisms used for simulation include MOSSIM of Bryant (1986) and CSA of Hayes (1982) while SPICE (Nagel, 1975) is a well-known transistor-level simulator.

One of the ever-present issues in modelling hardware is producing a faithful representation of the inherently continuous analogue behaviour produced by electron flow in materials. The device physics level of modelling is far too detailed for the design analysis tasks that are required, and elegant approximations within a discrete model such as a switch-level model are constantly being investigated and discovered.

1.11 SPECIFICATION PRINCIPLES: CONSTRUCTING A MODEL

In Sec. 1.8 a number of fundamental properties required of a model were mentioned. Central to the construction of a model is the use of a *descriptive language* in which to express both the structure and the behaviour of the hardware being modelled. This language *syntax* should also possess a *semantics*, and it is this semantics which allows us to reason about the behaviour of the physical hardware using its interpretation in the model.

This brings us to a fundamental requirement when modelling: the need to translate between the physical world and the model which should accurately capture the relevant phenomena of the physical world. This relationship is pictured in Fig. 1.8.

The hardware devices which are to be modelled may be of great complexity—consider a VLSI circuit with 200 000 transistors, for example—a rigorous and well-structured approach is needed to aid the translation process. A 'good' model of hardware, particularly of hardware behaviour, should capitalize on the following two observations:

- While the overall behaviour of a large circuit may be exceptionally complex, the behaviour of the basic 'building blocks' used to construct it, the transistors and the logic gates, is fairly simple.
- These simple building blocks are usually assembled into the complete device in some particular, modular way.

These hardware features require a model to be both *constructive* and *hierarchical*.

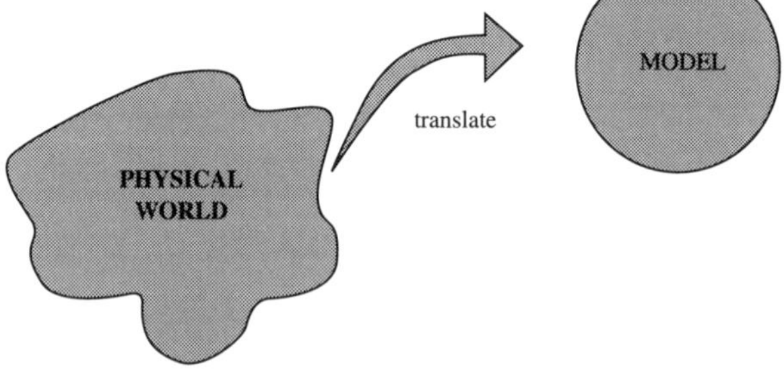

Figure 1.8 Model in relation to the physical world.

Because of the complexity of the digital hardware being specified, design description must be conducted constructively. Here a particular hardware design is represented in terms of its components. The components, such as those pictured in Fig. 1.3, have their behaviour and structure individually specified in the formalism. The behaviour of the constructed hardware is then obtained by a suitable *construction* of the behaviour of the component parts. For example, the behaviour of transistors can be used to construct the behaviour of CMOS logic gates, while these gate behaviours can then be used to obtain the behaviour of memory components such as latches which may be built up from the gates. Hence the constructive properties of a model should mimic the actual manner in which designs are constructed bottom-up, as pictured in Fig. 1.2. In practice these components would exist in a library of predefined components, which could be used to construct larger modules.

Figure 1.2 also illustrates an additional required feature of a model: it should allow descriptions in the model to be constructed hierarchically. Since hardware frequently exhibits a hierarchical structure, we wish to avail ourselves of this implicit structuring and construct the representation of the model in a similar fashion. As a model is constructed hierarchically we can move both top-down and bottom-up through various levels of representation, or levels of abstraction.

To effect the constructive property a model should contain some *construction*, or *composition mechanism*, while the ability to represent hierarchy in a model is obtained by use of an *abstraction mechanism.* Switch-level models concern themselves with describing hardware at only a single level of abstraction, that of switches. Because of this, modelling formalism such as CSA (Hayes, 1982) and MOSSIM (Bryant, 1986) possess a construction mechanism but not an abstraction mechanism. Since designs cannot be represented at a more abstract level than the switch level, there is no need for a mechanism to map into these higher levels.

The core of this book is the presentation of two formalisms, one involving the use of higher-order logic and the other a process algebra in which composition and abstraction mechanisms have a pivotal role to play in the modelling process.

1.12 LIMITATIONS OF FORMAL SPECIFICATION AND VERIFICATION TECHNIQUES

The availability of formal techniques for the specification and validation of digital hardware should be thought of as additional firepower in the designer's armoury. Formal techniques, such as those presented in this book, do not in themselves provide a panacea for the traditional problems faced by a designer. However, taken along with the traditional CAD tools used by circuit designers, they increase confidence that the design task has been conducted correctly.

As in all formal techniques, the quality of the analysis can be severely reduced if any one step of the description and validation process is performed inaccurately. For example, how do you prove that the design requirements are faithfully represented by a specification against which an implementation is verified? The answer would be to simulate the specification itself carefully to increase assurance that it is indeed correct. At the other end of the design process a question remains as to whether the physical hardware which is built accurately realizes the design that the designer has created and validated. Here the answer is to test the physical hardware to build up confidence in this final step. This need to establish confidence in every stage of the design process, including the formal techniques presented in the following chapters, is best achieved by the careful introduction of, and experimentation with, these design and analysis methods. For example, confidence in the correctness of hardware verification proofs is achieved by the careful construction of the mathematical formalisms, such as higher-order logic or process algebras, in which hardware models are created, by building up experience in modelling using these formalisms, and by the careful realization of verification techniques in mechanical proof systems. The extensive application of hardware verification systems such as the HOL and Circal systems contributes to our understanding of the usefulness of these formal techniques as additional aids to improving design correctness.

CHAPTER

TWO

SPECIFYING HARDWARE STRUCTURE

Digital hardware is inherently structural; an electronic system is a physical device which is constructed from components by wiring them together according to a set of rules, the prescribed design specification. This creates a structure where the component modules constitute the building blocks and wires take the role of the mortar which is used to join the blocks (modules) together. Whether the component modules are gates on an integrated circuit, chips mounted on a printed circuit board or the boards themselves which constitute a computer, the structure of the constructed system is readily apparent.

The design of a digital system indicates to the manufacturer the structure which is to be constructed. This is achieved by specifying the type of building block components to be used and the exact manner in which they are connected. The specification of the wiring information entails describing how particular connectors, or ports, of one component are directly attached to connectors belonging to other components.

In this chapter we describe the underlying concepts necessary for both graphical and language representations of hardware structure. Traditionally, the structure of a hardware design has always been specified by graphical means, using a circuit diagram for example. The two-dimensional nature of most digital systems and the ability of human designers to conceptualize in terms of pictures makes this graphical approach appropriate.

Recent developments in circuit design techniques have seen the emergence of hardware description languages or HDLs. In this chapter we discuss and develop languages for specifying design structure and introduce the key language features necessary for such structural specification. A particular description language called VHDL (IEEE, 1988), now an IEEE standard and finding increasing favour in the design community, is used in part to illustrate these structural specification issues.

Two hardware modelling formalisms designed for the purpose of rigorous hardware specification and its subsequent verification by mathematical proof are introduced in Chapters 5 and 7. The key features of process algebras and higher-order logic which make them applicable to digital hardware are presented there. The properties of the two formalisms which are used for structural specification are consistent with the principles established here and follow naturally from the concepts presented in this chapter.

In Chapter 3 we show how to specify the behavioural properties of digital hardware using these two formalisms. This then leads to the presentation of formal verification techniques for digital hardware using higher-order logic and the proof techniques developed for process algebras.

2.1 DESCRIBING HARDWARE

Programming languages provide us with a syntax in which to rigorously describe algorithms and encode sequences of actions. These actions, such as assignment, are ordered using the sequential composition of commands, which in Pascal-like languages is denoted by a semi-colon. Procedural programming languages also have the facility to encode an algorithm as a program in a structured way. This means that a complete algorithm is not programmed monolithically but is divided into self-contained sub-parts, each of which is programmed as a separate sub-program or procedure. This is exactly the way to describe and design a large and complex VLSI system. The rationale for this is quite clear; if we were given the task of describing a 100 000-transistor chip it would be impossible unless we adopted some form of structuring.

Constructive Specification

Suppose our 100 000-transistor chip is a microprocessor and we want to describe both its behaviour and its structure.

The structure would initially be split into logically distinct parts such as the data path and control unit of the microprocessor pictured in Fig. 2.1. Each of these components is then further split into smaller components until the blocks are small enough that they either exist in a design library or can be implemented to produce a new library ‘cell’. A description of the behaviour of the whole device is then established by *composing* the behaviour of the blocks to obtain the behaviour of larger components. This higher-level component behaviour is then composed to establish the behaviour of an even larger component, and the process is repeated until the complete behaviour of the device has been configured.

This form of specification is called *hierarchical* or *constructive* specification. It permits a large device to be described in a rigorous way by splitting

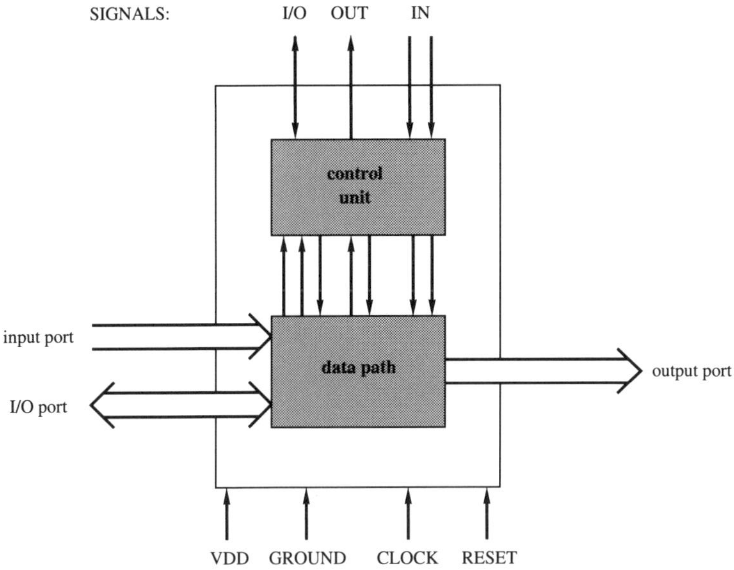

Figure 2.1 Data path and control unit.

the overall descriptive task into many smaller descriptive tasks. This 'divide-and-conquer' methodology is common to many branches of computer science, and its advantages are well known. In contrast to this approach, switch-level models are not hierarchical, for example, as they lack the ability to describe digital hardware at anything other than the basic transistor level, so requiring a complete circuit to be described totally at the most primitive level.

Descriptive Abstraction

Suppose we wish to model and analyse a digital design at a less detailed level than the transistor level. We may be interested in modelling a processor at a *register transfer level*, for instance, where the basic unit of information being manipulated is a vector of Boolean values rather than a single logical value taken from some multivalued logic, as is the case at the switch or transistor level.

Some distinct representation levels are given in Fig. 2.2. These representation levels allow a digital system to be described or modelled at varying levels of detail, with different amounts of information being represented. A good rule of thumb is that a circuit should be modelled and analysed using as little descriptive information as possible while presenting a faithful and accurate representation for the purpose under consideration. If a circuit is modelled in more detail than is necessary, this becomes an overhead without contributing to the quality of the analysis. A good modelling formalism should allow for different levels of representation within the one model with a rigorous *abstraction* mechanism

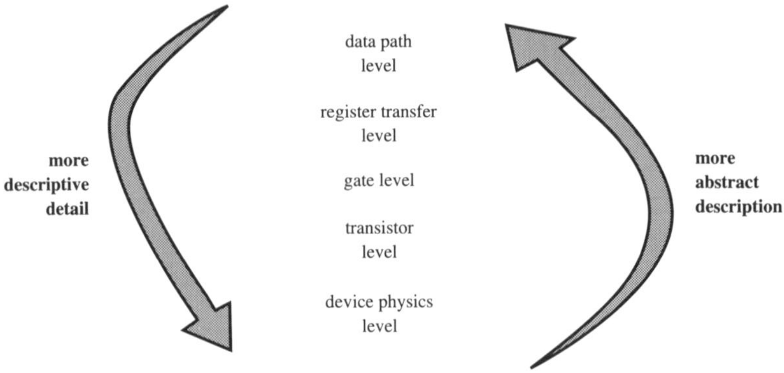

Figure 2.2 Distinct representation levels.

to allow information to be discarded from a detailed description to produce a coarser representation.

We have now informally introduced the two main descriptive concepts required by a formalism for modelling digital systems; the hierarchical *construction* of a description together with the *abstraction* of detail. These two properties are fundamental to the task of modelling circuits of the complexity found in VLSI. In the two hardware verification formalisms presented in detail in this book, HOL and Circal, behaviour and structure are both described hierarchically using the notion of composition and abstraction.

2.2 REPRESENTING STRUCTURE

The general features of structure and behaviour which any digital hardware modelling framework should rigorously represent are presented in this and the following chapters.

Structural Features

A number of significant concepts relating to the structure of complex digital systems and the manner in which they are constructed can be isolated. These concepts arise primarily from the two-dimensional nature of digital systems. Their structure, although not their behaviour, can be naturally described and designed in a graphical or pictorial manner. Any modelling formalism therefore requires primitives which correspond to a natural pictorial representation of structure. In what follows we informally introduce a simple subset of the XCircal hardware description language to illustrate the necessary underlying features of structural description. To illustrate these language concepts it is natural to use the corresponding pictorial representations of the structure of the digital system being described.

The structural properties that have to be described include:

- definition of new generic components
- creation of instances of generic components
- interconnection of components in a well-defined way
- 'black-boxing' of a system of interlinked components by hiding their internal connections
- naming of a complex of interlinked components as a single distinct component

The interconnection of components can be described in a natural and rigorous way by using the notion of *labelled ports* and by following the convention that only similarly labelled ports may be joined or wired together.

Components may be represented pictorially as named *boxes* with distinct labelled ports on their periphery. Figure 2.3 illustrates a component called `Add` with three ports labelled by `a`, `b` and `result`.

Every component box in a complex system may be represented as a box of a given *generic type* and a given *port-list.* The type corresponds to the name used to identify a box, `Add` in the above, while the port-list is the set of labels used to name the ports. The port-list of the box in Fig. 2.3 is the list `(a,b,result)` and this denotes the only legitimate connections through which other components can interact with the `Add` device. A type/port-list pair gives a unique identity to every component, and the box in Fig. 2.3 can be denoted linguistically by

```
Add(a,b,result)
```

where we concatenate the type name with the port-list information.

This syntax resembles that of the procedure concept in programming languages, with its use of formal and actual parameters. Here we use something similar to a procedure name followed by a list of parameters. Structurally, we adopt a similar convention; a component or box name followed by a list of formal port names is used to *define* a generic box. After this definition phase if a box name is followed by a list of actual port names, then this particular instance of a box is *created.*

A typical circuit is constructed from inter-linked components, possibly a large number of them. The convention that similarly named ports, two or more,

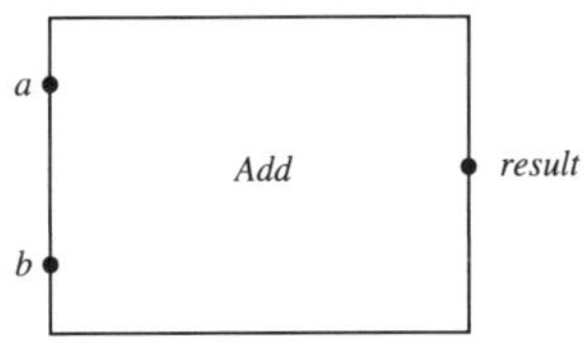

Figure 2.3 An add component.

can be joined together may be adopted, and this connection rule allows any design to be represented in this abstract pictorial form.

Figure 2.4 pictures a typical but small programmable logic array, a PLA, represented at this abstract *box level* and constructed out of an AND and OR plane and an input and an output register `InReg` and `OutReg`. It is the specific labels on the boxes which allow the components to be correctly connected in such a way as to model accurately the structure of the physical PLA. The two register components may be instanced from a generic `Reg` using a relabelling instantiation function, described below, if they have identical structure: in other words the same number of input and output ports.

Composing Structures

The hierarchical and constructive philosophy adopted allows large structures to be built up rigorously from smaller components. This idea is frequently used in the design of complex digital systems, such as those made possible by VLSI technology advances, and is one of the cornerstones of the approach presented in this book.

A *composition operator* is used to put structures together to make larger structures, and this operator can be imagined as implementing the wiring together of similarly labelled ports. This binary operator is applied to two type/port-list pairs and creates links according to the labels belonging to the intersection of the component port-lists. Composition is an associative and commutative operator, since no significance should be attributed to the order in which a number of components are linked together.

A simple circuit may be constructed out of the `NOR` and inverter (`INV`) components pictured in Fig. 2.5.

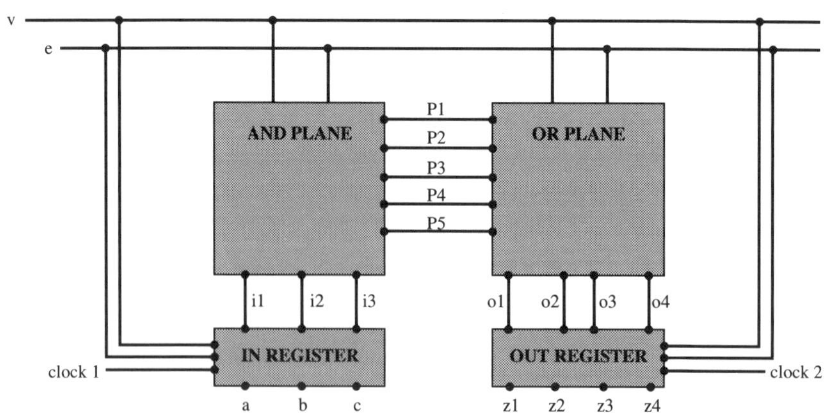

Figure 2.4 A typical programmable logic array (PLA).

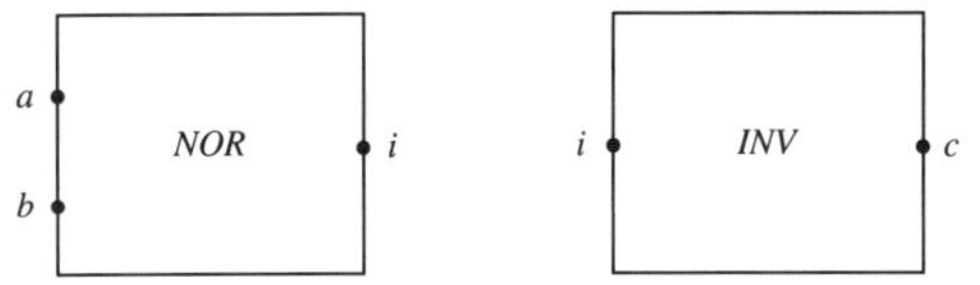

Figure 2.5 Components.

The components in Fig. 2.5 have one label in common, and the composition operator joins the ports labelled `i` as in Fig. 2.6, placing the label on the connecting node. It thus has the effect of wiring the two `i` ports together.

Composition can be represented in the XCircal language using the product operator '∗'. Taking `NOR` and `INV` components with appropriate port-lists, the following expression captures the same structural information as the graphical representation in Fig. 2.6:

```
NOR(a,b,i) * INV(i,c)
```

This new structure will itself have a port-list, the union of the component port-lists, indicating how to attach other components to the simple NOR/INV circuit. In this way large structures can be rigorously built up from primitive components by repeatedly producing larger and larger structures.

The four-component PLA of Fig. 2.4 can now have its structure expressed by

```
AndPlane(v,e,i1,i2,i3,p1,p2,p3,p4,p5)*
OrPlane(v,e,o1,o2,o3,o4,p1,p2,p3,p4,p5)*
OutReg(v,e,o1,o2,o3,o4,z1,z2,z3,z4,clock2)*
InReg(v,e,i1,i2,i3,a,b,c,clock1)
```

The intersection of the port-lists of the four PLA components denotes where the links are inserted. Note that all four components have power and ground ports `v` and `e`, since they all connect to a power source and to ground.

This idealized description of a PLA structure contains no geometrical information; it is an abstraction of a real design expressed at a given level of representation. At a more detailed level of representation, individual gates and transistors in each of the components would require to be structurally described; at an even more detailed level actual geometrical information would be included. In contrast, at a higher level of representation the complete PLA constructed out of the `AndPlane`, `OrPlane`, `InReg`, and `OutReg` components could be described as a single box.

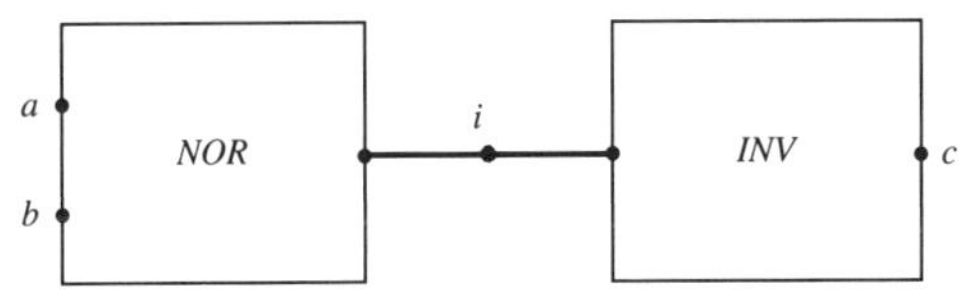

Figure 2.6 The composed circuit.

Figure 2.7 represents the four-component structure after it has been 'black-boxed' as the single box of type PLA by removing reference to the interconnected, internal ports. The structure shown in Fig. 2.7 results from the 'hiding' or internalization of the `i`, `o` and `p` wires used to construct the composite system. These three sets of lines are taken to be local to the PLA and as such should not be available for linkage to other components. The other *external* ports will not be internalized because they will be used to connect further devices to the PLA.

Abstraction

The hiding operator `-a` of the XCircal language explicitly removes the `a` labels from a port-list, and we may then define a new generic type called `P` to be the constructed system with the `i`, `o` and `p` lines hidden. Hence

```
P(v,e,clock1,clock2,a,b,c,z1,z2,z3,z4)←

(AndPlane(v,e,i1,i2,i3,p1,p2,p3,p4,p5)*
OrPlane(v,e,o1,o2,o3,o4,p1,p2,p3,p4,p5)*
OutReg(v,e,o1,o2,o3,o4,z1,z2,z3,z4,clock2)*
InReg(v,e,i1,i2,i3,a,b,c,clock1)) -(i p o)
```

The hiding operator is used to abstract away from internal information and allows a composite structure to be represented only in terms of how it interfaces externally with other structures. Internal structural details are irretrievably lost when a system has its structure represented using the hiding operator, because of the abstraction it introduces. Note that `( )-i` is actually a shorthand notation for `( )-(i1 i2 i3)`, the hiding of all the indexed `i` lines. Similarly `( )-p` and `( )-o` are also shorthand notations. In fact the ∗ composition operator binds more strongly than the `( )-i` abstraction operator, making the parentheses redundant, but they will sometimes be used to increase readability.

The definition operator ← introduces a new *type name* and its port-list in terms of an existing system of linked boxes with the hiding operator applied to it to internalize certain wires and ports. The port-list of the defined box should be identical to the constructed port-list on the right-hand side of the ← symbol.

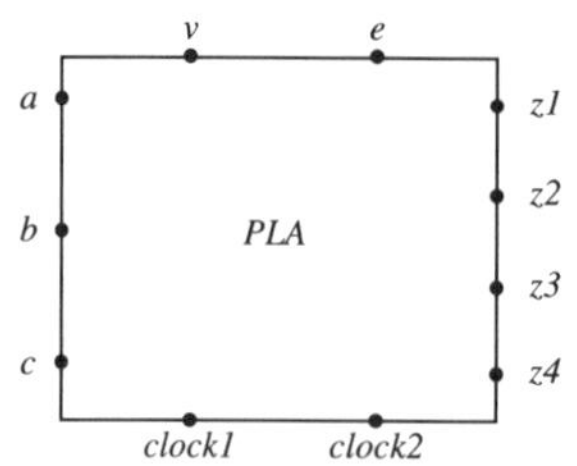

Figure 2.7 The PLA as a single unit.

The composition operator causes component port-lists to be unioned together, while the hiding operator removes the appropriate label from the port-list of the component to which it is applied.

The degenerate use of the definition operator involves a system of only one component with no hiding, and the definition operator can be used to simply define a new component type in place of an old component: for example

```
Inverter(i,c) ← INV(i,c)
```

Given a generic `Add` component, unique instances can be created by relabelling into a different port-list. A one-to-one relabelling function produces a new port-list and so also a new type/port-list pair. A relabelling mapping `a` to `x`, `b` to `y` and `result` to `res` produces a new `Add` component, as pictured in Fig. 2.8, from that pictured in Fig. 2.3.

The postfixed relabelling function `[x/a]` replaces label `a` by `x` in the port-list of the component type to which it is applied. The `Add` component with the new sort is defined by

```
Add(x,y,res) ← Add(a,b,result)[x/a,y/b,res/result]
```

In the definition of the PLA component above we have to ensure that the port-list of the defined PLA matches the union of the component port-lists with the appropriate hidden labels removed. Thus the port-list information on either side of the definition symbol ← must be consistent, and acts as a syntactic check on the accuracy of any structural definition. While we have an explicit postfixed operator to relabel ports and create a new instance of a component, we could also adopt an implicit relabelling convention using the *scope* of a component identifier. When a component name is first used it defines a new generic component. When used subsequently, within the scope of the identifier, it refers to a new instance of that particular component being created with the particular named port-list replacing the port-list used in the original generic definition. Hence if `Add(a,b,result)` was previously defined, then `Add(x,y,res)` creates a new `Add` component consistent with the previous port-list relabelling convention.

This completes our introduction of the primitive structural description operators and their associated graphical interpretation. They constitute a subset of the XCircal language which allows us to represent rigorously the idealized structure of any complex of components in terms of labelled box definition, box

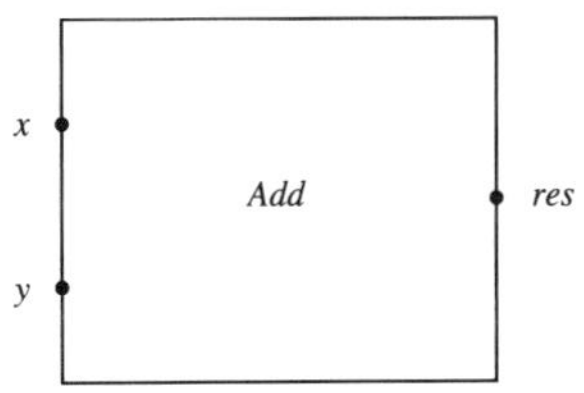

Figure 2.8 Relabelled `Add`.

instantiation, box composition, and label hiding. These operations have a graphical counterpart, and both linguistic and graphical representations of the inherent structure may be used.

Given a VLSI system pictured graphically using representations such as logic diagrams or even a sticks diagram (Williams, 1968) we can then represent it in terms of boxes by throwing away any geometrical information to generate a language description of its structure using the above operators. In this way any existing hardware system or design may have its structure described as an expression in the language. We can also use the language directly to create designs, and so we can consider our description language as the basis of a VLSI design language; with a few slight modifications this language can form the basis of a structural design language such as that presented in Sec. 2.4.

2.3 HIERARCHICAL DESCRIPTION

Digital hardware design lends itself to the repeated use of a standard set of components connected in regular ways. At the transistor level this replication can be seen in a dynamic shift register, Fig. 2.9, which is constructed from pairs of inverters and pass transistors. The shift register can be described either structurally or behaviourally, but here we specify its structure using only the XCircal language constructs presented so far. Indeed, a number of still more detailed behavioural descriptions may be produced, even for a simple circuit.

An XCircal specification can be built up hierarchically in terms of its replicated components, in this case in terms of a `Cell` component. If a `Cell` is taken to be a transistor/inverter pair we must first of all describe this component and then describe the register in terms of four cell components.

Before defining the *generic* `Cell` component we will describe a transistor/inverter pair by

```
PassTran (p,g,q) * INV(q,r)
```

This expression defines the cell structure of Fig. 2.10 where `p` and `q` are the input and output ports of the pass transistor, `g` is its gate and `q` and `r` are the input and output ports of the inverter. While a pass transistor is in principle

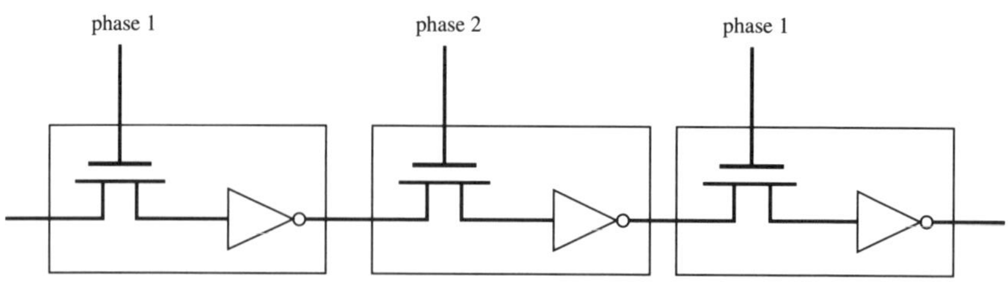

Figure 2.9 Dynamic shift register.

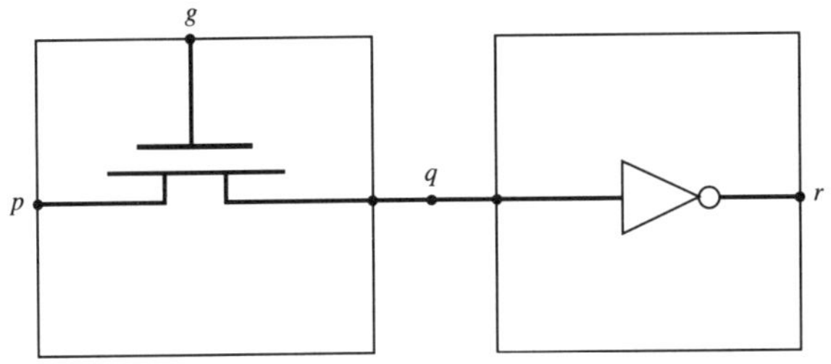

Figure 2.10 Cell structure.

bidirectional, when composed with an inverter directionality is forced on to it so allowing us to talk about *input ports* and *output ports*. Notice that the XCircal syntax does not distinguish input and output ports, but the context in which ports are used usually allows us to infer directionality.

The connection labelled by `q` joins the two components together. This dedicated wire is only used by these two components, and must be hidden to remove the possibility of other components attaching themselves to it. The hiding operator is used to hide out the `q` line and the module `Cell` can be defined as follows:

Definition

```
Cell(p,g,r) ← (PassTran(p,g,q) * INV(q, r) )-q
```

Notice that `Cell` has port-list `(p,g,r)`, using the convention that the composition operator unions port information together while the hiding operator removes labels from the port-list.

Four *instances* of the generic component `Cell` can now be created and composed to form the register pictured in Fig. 2.9. The relabelling operator is used for this instantiation, creating four cells with port-lists `(p1,g1,p2)`, `(p2,g2,p3)`, `(p3,g3,p4)` and `(p4,g4,p5)` respectively.

For $1 \leqslant n \leqslant 4$, `Cell[n]` is obtained by relabelling as follows:

Definition

```
Cell[n] ← Cell[pn/p,gn/g,pn+1/r]
```

The four cells can then be composed, their internal `pi` lines hidden for $2 \leqslant i \leqslant 4$, leaving a four-cell register with external ports given by port-list `(p1,p5,g1,g2,g3,g4)`. The following definition names this four-cell register `RegFour`:

Definition

```
RegFour (p1,g1,g2,g3,g4,p5)←
(Cell[1] * Cell[2] * Cell[3] * Cell[4])-(p2 p3 p4)
```

Constructing Behaviour Hierarchically

The above example indicates how an existing structure, a shift register, may be described hierarchically.

A top-down structural decomposition allows the *structure* of the complete system to be described in terms of the sub-components. The *behaviour* of these components may also be defined if we use a formal system such as the process algebra or higher-order logic formalisms which will be introduced in Chapter 3, or they may be taken directly from a library of component/behaviour pairs. Finally, the behaviour of the complete structure can be established bottom-up by constructing the behaviour of repeatedly larger structures using behavioural variants of the composition and abstraction operators until the topmost level is reached. Bottom-up design starts with the primitive components, and the structure and behaviour of the complete design may then go on hand-in-hand.

Hierarchically constructing the behaviour of the shift register involves composing the most primitive components, pass transistors and inverters, and then hiding or localizing their communication link. This forms a `Cell` component of which any number of distinct instances may be created by using a *unique* relabelling. These individual cells may then be composed and their internal wires hidden to form the appropriate register structure. Figure 2.11 illustrates this hierarchical or constructive approach to description. In this way the structure *and* behaviour of any existing circuit may be described in a constructive manner. While the definition of `RegFour` represents the structure of a shift register constructed out of four cells, it also represents the *behaviour* of the register in terms of the behaviour of its components if this component behaviour is available and if appropriate construction and abstraction operators exist in the formalism, acting as behavioural analogues to the structural composition and abstraction seen so far.

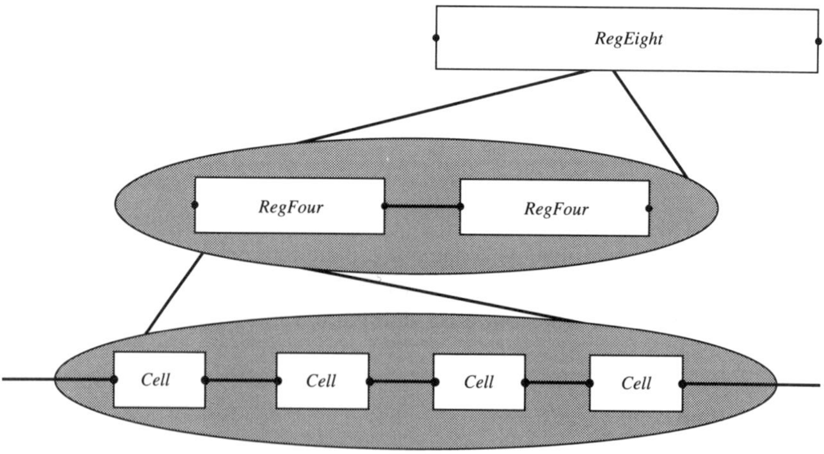

Figure 2.11 Constructive approach to description.

Various methods for describing hardware behaviour will be introduced in the next chapter.

Representing Replicated Structures

The shift register example illustrates how design structure can be rigorously described, and this description task is greatly aided by any structural *regularity* found in the design. The task of designing complex VLSI circuits is made easier if existing components can be replicated and composed in a regular way. Similarly, the description task directly mirrors the design specification task and these regular designs greatly help the description and analysis tasks. We can use the shift register example to illustrate this approach.

The basis of generating descriptions of regular hardware structures is still dependent on relabelling generic components to create instances which will be labelled in such a way that the appropriate structure is created when the instances are composed.

Definition

```
RegEight(p1,g1,g2,g3,g4,g5,g6,g7,g8,p9)←

    (Cell[1] *Cell[2] *. . .* Cell[8]) - (p2 p3 p4 p5 p6 p7 p8)
```

The associativity of the composition operator allows regular structures to be constructed in various ways by alterning the *order* in which the components are joined. As the associativity *rule* can be proved to preserve the integrity of the behavioural description using the underlying formalism, as in the Circal process algebra, the formalism which underpins the XCircal language, we can construct equivalent descriptions of the eight-cell register first presented in Fig. 2.9. For instance, the eight-cell register may be formed out of two four-cell registers as in Fig. 2.12. Creating another instance `RegFourA` of `RegFour` by relabelling gives:

Definition

```
RegFourA(p5,g5,g6,g7,g8,p9) ←
RegFour[p9/p5,p5/p1,g5/g1,g6/g2,g7/g3,g8/g4]
```

`RegEight` may be created by composing `RegFour` and `RegFourA` to generate

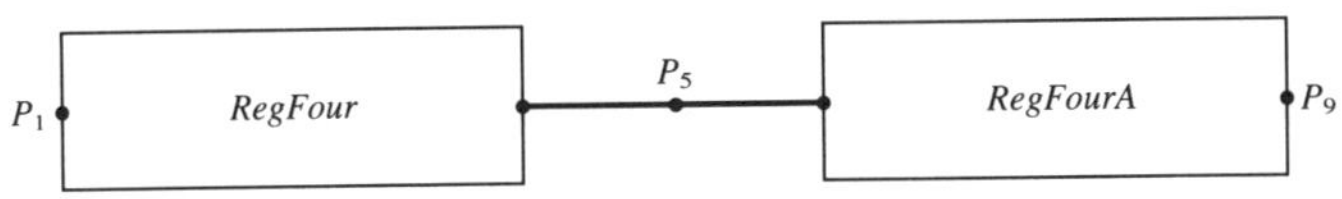

Figure 2.12 Eight-cell register.

the structure in Fig. 2.12 followed by the hiding of line `p5`. The following definition is structurally (and behaviourally) equivalent to the previous definition of `RegEight`.

Definition

```
RegEight ← (RegFour * RegFourA)-p5
```

Iterative Language Features

This hierarchical definition of `RegEight`, in terms of `RegFour`, which is itself constructed from the `Cell` component, and the re-use of previously defined components, is one approach to simplifying the description of replicated structures. Alternatively it may prove more convenient to use `FOR` and `WHILE` structures as found in most programming languages. A `FOR` construct could be introduced to the XCircal language to define `RegEight` as follows:

Definition

```
RegEight ← * (FOR i=1:8 CYCLE Cell(pn,gn,pn+1) REPEAT)
                - (p2 p3 p4 p5 p6 p7 p8)
```

The `FOR` construct generates eight instances of the `Cell` component suitably relabelled. The * composition operator now appears only once as a single prefix operator to the eight cell instances. Again the hiding operator is used to hide local interconnection information. This description is if anything syntactically more complex than the original definition of `RegEight`, but as it is taken to be equivalent then what syntax is used is only a matter of descriptive convenience.

Perhaps a more significant change to the existing syntactic conventions adopted so far is to explicitly define the desired external ports of a constructed system rather than explicitly indicate the local, internal lines to be hidden. We can utilize the port-list concept to implement this, with port information occurring on both sides of the symbol ← in a definition. The newly defined structure and its port-list is named on the left-hand side and the composition of the existing components together with their port-lists appears on the right-hand side. Since the port information must match, we may imply that the abstraction operator must be used to balance the port-lists. For example, we take the following expression as the definition of the cell component:

Definition

```
Cell(p,g,r) ← PassTran(p,g,q) * Inv(q,r)
```

Since the port-list of the right-hand side involves unioning together the component port-lists, we see that label `q` appears in the port-list of the right-hand side but not on the left. We therefore assume that `q` is hidden to obtain the structure `Cell(p,q,r)`.

This convention of explicitly representing the port-list of a constructed component can be continued as a mechanism for implicitly defining relabelling where we can assume relabelling has occurred whenever an *instance* of a component appears. For instance the expression

```
Cell(pn,gn,pn+1)
```

relabels the generic component `Cell` and is equivalent to our previous use of the relabelling operator with `pn` replacing `p`, `gn` replacing `g`, and `pn+1` replacing `q`. We therefore have that

```
Cell(pn,gn,pn+1) = Cell(p,g,q)[pn/p,gn/g,pn+1/g]
```

These *implicit* composition, hiding and relabelling constructs can be combined to produce the following definition of `RegFour` which is equivalent to that given previously:

Definition

```
RegFour(p1,g1,g2,g3,g4,p5) ←
* (FOR i=1:4 CYCLE Cell(pi,gi,pi+1)REPEAT)
```

This syntax, with minor modifications, is that of a commercial design language for use with a gate array and standard cell design system. This structural specification language is called MODEL, and appears in the next section.

2.4 A DESIGN LANGUAGE FOR STRUCTURAL SPECIFICATION

In the previous section we commented on the similarity between describing an existing digital system and designing or prescribing a new one. The necessity of performing specification in an hierarchical manner has also been stressed, and this led us to consider an abstraction feature such as that found in the structural subset of the XCircal description language.

Let us take language constructs similar to those developed above for the XCircal language but with composition, abstraction and relabelling operations being expressed implicitly rather than as explicit language constructs. These implicit language features, together with replication constructs, provide us with the basis of a syntactically elegant structural design language which is in commercial use today. This powerful hierarchical design language is called MODEL (European Silicon Structures, 1990) and it is used by European Silicon Structures, an ASIC chip manufacturer.

Component Parts

The primitive design component in the MODEL language is a *part*. A part is identical to the named box used in the XCircal language, with named ports being used to indicate how the part is connected to other parts. MODEL differs slightly from the XCircal subset in that input and output ports are distinguished from each other and called *input signals* and *output signals*. A part represents a bidirectional port as two separate signals, an input and an output signal.

As with XCircal boxes, a generic part can have relabelled instances created, in this case by implicit relabelling. Similarly, rather than use an explicit operator, composition and abstraction is treated implicitly, with a *part definition* specifying the internal structure of the component in terms of interconnected instances of simpler parts. Design will proceed top-down until a level is reached which contains predefined primitive parts such as NOR and NAND gates held in a parts library.

Part definition corresponds to naming and defining the structure of components in XCircal using an almost identical syntax to that introduced in Sec. 2.3. The MODEL language syntax is somewhat Pascal-like, and the definition of a part mimics the definition of a Pascal procedure. The component is named by the part name, and its formal parameters are the input and output signal lines used to connect it to other parts. These formal parameters are specified in the declarative head of the part, while the body describes how smaller parts are interlinked to *implement* it. Reference to these smaller parts can be thought of as procedure calls to the appropriate parts: a part description must only make reference to previously defined or predefined parts. While this ordering of part definitions implies that a design in MODEL is written in a somewhat unnatural bottom-up way, design usually entails a mixture of bottom-up and top-down techniques. The designer knows what predefined parts are available as the basic building blocks, and in this way a complete circuit design, itself a single part, will result.

The general syntax of a part definition is as follows:

```
PART partname[input-signals] → [output-signals]
     SIGNAL internal-signals
     smaller part instantiation
           ⋮
     smaller part instantiation
END  partname}
```

The keywords PART and END are used to delimit a part definition. The newly defined part is called 'partname' and it has its externally visible input signals named by the *formal parameters* listed by 'input-signals'. Similarly, 'output-signals' lists the formal parameters used to denote the externally visible output signals. These parameters correspond both to the parameters used in a Pascal-like procedure definition and to the port-list information captured in the definition of a generic XCircal component.

Constructing Instantiated Parts

MODEL requires internal communication lines to be named and declared prior to their use, and the keyword SIGNAL indicates the definition of 'internal-signals' as a list of internal lines. The internal signal declaration is then followed by a list of instantiations of previously defined parts. These are instantiated by replacing the formal parameter by the *actual* input signal parameter taken from 'input-signals' and 'internal-signals', and the actual output signals taken from 'output-signals' and 'internal-signals'. These parts are composed according to the convention used by XCircal, with identical signal names being used to wire up the appropriate signal ports. Unlike the XCircal syntax, composition is indicated implicitly without using an actual composition operator. This is effected by simply missing out the '$*$' composition operator from the XCircal syntax.

The need to represent the internal lines explicitly by a SIGNAL declaration is in fact redundant. This can be seen by comparing it with the treatment of implicit hiding, or abstraction, given by the port-list of a defined XCircal component as in the previous section. This redundancy and the need to declare parts prior to their instantiation are implementation issues and are not fundamental to the language design.

Hierarchical Design Using MODEL

The design of a dual D-type flip-flop illustrates how part instantiation, together with the MODEL counterparts of the XCircal composition and abstraction language features, allows designs to be generated hierarchically.

Taking two instances of a three-input NAND gate from the library of predefined parts, we can generate the flip-flop called `block` pictured in Fig. 2.13.

The `block` component is composed from two instances of a generic NAND with their signal lines named in such a way as to create the structure in Fig.

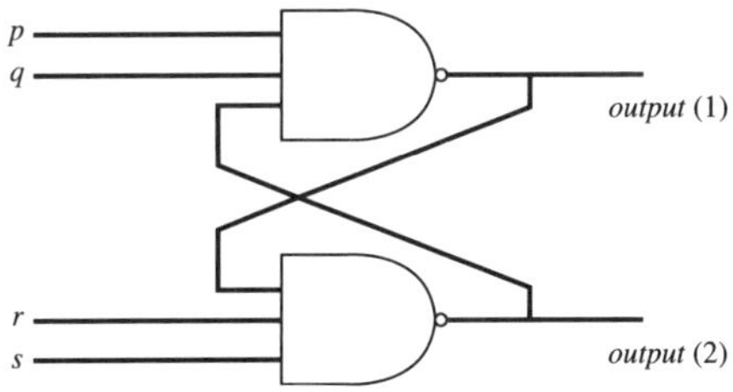

Figure 2.13 A flip-flop called `block`.

2.13. There is no opportunity to perform abstraction at this point, since the feedback lines are also projected outwith the `block` as output signal lines. Three `block` instances may now be generated with their signal lines named to allow the structure in Fig. 2.14 to be designed.

This D-type flip-flop is constructed from three of the previously defined `block`s which are composed together and have their internal connections hidden. This leaves four input signals, the data line `d` together with a `clear`, `preset`, and `clock` line, and a `q` and `qbar` output line.

The following MODEL definition specifies both the `block` and the complete D-type flip-flop:

```
PART block[p,q,r,s] → output(1:2)
     NAND [p,q,output(2)] → output(1)
     NAND [output(1),r,s] → output(2)
END  block}

PART flip-flop[reset,clear,clock,d] → q,qbar
     SIGNAL aout,bout(1:2)
     block[reset,bout(2),clear,clock] → -,aout
     block[aout,clock,clear,d] → bout(1:2)
     block[reset,aout,clear,bout(1)] → q,qbar
END{flip-flop
```

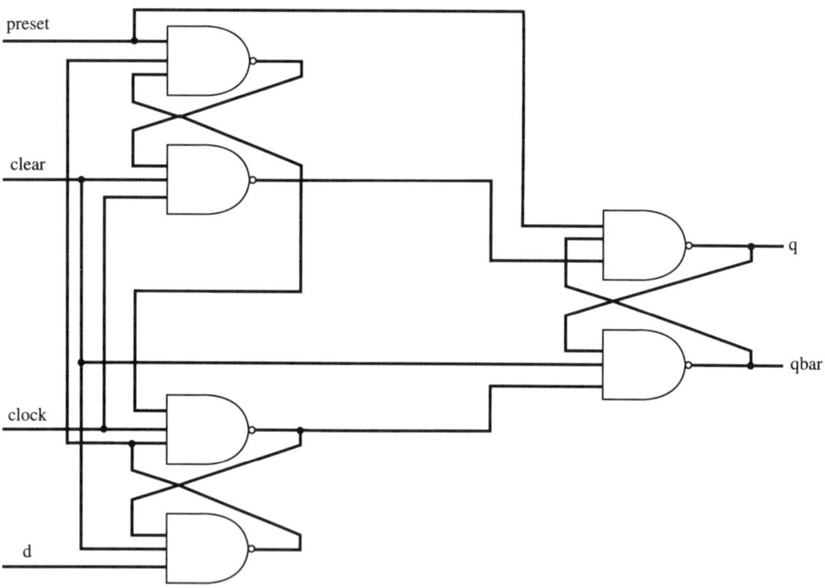

Figure 2.14 D-type flip-flop.

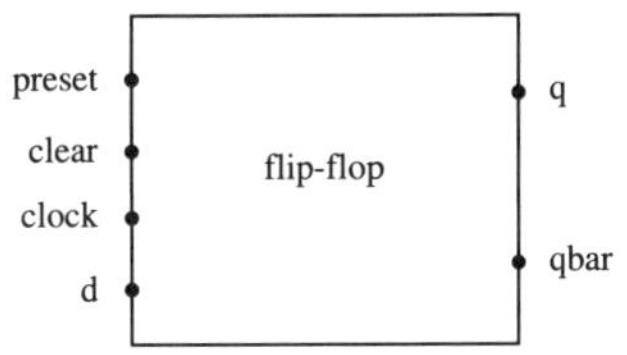

Figure 2.15 Example of a flip-flop.

The topmost block in Fig. 2.14 has only one output signal; its output corresponding to output(1) in Fig. 2.13 remains unconnected. This is described in the flip-flop definition where the first instance of `block` has its first output represented by the *blank signal* '–' to indicate its unconnected status.

The local signals used to connect the three blocks together are `aout`, `bout(1)` and `bout(2)`. These are hidden from the outside world, resulting in a flip-flop with the topmost structure pictured in Fig. 2.15.

Specifying Multiplexer Structure

The multiplexer shown in Fig. 2.16 is taken from a gate array design system handbook, and we intend to describe it using the MODEL language. This example circuit can only be translated into a MODEL program in a single way. Usually a *choice* can be made as to how to partition an existing block diagram into distinct logical units before translating into the language. Using the language to describe an existing schematic design is helpful for illustrative purposes, although it is obviously intended that designs will be directly produced in MODEL.

The eight lines named `data(1)`, `ctrl(1) . . .`, `data(4)`, `ctrl(4)` are used to name the input lines through which other parts, representing the environment

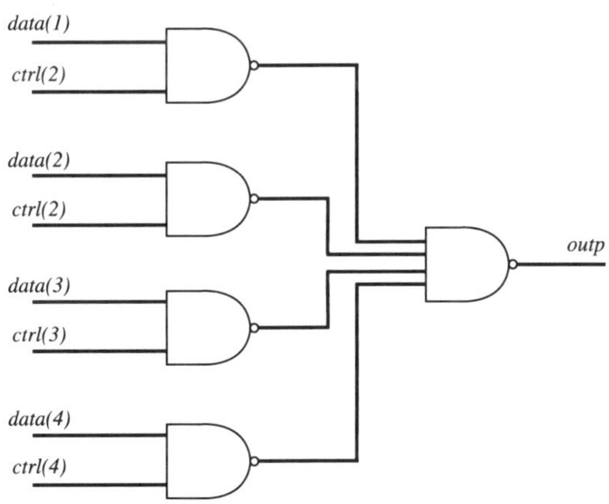

Figure 2.16 Example of a multiplexer.

that the multiplexer is to be used in, can be attached. The multiplexer has only one output, `outp`. The model definition of the multiplexer part is given by:

```
PART mux[data(1:4),ctrl(1:4)] → outp
     SIGNAL temp(1:4)
     NAND [data(1),ctrl(1)] → temp(1)
     NAND [data(2),ctrl(2)] → temp(2)
     NAND [data(3),ctrl(3)] → temp(3)
     NAND [data(4),ctrl(4)] → temp(4)
     NAND [temp(1:4)] → outp
END  {mux}
```

The part is identified by `mux` with four input signals named `data` and four input signals named `ctrl`. For notational convenience they are each treated as a signal vector with a parameter identifying each signal within the four-signal vector. Note that in the declaration heading `data(1:4)` could have been written as `data(1), data(2), data(3), data(4)`: vectors have obvious uses at the register-transfer level as well as this gate level of description. The declaration heading also declares `mux` to have a single output named `outp` to the right of the →. The `SIGNAL` declaration names signal lines to be used internally in the part; they will not be visible outside the part as only the `data, ctrl` and `output` lines will pass through the part boundary.

The body of the part definition follows the declaration headings. It is here that the components of the part and their interconnections are specified. These sub-parts must have been previously defined or must belong to a system part catalogue. They use the same signal names as the formal parameters introduced in the declarative heading. In MODEL, part instantiations are wired together using signals with outputs joined to inputs with the same name, following the convention introduced in the XCircal language. In the `mux` example the outputs from the first four NAND gates, called `temp`, join with the `temp` inputs of the last gate, the ordering of the part instantiations being unimportant.

The NAND gates used in `mux` are instances of a generic, previously defined gate taken from the system library. The formal parameters of the generic definition are replaced by the actual signal parameters, as indicated by the instances of NAND gates in `mux`.

Replicated Structures

Many components are built out of common sub-components replicated in various uniform ways. Common programming control statements are incorporated in MODEL to facilitate the description of these regular structures without the need for instantiating every component in a design. This corresponds with the introduction of the `FOR` construct in the presentation of XCircal in Section 2.3.

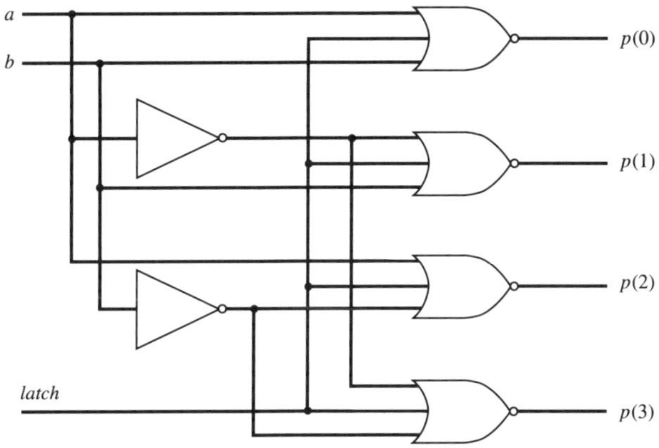

Figure 2.17 A decoder circuit.

A decoder circuit constructed from four identical three-input NOR gates is pictured in Fig. 2.17.

A FOR loop is used to generate the four instances of the NOR gate with the appropriately named input signals. If the input signals are not named correctly, then the sub-components will not wire up as required.

The primitive NOR parts are indexed from 0 to 3, and each has an output signal named `p(0), . . . , p(3)`. The conditional IF statement is used in the input parameters to ensure that the first input to two of the gates is an `a` while the remaining two gates receive an inverted signal. The second input to the NOR gates is either `b` or an inverted `b` with the third input being an 'unadulterated' latch. The three input signals of the complete decoder are `a`, `b` and `latch` while the four output signals are `p(0), . . . , p(3)`.

The following MODEL program defines the decoder of Fig. 2.17. Other encodings of the same device are, of course, possible.

```
PART decoder [a,b,latch] → p(0:3)
    SIGNAL abar,bbar
    INTEGER i
    NOT[a] → abar
    NOT[b] → bbar
    FOR i=0:3 CYCLE
        NOR [IF i&1=0 THEN a ELSE abar ENDIF,
             IF i&2=0 THEN b ELSE bbar ENDIF,
             latch] → p(i)
    REPEAT
END {decoder}
```

The following features of the above PART definition should be noted:

- The { } brackets enclose a comment.
- The loop variable `i` must be introduced in the declarative portion of the definition prior to its use.
- `NOT` is the primitive inverter component taken from the part library.
- `abar, bbar` are internal signals and are introduced in the declarative heading.
- Indentation is used to aid understanding of the code, for instance in the `FOR` loop.
- The `IF` statement uses a predicate which tests the binary representation of `i` to see if the last or second last bit is `0` or not. For instance, `(01& 1=0)` is false while `(01&2=0)` is true. `IF` statements are delimited by the keyword `ENDIF` and are used inside a part instantiation to generate the appropriate signal parameter.

The last property ensures that `a` is an input to the zeroth and second NOR parts with `abar` (the inverted `a`) as input to the first and third NOR part. The zeroth and first NOR also have `b` as input and the second and third have `bbar`.

Parametrized parts

The four-way multiplexer illustrated in Fig. 2.16 can be generated as a specific instance of a parametrized part definition where the number of components is a variable. This 'higher-order' definition would define an `n`-way multiplexer which would be instanced by allocating an integer to it to determine both the number of inputs and the number of primitive components.

The following is a parametrized definition of an `m`-way multiplexer:

```
PART varimux(m) [input(1:m),control(1:m)] → output
     SIGNAL temp(1:m)
     INTEGER i
     FOR i=1:m CYCLE
     nand [input(i),control(i)] → temp(i)
     REPEAT
     nand [temp] → output
END  varimux}
```

The following call to `varimux` instances the four-component multiplexer:

```
varimux(4)[p,q,r,s,select(1:4)] → result
```

The formal parameter `m` is replaced by `4` in this example. It is used both to specify the upper bound on the number of internal signals and to control the number of cycles around the `FOR` loop, laying out a NAND gate every time. The ability to define parametrizable parts helps the overall design process by allowing a *family* of parts to be defined using a single definition, so avoiding the need to define each part separately.

2.5 DESCRIBING STRUCTURE IN VHDL

In 1983 the US Air Force contracted a consortium involving Intermetrics, IBM and Texas Instruments to produce a hardware description language to support the design, description and simulation of VLSI and VHSIC (Very High Speed Integrated Circuit) devices. Known as VHDL, for VHSIC Hardware Description Language, it constituted part of a military-funded research programme into VHSIC component design. VHDL evolved through various versions until an IEEE standard hardware description language was reached (IEEE, 1988). The aim was to produce an industry-wide standard language whose syntax and semantics are completely described. This will aid the communication of hardware design data such as that between a design house and a customer, and will support human and mechanical design and validation of integrated circuits. VHDL syntax has been well defined, but a rigorous formal semantics has yet to be produced.

In this section we present the core structural features of VHDL version IEEE-1076 (IEEE, 1988). Like all languages designed by committee, including ADA, to which VHDL is related, the current standard version of VHDL differs in many ways from the original proposal. Most of these differences are in nomenclature and other syntactic details and do not affect the conceptual core of the language which, with respect to structural description, relates closely to the XCircal and MODEL languages presented above.

VHDL Concepts

Before looking at how to specify structural information in VHDL, it is useful to mention some of the underlying concepts of the language and present some of the terminology that is particular to it.

VHDL is a *fully typed* language, in the sense of programming languages such as Pascal and ADA. All data used in the description of a hardware component must therefore be given an explicit type, and this allows certain consistency checks to be made on the syntax of the descriptive programs.

The basic building block of VHDL descriptions is something called a *design entity*. The language can be used hierarchically to describe components of any size and at any level of abstraction, so a design entity may range across the complexity spectrum from a single gate to a system implemented using a multitude of interconnected integrated-circuit chips. Each design entity consists of an *entity declaration* and an *architecture body*. The entity declaration describes the interface between the entity and its environment, that is other design entities, in terms of input and output *ports*. The architecture body describes the function of the entity, that is, the generation of data on output ports from data on input ports.

The architectural body, the core of the description of any portion of hardware, gives the internal details of a design entity in terms of its structure or its behaviour or a combination of the two. A *structural* description describes the architecture in terms of the interconnected components from which the entity is built. A *behavioural* description represents the functionality of the design entity using well-understood high-level programming language constructs. In general, architectural bodies contain a mixture of structural instantiations of previously designed components together with the behavioural description of components which remain to be designed.

Language Features for Structural Specification

The basic unit for describing structure in VHDL is the *component*, which corresponds to a box in XCircal or a part in MODEL. A component corresponds to any unit of hardware: a gate, a microprocessor, a chip, or even a number of chips on a printed circuit board. As with XCircal and MODEL, the concept of a *port* is used to indicate how one component connects structurally to other components.

The VHDL treatment of connection differs from the convention established in the earlier parts of this chapter with the introduction of a *signal* primitive. Signals have both a behavioural and a structural interpretation; as structure they correspond to the actual wires used to join two ports together, while behaviourally they represent the sequences of data values, of the appropriate data type, which passes across the wire as time progresses. This behavioural treatment is discussed in Chapter 3.

The interconnection of components is effected in VHDL by declaring signals and explicitly connecting these signals to the ports of the subcomponents which require to be wired together. To illustrate this approach to component connection, we use a simple adder example. Here we wish to specify the structure of a full-adder constructed from the appropriate interconnection of two half-adders and an OR gate as in Fig. 2.19.

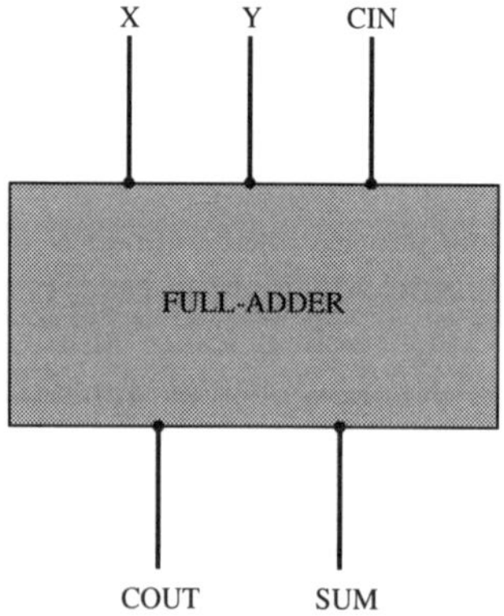

Figure 2.18 Full-adder interface.

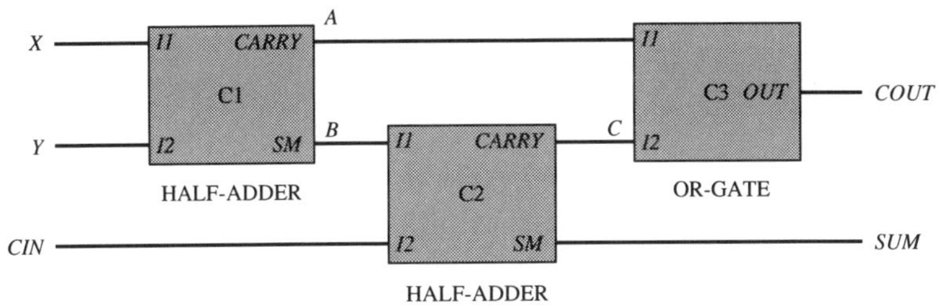

Figure 2.19 Full-adder structure.

Describing Adder Structure

In the VHDL language fragment below we represent the interface of the complete design entity called `FULL-ADDER`. The three input ports `X`, `Y` and `CIN` and the two output ports `COUT` and `SUM` are used to connect instances of the `FULL-ADDER` when constructing larger designs.

The interface information described in Fig. 2.18 is captured by the interface header of the `FULL-ADDER` entity description given below.

```
entity FULL-ADDER is
   port (X,Y,CIN : in Bit;SUM,COUT:out Bit)
end FULL-ADDER

architecture structure of FULL-ADDER is
signal A,B,C : Bit;
component HALF-ADDER
port (I1,I2 : in Bit;CARRY,SM : out Bit);
end component;
component OR-GATE
port (I1,I2 : in Bit; OUT : out Bit);
end component;

begin

C1 : HALF-ADDER
   port map (I1 ⇒ X, I2 ⇒ Y, CARRY ⇒ A, SM ⇒ B);

C2 : HALF-ADDER
   port map (I1 ⇒ B, I2 ⇒ CIN, CARRY ⇒ C, SM ⇒ SUM);

C3 : OR-GATE
   port map (I1 ⇒ A, I2 ⇒ C, OUT ⇒ COUT);

end structure;
```

The interface declares `X`, `Y` and `CIN` as input ports of type `Bit` and `COUT` and `SUM` as output ports, also of type `Bit`.

The architectural body of the entity definition is a structural one describing the FULL-ADDER component in terms of simpler components. The structure defined in the above entity specification is pictured graphically in terms of these smaller components, a HALF-ADDER and an OR-GATE, in Fig. 2.19.

The structural description of FULL-ADDER uses signals A, B and C to name internal interconnections between the ports of its components. The component declarations in the structural body name the local subcomponents to be used in the construction of the entity, along with the appropriately typed input and output ports. Particular instances of the subcomponents are generated between the **begin** and **end** brackets, and it can be seen from the entity specification that instantiation involves assigning a name for each component, in this case C1, C2 and C3, together with the introduction of particular port names. Here an actual port or signal name is associated with the local or formal port name given in the subcomponent declaration. This approach, using instances of standard components with their ports renamed, is analogous to defining and calling procedures in programming languages and has been described previously with the XCircal and MODEL languages. Entity definitions correspond to procedure calls with actual port names being assigned to the component ports just as actual parameters replace formal parameters.

The VHDL port naming convention used when creating particular instances of a generic component differs from that of the XCircal and MODEL languages, and from that of the HOL and Circal formalisms described in later chapters. Here a component instantiation statement involves an association list which follows the reserved words **port map**. For example the OR-GATE component C3 has signal A associated with local port name I1, signal C with port name I2 and output port COUT associated with local port OUT. A local port is therefore explicitly associated with a signal or a port using the ⇒ symbol. This form of port relabelling when performing component instantiation is notationally more clumsy than the elegant treatment shown previously with XCircal and MODEL. Fortunately, VHDL also permits this more elegant relabelling approach. This follows the standard procedural call convention of programming languages, where formal parameters, in this case local ports, are replaced by actual parameters according to their position in a parameter or port-list.

The simpler VHDL port naming convention, consistent with that adopted by the XCircal and MODEL languages, is illustrated in the following example. A four-bit ripple-carry adder, whose structure is pictured in Fig. 2.20 may be specified using four instances of the full-adder component. This example also illustrates the use of port vectors and iterative language constructs to generate regular replicated structures.

```
entity FOUR-BIT-ADD is
port (CIN : in Bit; X,Y : in Bit_vector(1 to 4);
      COUT : out Bit; SUM : out Bit_vector (1 to 4));
end FOUR-BIT-ADD;
```

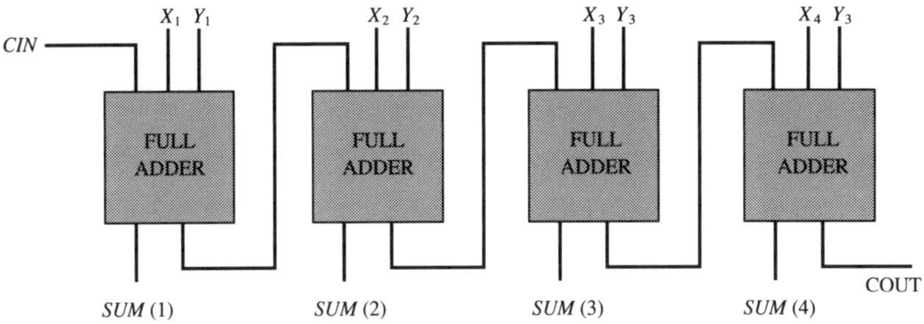

Figure 2.20 A ripple-carry adder.

```
architecture add-structure of FOUR-BIT ADD is
signal CARRY : Bit_vector(1 to 4);
component FULL-ADDER
port (X,Y,CIN : in Bit; SUM, COUT : out Bit);
end component;

begin
G1 : for i in 1 to 4 generate
  G2 : if i = 1 generate
    FULL-ADDER port map (CIN,X(1),Y(1),SUM(1),CARRY(1));
  end generate;
  G3 : if i > 1 and i < 4 generate
    FULL-ADDER port map (CARRY(i-1),X(i),Y(i),SUM(i),CARRY(i));
  end generate;
  G4 : if i = 4 generate
    FULL-ADDER port map(CARRY(4),X(4),Y(4),SUM(4),COUT);
  end generate;
end generate;
end add-structure;
```

A given design entity, such as the full-adder, may have a number of architectural bodies. In each case the description will have an identical interface header but the distinct architectural bodies will capture distinct design information, and even alternative implementations, at various levels of abstraction. This design information can be behavioural information, structural information or a mixture of the two. Behavioural VHDL specification is presented in Chapter 3.

Rather than instance each of the four full-adders individually, a **generate** statement is used in a manner similar to a loop in a programming language to generate the four individual components repeatedly. Notice that three **generate** statements are needed; one to generate the first stage, one to generate the last stage, and one to generate the other two stages with suitably named ports to allow appropriate interconnection. The first stage uses the external input carry to the complete component, while the other stages use internal carries between stages. As with any loop construct, a conditional statement is used to distinguish between the three cases.

As the structural body used to describe a four-bit full-adder is constructed from four full-adders, and as a full-adder is constructed from two half-adders and an OR gate, a hierarchical description of one possible implementation of a four-bit adder has therefore been constructed.

2.6 STRUCTURE IN HOL AND CIRCAL

Earlier in this chapter we developed the structural subset of the XCircal language to illustrate the use of explicit operators for composition and abstraction. Two formalisms for the formal description and verification of hardware are presented in detail in this text. These involve a particular use of higher-order logic, called HOL for short, and a process algebra called Circal. XCircal is a hardware description language which extends the syntax of the underlying Circal formalism; it is the Circal formalism which provides proof facilities for the XCircal language. The relationship between Circal and XCircal is described in detail in Chapter 7, and the properties of the Circal formalism which allow descriptions to be formally verified are discussed in Chapter 8.

Specifying hardware structure in both of these formalisms is also performed using a composition and an abstraction operator. From a behavioural point of view the actions of these operators are quite different, but from a structural viewpoint composition again corresponds to wiring together similarly named ports while abstraction is used to internalize wires and create an externally visible 'black-box' structure.

Composition and Abstraction in HOL

Given a half-adder and an OR gate component, the full-adder module pictured in Fig. 2.19 may have its structure specified in the HOL formalism by the FULL-ADDER HOL *predicate* which is defined below.

```
FULL-ADDER (x,y,cin,sum,cout) =
∃a,b,c.HALF-ADDER(x,y,a,b)∧HALF-ADDER (b,cin,c,sum)∧OR (a,c,cout)
```

Existential quantification on variable a, b and c (indicated by the symbol ∃) is used to effect abstraction, while the conjunction of the three component predicates via the logical AND operator '∧' corresponds to the use of the '*' operator in XCircal. Behaviour in HOL is represented by predicates, functions whose result is either true or false, which relate input values to output values. From a structural point of view the existentially quantified variables a, b and c are composed according to the structure pictured in Fig. 2.19 and then hidden while x, y, cin, sum and cout are the externally visible ports as in the VHDL FULL-ADDER definition.

Composition and Abstraction in Circal

In the XCircal language, and in the Circal formalism which underpins it and provides it with a formal semantics, each component is represented behaviourally by a *process* which describes behaviour in terms of actions and state evolution in a somewhat similar fashion to a finite state machine (Hopcroft and Ullman, 1969; 1979). Structurally, composition and abstraction is achieved using the $*$ and ( )–a operators, as presented earlier in this chapter.

The structure of the full-adder given in Fig. 2.19 is then given by the following XCircal process definition creating the process FULL-ADDER in terms of the HALF-ADDER and OR component processes.

```
FULL-ADDER (x,y,cin,sum,cout) ←
(HALF-ADDER(x,y,a,b) * HALF-ADDER(b,cin,c,sum) * OR (a,c,cout) )-(a b c)
```

An introduction to behavioural description in HOL and XCircal is given in Chapter 3. In later chapters HOL and XCircal are examined in detail. In particular, both of these languages and their underlying mathematical formalisms will be presented in terms of the description and verification of the behaviour of complex digital systems.

CHAPTER

THREE

SPECIFYING THE BEHAVIOUR OF HARDWARE

3.1 THE NEED FOR BEHAVIOURAL SPECIFICATION

The primary requirement of any circuit is that it performs a particular function and in so doing exhibits a certain *behaviour*. The design process should therefore concern itself with the behaviour of the circuit as well as with structural and geometrical layout issues. A designer will initially have some idea of what the circuit should do, i.e. what its behaviour should be. The design process can then be imagined as the formalization of an informal idea in the mind of the designer followed by the transformation of this *specification* of behaviour into a geometrical, mask-level circuit representation from which fabrication can proceed.

The behaviour of the completed design must be checked for correctness in some way prior to fabrication, preferably as a continuing exercise throughout the evolution of the design. The design process continues until the behaviour of the design can be shown to match that of its specification. So, while the design process may involve a great deal of manipulation of structural information, the ability to represent the behaviour of the circuit in a precise way is of central importance to the design process.

There are at least four main reasons why the *formal* description of behaviour is of importance to the complete design process. These can be summarized as follows:

- for system specification
- as an aid to designers
- as input to high-level design automation tools
- for design validation

The *description* of the actual behaviour of an existing hardware design or the specification of the intended behaviour of a circuit awaiting design is generally informal, and is usually done by means of natural language sentences, flow graphs, logic tables, Boolean formulae, or timing diagrams. Formal specification of the required behaviour of a design makes it possible to communicate these requirements unambiguously and completely to the designers, providing a precise statement of design requirements. The ability to describe behaviour formally in a design language allows the correspondence between specified behaviour and the behaviour of the constructed design to be established. As the primary aim in any design exercise is to produce an implemented system which satisfies the behavioural specification, that is, the design should be *correct*, this role of behavioural description is clearly an important one. In Sec. 3.3 we will see that the specification of increasingly smaller components occurs throughout the design process with a hierarchy of specifications corresponding to any natural design hierarchy.

The designer of a complex very-large-scale integrated (VLSI) system will use behavioural description languages as a *designer's aid*. The advent of *hierarchical* design requires the rigorous description of both the structure and the behaviour of design components at the various intermediate stages in the evolution of a complete design. The manipulation of the large amounts of descriptive data requires that the well-established techniques found in programming languages be used to aid the design process. The use of hardware description languages involving behavioural description as the medium in which a designer will work will increase steadily in the future, owing to the ever-increasing complexity of VLSI systems. Examples of languages developed with this purpose in mind are VHDL (IEEE, 1988), Verilog (Thomas and Moorby, 1991) and ELLA (Morison *et al.*, 1985).

Large designs are usually produced in segments with some parts of the design being produced 'by hand' and others being produced using *design automation tools*. An interface between the components needs to be specified, and this can be done most naturally using a design language which allows the description of structural, geometrical, and behavioural attributes. Input to design automation systems will need to contain behavioural information if designers are to work at a higher and more abstract level of design than that of pure structure or geometry. Most present-day design automation systems work in the structural or geometrical domains: examples of the latter are automatic placement and routing programs. Abstract behavioural descriptions are, however, being used as input by an emerging number of design synthesis systems as discussed by McFarland *et al.* (1990).

Finally, the most significant reason for specifying behaviour and for including behavioural description capabilities in a language is for *design validation*. Traditionally, validation techniques using simulation did not generally make use of behavioural description languages since they restricted themselves to describing circuits at a single level of representation such as the circuit level (Nagel, 1975), or the switch level (Bryant, 1986; Terman, 1983). Simulation then occurs monolithically over the complete device description after the design is complete, with the inherent problems of descriptive complexity and redesign effort when flaws are discovered. However, an integrated design and validation process allowing increasingly detailed descriptions of an evolving top-down design to be validated by simulation or verified by mathematical proof techniques breaks the design and validation tasks into manageable sub-tasks. This approach requires a behavioural description language in which to describe behaviour at different *levels of representation*, from the interactions among functional blocks down to the behaviour of primitive devices at the transistor level. The VHDL hardware description language has been produced for exactly this reason. Although its behavioural model does not support formal verification, it has been designed to support simulation. Behavioural description in VHDL will be introduced later in this chapter. However, before discussing the description of behaviour further it is appropriate to consider the precise meaning of the term in the VLSI design verification context.

3.2 TWO APPROACHES TO BEHAVIOURAL SPECIFICATION

Specifying the behaviour of a device is intrinsically a more complex activity than specifying its structure. This is because of the rich domain of behavioural properties requiring description, compared to the much less complex structure. As mentioned in Chapter 2, hardware structure can always be described, either textually or graphically, as a hierarchy of interconnected 'black boxes' in a standard, uniform manner satisfying the previously presented concepts of construction then abstraction.

The situation is, however, different in the case of behavioural specification. While the concept of constructing the behaviour of a large circuit from the behaviour of its distinct components, and the use of abstraction after construction, is necessary to deal with behavioural complexity, there appears to be no universal way to describe behaviour. While informal behavioural specification may utilize a range of descriptive techniques including natural language, graphical techniques, and programming-like notations, formal behavioural description may be classified in a fairly coarse way according to two distinct approaches. Behaviour can be described either *assertionally* or *operationally*.

Specifying Behaviour Assertionally

An assertional formalism represents hardware behaviour in terms of *predicates* whose arguments assert relationships between current and past values residing on each port. Predicates may be true or false, and the behaviour of a particular hardware device is specified by defining how the values on some ports, at some points in time, relate to others. In particular, the values on ports designated as output ports will usually be related to the values on input ports at some previous time. We will examine a particular assertional formalism, based on higher-order predicate logic, in detail in later chapters. The HOL formalism has been introduced briefly in the previous chapter in the context of structural specification, and we will give an informal introduction to some of its underlying behavioural concepts here.

In Chapter 1 we discussed the shortcomings of Boolean algebra as a formalism for the accurate description of hardware behaviour. The main deficiency of Boolean algebra is the lack of a mechanism for describing *time*. Timing is central to digital hardware, because its design and specification is concerned not just with *what* particular function is computed but also with *when* it is computed. The treatment of time in the HOL formalism has time proceeding in discrete *time steps*, and the arguments of the predicate which express the behaviour of a hardware module are *functions* over time. That is, they are functions from points in time to values. As the predicate arguments are functions over values rather than just values, we have a *higher*-order logic rather than a *first*-order logic. For example, a NAND gate with a propagation delay of 1 time unit between input and output may be defined in the HOL formalism by a higher-order logic formula defined as follows.

Definition

```
NAND(i,j,out) = ∀ t.out(t + 1) = ¬(i(t) ∧ j(t))
```

This assertional approach to behaviour involves describing *snapshots* of the behaviour of the hardware being specified at discrete points in time. In the above NAND gate example we utilize a predicate, also called `NAND`, taking the arguments `i`, `j` and `out`. These arguments correspond to two input ports, `i` and `j`, and an output port `out`. That is, we are describing a standard two-input NAND gate with the abstract structure and logic symbol given in Fig. 3.1.

As mentioned above, the arguments are themselves functions from integer values representing the points in time, to the discrete values associated with a particular model of a logic gate. This domain of logic values may be the Booleans {0, 1} or may be a multivalued logic such as that used by Hayes (1986) or Bryant (1984). The `NAND` predicate is itself a special function, for that is what a predicate is, taking the time-to-value functional arguments and returning *true* or *false*. In fact the above specification of the behaviour of a NAND gate asserts that for all points in time, described by the *universal quantifier* ∀ over variable

Figure 3.1 Abstract structure and logic symbol for NAND gate.

`t`, then the Boolean value at the output port `out` at time `t + 1` is the negation of the logical conjunction, or anding, of the Boolean values at both inputs `i` and `j` at the previous point in time `t`. Thus a propagation delay of 1 time unit is described.

The granularity of time, in other words the interval of time between two adjacent points in time `t` and `t + 1`, can be chosen to enable all gate propagation delays to be modelled by integer multiples of the intervals. For example, an inverter might need 2 units, or intervals, of time to propagate a change on the input to a change on the output. The output then appears at time `t + 2` relative to the input at time `t`. A substantially coarser grain of time would prevent this gate from being modelled realistically.

The application of existing logic theories to the task of behavioural description and verification is a standard approach to creating a hardware verification system. The HOL system of Gordon and Melham (1993), which we examine in detail in this book, the VERITAS system of Hanna and Daeche (1985), the use of the Boyer–Moore system (1988) by Hunt (1986) and the development of temporal (Moszkowski, 1983) and modal logics (Clarke *et al.*, 1991) are examples of this approach. They have the advantage of giving access to an existing logic theory in which to conduct verification proofs, and they are fairly general in terms of the various types of data which can be described, but they have certain shortcomings. These include the possible lack of an intuitive way of describing hardware behaviour, an inability to support simulation and the fact that they utilize *theorem proving* to perform hardware verification proofs. Theorem-proving systems are inherently interactive and require significant user control: what designers require, on the other hand, is a fully automatic system to determine whether their hardware design is correct or not, and if not why not. Some of these deficiencies are addressed in the alternative approach to behavioural description which we now consider.

Specifying Behaviour Operationally

As an alternative to using an existing logic theory and expressing behaviour via predicates, an operational treatment corresponds to the *event/next state* approach as found in automata theory (Hopcroft and Ullman, 1979). Behaviour is described as a dynamic process, which indeed is just what hardware behaviour is. Every hardware module is in a particular state which then may evolve to a new state as a result of interaction between modules. This approach allows for the ready construction of intuitively understandable descriptions, since the event/state descriptive concept is well understood and in common usage.

An *action* or event is a dynamic concept, such as the change in voltage on a line or the communication of data over a bus. Actions will be assumed to occur on named ports belonging to a *design component* where a complete design is itself called a component. The behaviour of a component is then taken to be a sequence of actions occurring through time, with some actions possibly occurring simultaneously because of hardware concurrency. Actions may have a causality relationship imposed on them, and this is represented by the sequential ordering of the actions. This causality property occurs when one action *causes* another action, such as a change on gate input causing an output change at some later time as in the NAND example above. As can be clearly seen, this event-based approach to behaviour introduces a relativistic view of time with the sequencing and simultaneity of actions capturing the time-related behaviour of devices. These properties of actions need to be captured realistically together with the notion of absolute time. This further requirement is due to the need to describe and reason about timing properties such as propagation delays and clocking schemes using real measures of time, and it depends on the level of detail that has to be represented.

The dynamic approach to behaviour in terms of action sequentiality and simultaneity as proposed above is familiar to computer scientists and hardware designers alike. If we further introduce the notion of the *state* of a design component, then we can imagine that the occurrence of actions causes the current state to evolve to a new state. This then leads us to a general form of behavioural description not unlike that found in finite-state automata.

Let us take a simple example and use it to exhibit the intended meaning of concepts such as component, state, action, sequentiality and simultaneity. An *inverter* may be pictured as a design component containing two ports, as illustrated in Fig. 3.2.

The only information captured in Fig. 3.2 is the component name `INV` and the presence of two ports, named `a` and `b`. This treatment of *structural* information corresponds to that presented in the previous section.

The *state* of an inverter at some point in time may be given by an assignment of values, taken from some value set, to ports. Multivalued logics are traditionally used to represent both voltage and charge, and the rationale for using different value sets is well presented by Hayes (1982). Let us just assume the Boolean values {0,1} and take the state of the component to be represented by the juxtapositioning of component name to a vector or list of port values. Assuming a port ordering `ab`, the four states of the inverter may be denoted by the following identifiers:

```
INV00, INV01, INV10, INV11
```

The state `INV01` is a stable state where the values on the ports are the inverse of each other. The state `INV00` represents an inverter where one port has been

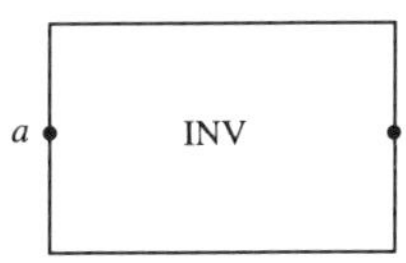

Figure 3.2 Inverter.

changed by an *external stimulus* or externally generated interaction but the output change caused by this has yet to propagate through. Notice that we do not distinguish between input and output ports. The behavioural description will restrict one port to be an input and one to be an output. The reasoning behind this is that ports belonging to some components such as a wire may be used for both input and output.

The behaviour of an inverter can then be described by the state transition graph in Fig. 3.3. The nodes correspond to the four inverter states, while the arcs are labelled by the actions which cause the states to change. Using Boolean logic, two actions are possible on any port `a`, namely `a0` and `a1`. The action `a0` corresponds to the `a` port taking value 0 with the assumption that it was at 1 to start with. If an `n`-valued logic were used to represent continuous behaviour discretely, then `n` actions would be possible at each port.

A multiple action such as the action pair (`a0 b0`) corresponds to the simultaneous occurrence of actions `a0` and `b0` with the `a` and `b` ports both changing to 0 simultaneously.

Notice that this event-based view of the world generates no actions if a circuit is dormant, as we would expect. Thus if the inverter were in a state `INV01` and no action on port `a` was forthcoming from other components in the surrounding environment which are 'wired up' to the inverter via the `a` port, then the inverter remains indefinitely in this state. This dynamic, event-based approach to the representation of behaviour contrasts with that adopted by the assertional technique described previously.

The state transition diagram in Fig. 3.3 represents a potentially infinite behaviour, since there is no designated terminal state. Most hardware components have potentially infinite behaviour, and hardware verification formalisms based on the two contrasting approaches discussed here all permit the description of such infinite behaviour usually via recursive constructs in the appropriate formalism.

The XCircal language may be used to describe the behaviour of this inverter in a textual way. XCircal and the underlying Circal formalism have been created for the express purpose of hardware description and verification, and are presented in detail in Chapter 7. As with the HOL formalism, XCircal has been used extensively for analysing digital systems. The higher-order logic and Circal formalisms, the HOL and XCircal languages derived from them, and their realization as the HOL system and the Circal system respectively, are used in this book to present two contrasting and, to some extent, complementary state-of-the-art approaches to hardware verification. Other authors who also adopt an operational approach to hardware verification include Subrahmanyan (1983), Gopalnakrishnan (1989) and Larsson (1988).

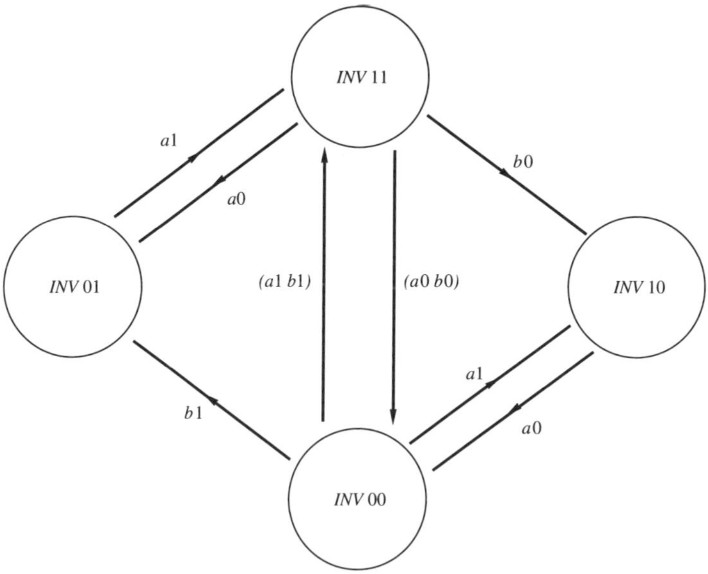

Figure 3.3 State transition diagram for inverter.

3.3 THE COMPOSITION AND ABSTRACTION OF BEHAVIOUR

Whether behaviour is to be described assertionally or operationally, two fundamental concepts are common to both forms of behavioural description: *behavioural composition* and *behavioural abstraction.* These concepts were met in the previous chapter where they were introduced from a structural point of view. We indicated there that these concepts are necessary to describe the structure of large, complex hardware systems in a hierarchical fashion. These concepts are also necessary to enable the behaviour of complex circuits to be described and then formally verified.

Behavioural composition

Suppose we wish to verify the correctness of a circuit such as the control circuit of Fig. 3.4. Verification, unlike simulation, will usually entail establishing a relationship between a specification of the desired behaviour of the circuit and the behaviour of its implementation. If the design or implementation is not cor-

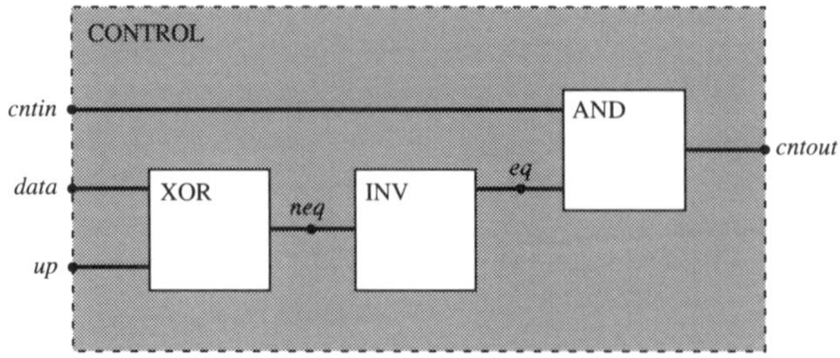

Figure 3.4 Internal structure of control circuit.

rect with respect to the specification, the equivalence of these two behaviours cannot then be established with the particular formalism used. In this example we would wish to show that

```
ControlSpec ≡ ControlImp
```

where the symbol ≡ indicates behavioural equivalence according to some definition of equivalence. The specification `ControlSpec` would be written directly in whatever formalism we were using, while the implementation behaviour named `ControlImp` is *constructed* from the behaviour of its constituent parts. That is, the behaviour of the `XOR`, `INV`, and `AND` components are composed using the appropriate *composition operator*.

In the preceding section we specified the behaviour of an inverter in a particular higher-order logic formalism called HOL, by way of example. If we also have HOL descriptions of the behaviour of an `XOR` and an `AND` gate we are then in a position to construct the behaviour of `ControlImp`.

This is achieved by the following HOL formula:

```
XOR(up,data,neq) ∧ INV(neq,q) ∧ AND(eq,cntin,cntout)
```

Logical conjunction, denoted by the symbol ∧, is used to compose the three behaviours, logical predicates remember, called `XOR`, `INV` and `AND`. Notice that this is a description of the structure of the control circuit pictured in Fig. 3.4, which also establishes its behaviour from behavioural descriptions of its components.

If the behaviour of the control implementation was being constructed in the XCircal language, then the behaviour of each of the three components would be expressed as the appropriate *process*, a process being inherently the textual description of the behaviour of a finite-state machine. In this case a particular composition operator needs to be defined which has the effect of combining the behaviour of component processes into the single process which captures the behaviour of finite-state machines interacting over their interconnecting wires. The XCircal formula describing how behaviours are composed is given by

```
XOR(up,data,neq) * INV(neq,eq) * AND(eq,cntin,cntout)
```

By application of the Circal (and XCircal) composition operator, presented in Chapter 7, this formula is replaced by the *behavioural description* process which corresponds to the complete control circuit. Notice that this behaviour has been *constructed* or *synthesized* from the component process behaviours using the composition operator. In the HOL formalism, logical conjunction between the predicates takes on the same role.

Behavioural Abstraction

One thing is missing from this constructive approach to establishing the behaviour of an implementation. This is performing *abstraction* on the wires which are *internal* to the control circuit, the `neq` and `eq` connections.

In Chapter 2 we introduced an abstraction, or *hiding*, operator to 'black-box' a design which was previously constructed using the structural composition or 'wire-up' operator. The abstraction operator allows a composite structure to be represented only in terms of how it interfaces externally with other components. Internal structural details are irretrievably lost when internal wires such as `neq` and `eq` are hidden to create the structure pictured in Fig. 3.5. After abstraction these ports cannot be used to wire up to other components from the environment, so internalizing communication channels. If a multicomponent wire-up is required, for example for fan-out, then abstraction should not occur until all the components have been suitably composed.

When behavioural abstraction is performed on the interactions which occur between the components over the shared wires, behavioural information is also irretrievably lost from the description of the implementation. The environment, that is other circuits to which the control circuit may be connected at some later date, will no longer be able to interact with the `neq` and `eq` ports and these interactions will be internalized and hidden. In this way, point-to-point communication can be achieved; the usual wiring convention in digital hardware. Again, notice that if fan-out were required, abstraction would not be performed over that particular communication link until after all components were attached.

Abstraction is achieved in the HOL formalism using existential qualification. The description of the control circuit in Fig. 3.4 is given by the formula

```
∃ neq, eq .XOR(up,data,neq) ∧ INV(neq,eq) ∧
           AND(eq,cntin,cntout)
```

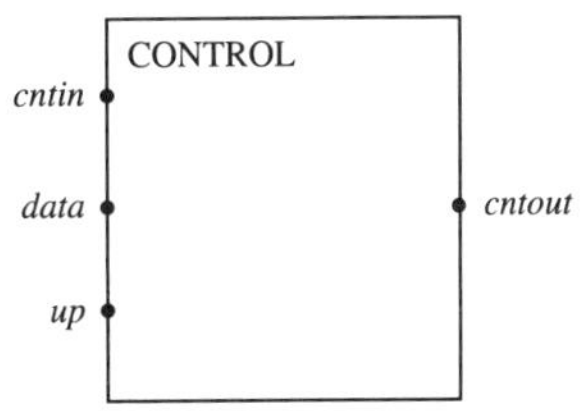

Figure 3.5 Control structure after hiding.

How the existential quantifier effects behaviour abstraction over HOL predicates will be discussed in Chapter 5.

Behavioural abstraction is performed in XCircal using an operator which removes reference to the particular actions occurring over the ports and wires being hidden. In the control example, all `neq` and `eq` actions will be removed. Details of the abstraction operator used in such an operational, process formalism will be given in Chapter 7.

3.4 BEHAVIOURAL DESCRIPTION IN VHDL

HOL and XCircal have been developed as frameworks in which to perform rigorous hardware description and verification. They may be used as conventional hardware description languages, in which hardware may be designed, or as vehicles for proof, where existing designs have their behaviour described. XCircal, although not HOL, also supports the simulation of descriptions; this distinction is due to the operational basis of the underlying Circal formalism of XCircal. In this respect XCircal resembles a hardware description language such as VHDL; VHDL was produced from first principles as a hardware description language where the descriptions are directly exercised by an appropriate VHDL simulator.

VHDL differs from many other HDLs in that it permits behavioural specification as well as structural specification. This concept of behavioural description is closely associated with the desire to perform simulation on VHDL design descriptions. Like all languages, programming languages and hardware description languages, the syntax of VHDL is rigorously described using Backus Naur Form (BNF), in this case in the VHDL manual (IEEE, 1988). Such a formal syntactic definition of a language describes how to construct legitimate programs in the language; what it does *not* do is indicate the meaning, behaviour, or *semantics* of the language. Unlike HOL and XCircal, VHDL has not been provided with a formal semantics. The availability of a formal semantics, or underlying formalism, is necessary to verify designs constructed in an HDL. However, the informal description of the meaning of syntactic constructs of VHDL and their interpretation within a simulation model of behaviour is considered adequate for most purposes other than verification.

Behavioural Concepts in VHDL

In Chapter 2 we discussed VHDL from a structural design perspective. We showed how a design entity consists of an interface to the outside world in terms of named ports together with a *structural architecture* body. This structural body of a VHDL design component, or entity, indicates which subcomponents were used to construct the entity and the particular way in which they are interlinked.

Design entities in VHDL may have more than one structural architecture indicating different ways in which a design may be constructed, although validation techniques would be required to demonstrate that all alternative designs have the same, or equivalent, behaviour.

Design entities may also have *behavioural bodies* which indicate *what* function the hardware module should have rather than *how* it is constructed, as with a structural body. No structurally smaller components are therefore used, and the behaviour of the body is expressed directly in terms of sequence of actions, basic functions and commands, and timing attributes. Such behavioural constructs are known in VHDL as *process statements.*

To illustrate the concept of a behavioural architecture and the implied use of a simulator to give the semantics of the behavioural process statement, we use the full-adder as an example. The VHDL description of the structure of the full-adder pictured in Fig. 3.6 was given in Chapter 2, but here we wish to express its behaviour.

The design entity header and the behavioural architecture of the full-adder is given by the following VHDL program:

```
entity fulladder is
        port (X,Y,Cin: in Bit ; Sum,Cout: out Bit)
end fulladder;
architecture behavioural-body of fulladder is
        signal S1,S2,S3: Bit ;
        process
        begin
          S1    ⇐ X xor Y;
          Sum   ⇐ (S1 xor Cin) after 5 ns;
          S2    ⇐ X and Y;
          S3    ⇐ S1 and Cin;
          Cout  ⇐ S2 or S3 after 6 ns;
          wait on X,Y,Cin;
        end process;
end behavioural-body;
```

The process statement describes a series of actions which will occur when this program is run on a VHDL simulator. The sequence of *signal statements,* such as S1 ⇐ X **xor** Y, indicates the assignment of values to the entity ports as time passes. In a behavioural body ports correspond to signals where a signal is a stream of values occurring at the port through time, in much the same way that the HOL formalism uses functions from time to values. The meaning, or semantics, of these signal statements is given (informally) in terms of how a VHDL simulator reacts to such statements.

Two classes of signal appear in this example; internal signals such as S1 which correspond to variables local to this program, and the input and output ports such as X and Y, which are themselves treated as value streams. When a

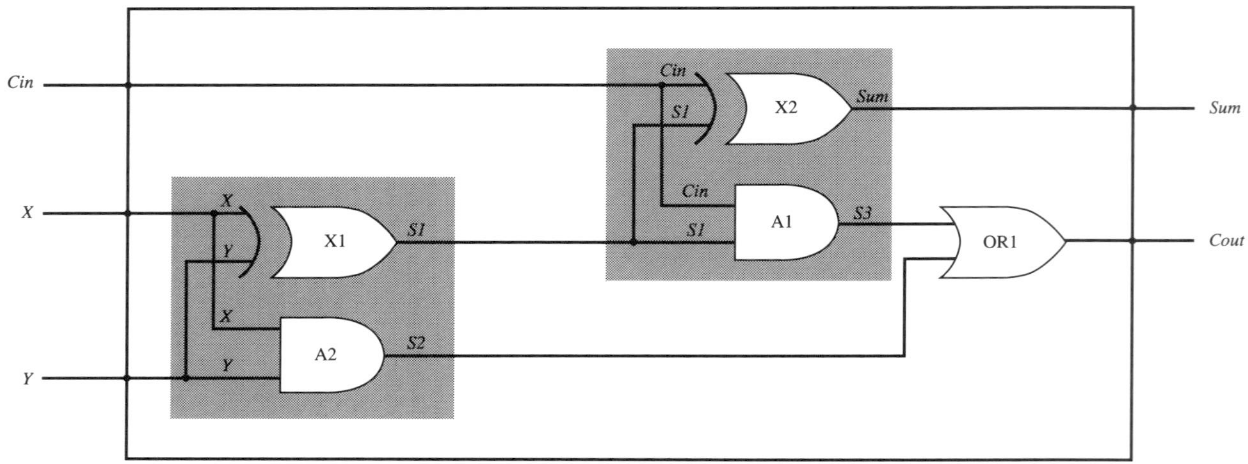

Figure 3.6 The structure of a full-adder.

simulation starts it is normal to initialize all signals of type `Bit` to logical `0`. The **process** keyword then causes the simulator to execute the five signal assignment statements in turn.

The first signal assignment, `S1 ⇐ X` **xor** `Y`, assigns the exclusive or of the values currently at the `X` and `Y` input ports to local signal `S1`. The simulator then executes the second statement, `Sum ⇐ (S1` **xor** `Cin)` **after** `5 ns`. But here the output signal `Sum` is updated 5 nanoseconds *later*, with the **xor** of the *current* values of signal `S1` and input `Cin`. That is, the simulator keeps track of a 5 nanosecond propagation delay between input and output.

When the final signal assignment statement in the process has finished, the process becomes passive and suspends itself. It stays in this suspended state until any of the signals mentioned in the **wait on** statement changes value. These happen to correspond to the input ports, so the simulator will perform no further execution of this architectural body until at least one of the input ports receives a change in value from its environment. Such an input change will cause the process to become active again, and the execution cycle repeats from the beginning of the process body. This is commonly known as *event-based* simulation and is discussed briefly in Chapter 4.

Mixing Structural and Behavioural Description

As the VLSI design process involves both *top-down* and *bottom-up* design, architectural bodies will generally contain a mixture of structurally described instantiations of previously designed components and behavioural descriptions of components which remain to be designed.

The following architectural body for the same full-adder entity mixes behavioural and structural information:

```
architecture mixture of fulladder is
 component XOR(A,B: in Bit;C: out Bit);
 component OR (A,B: in Bit;C: out Bit);
 signal      S1,S2,S3: Bit;
 begin
       X1: XOR(X,Y,S1);
       X2: XOR(S1,Cin,Sum);
       S2 ⇐ X and Y after 2 ns;
       S3 ⇐ S1 and Cin after 2 ns;
       OR1: OR(S2,S3,Cout);
 end mixture;
```

It can be seen that the full-adder is being described directly at the gate level without the use of the intermediate hierarchy which involves half-adder components. In this example components `XOR` and `OR` exist but a component which implements logical and remains to be designed.

Describing Time in VHDL

The representation of timing properties is one of the major roles of any hardware description language. This is because hardware is designed not just to compute a certain function or perform particular actions but to perform the actions at a certain point in time. Usually timing characteristics involve the maximum delay that is acceptable between the arrival of some input data or control signals and the generation of some output. This maximum *transport delay* is usually dependent on the requirements of the other components in the surrounding environment; they will require data to be available to them at certain predefined times.

The delay across a component may be specified using actual timing values, and an output event which is caused by an input event can be defined to occur a particular period of time later than the input which caused it. In the behavioural architecture for the full-adder, output on `Sum` is defined to occur 5 nanoseconds *after* the input actions on `S1` or `Cin` which cause the output to change. VHDL uses two time scales or grains of time in a way that is similar to that adopted by the CONLAN HDL (Piloty *et al.,* 1983). A macro time scale in terms of nanoseconds, microseconds, etc., is used to represent real timing information by breaking the time axis into discrete equidistantly spaced points in time. Within this macro time scale the micro time scale is used to specify the causality relationship between input and output events, such as between `X` and `Y` and signal `S1`. Figure 3.7 pictures the two time scales, where it can be seen that any number of micro time units can occur within one macro time unit.

The rationale behind these two distinct ways of representing time follows from a requirement to use VHDL descriptions for the simulation of discrete design behaviour at any level of abstraction down to the gate level. There is an apparent need to allow for two types of event ordering in simulation; by using real-time information on an absolute time scale (the macro time scale) and by the relative ordering of event occurrences (the micro time scale).

The two forms of time representation are featured in the clocked path pictured in Fig. 3.8. Macro time is used to specify the clock period controlling the flow of data between the latches `REG1` and `REG2`. Micro time is then used to specify the propagation delay as the data passes through the combinational logic between the registers.

As mentioned previously, the meaning ascribed to VHDL syntax is based on an assumption of how an event-driven simulator would evaluate the behaviour

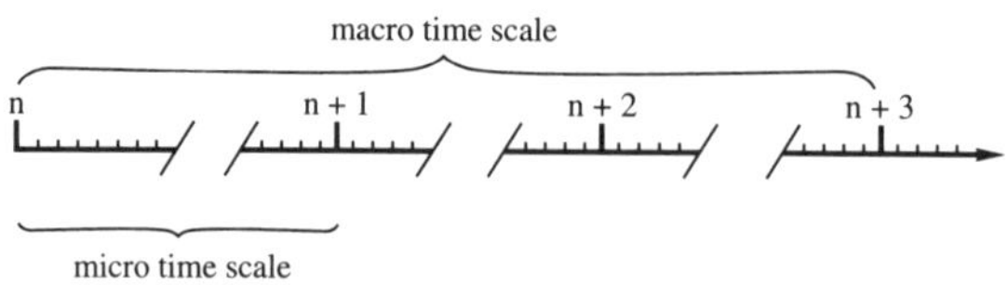

Figure 3.7 Macro and micro time.

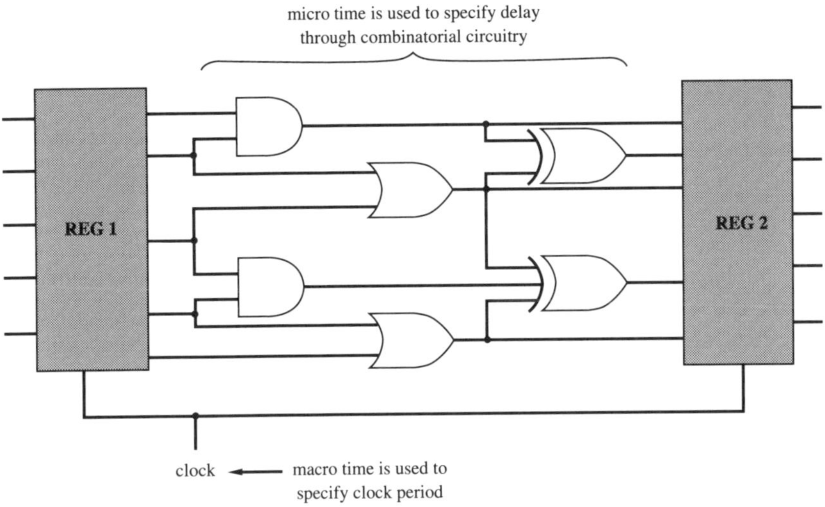

Figure 3.8 A clocked data path.

described by the architecture bodies of VHDL design entities. The lack of a formal semantics for VHDL, specifying the intended meaning of syntactic constructs independently from how the behaviour may be mimicked by a simulator, is one of the major omissions in its development. One of the consequences of this orientation towards simulation is that certain language concepts such as the treatment of time have been built with a bias towards evaluation.

Validation in VHDL

The orientation towards simulation overlooks the requirement of other validation techniques. In particular, no thought has been given to the use of formal verification techniques within a VHDL design and analysis environment. Later chapters will present a number of frameworks and techniques for the formal verification of design correctness. This has particular reference to future uses of VHDL, where new techniques will be developed to show the behavioural equivalence of alternative design entity bodies, for example.

Behavioural equivalence is a significant feature because of the way in which it is intended to be used in the design process. During a design exercise different design choices may be made, resulting in a number of different bodies being associated with a single design entity interface. Alternative architectural bodies give different implementations of a design whose behaviour may be specified by a pure behavioural body. These alternative implementations permit a designer to experiment with different design styles, different implementation algorithms, and different structured decompositions such as a carry lookahead implementation of an adder rather than a 4-bit ripple carry implementation. The intention is that all alternative architectures will compute the same function and that they will all be satisfactory implementations of the specified behaviour, also given as an architectural body of the entity. The alternative implementations will be described at a lower level of abstraction than the specification, as was previously demonstrated using our 4-bit adder example, but this behavioural equivalence property must be established somehow. The intention of VHDL is that the architectural bodies will have their behaviour established by use of a simulator and the correctness ascertained by simulating *all* the bodies to ensure that they correctly implement the specified behaviour. In future it is hoped that this validation process can be performed more rigorously and in a 'simulator independent' manner, using formal verification techniques such as those presented later in this text. Work by Van Tassel (1992) towards formalizing the VHDL simulation cycle and by Borrione *et al.* (1991) on VHDL verification represents progress in this direction.

CHAPTER

FOUR

DESIGN VALIDATION: VERIFICATION AND SIMULATION

Validation is the process used to demonstrate design correctness. It is part of the procedure used to establish confidence that the design will operate as intended when it is manufactured and then put into use.

There are many ways of establishing whether a design is correct, but the common feature is that the behaviour of the design is represented as a model in some descriptive formalism. Distinct models may capture the different features requiring validation with varying degrees of accuracy, depending on the descriptive power of the particular formalism and the validation techniques which are applicable to a model created in it.

The significance of performing validation within a modelling formalism, as opposed to constructing the actual hardware and testing to see if it behaves correctly or not, is directly associated with the cost and effort of fabricating and testing the design. Two aspects require validation; the design must compute the function intended of it and this must be completed within certain time bounds. The functionality may also depend on subtle timing properties of the design such as whether a spike is produced by a latch. If there are such functionality and timing problems in a design, they must be detected before the design is built. Computer time is far cheaper than manufacturing costs, so we need a representation of the modelled design held as some form of data structure, coupled with software which implements the validation techniques by application of that data structure, to allow designs to be validated before manufacture. Not only can the validation tools be applied to detect design flaws, but design changes which have to be effected to eliminate the errors can readily be made.

A further advantage of this approach is that a clear distinction can be made between errors introduced by the fabrication process and those generated during the design cycle. If a design has been thoroughly validated before fabrication, then if actual chips are found to be faulty by testing after manufacture, we can tell that the manufacturing process itself must have introduced them. This assumes that the description and validation process does not itself introduce the fault. Confidence in this can only be achieved by careful creation of the theory and the models, and their continuing successful use.

In this chapter we distinguish between the two distinct approaches to design validation, namely formal verification by mathematical proof and the more experimental process of simulation. The distinct roles of each which contribute to the process of creating a correct design will be isolated and discussed, and the common features, such as the use of an underlying model, will also be presented. Simulation, the most commonly used approach to design validation, is also discussed and its underlying principles are presented. As an alternative to post-design validation the need to incorporate validation techniques into the design process is introduced, and the chapter concludes with a discussion of the use of simulation and verification techniques in a digital design framework.

In subsequent chapters formal verification is presented as an alternative to simulation, with two complementary verification frameworks being introduced. The underlying concepts of both approaches are given, and a number of examples are used to indicate the significant features of the two frameworks. These two approaches, using higher-order logic and process algebras, are developed in detail in Chapters 6 and 7.

4.1 DISTINGUISHING BETWEEN SIMULATION AND VERIFICATION

The terms simulation and verification are often used interchangeably in the electronics industry. In this book the two concepts are differentiated: *simulation* is the experimental process which aims to mimic the dynamic behaviour of hardware as it evolves through time, while *verification* refers to the process of demonstrating design correctness using mathematical proof techniques.

In formal verification, mathematical proof techniques are used to establish the correctness of a design with respect either to some particular behavioural criteria, such as a given timing property, or in terms of its equivalence to a fairly complete specification given at a more abstract level. Proof of such correctness properties is performed using a variety of proof techniques which may be available to a given formalism. Examples of such techniques include the use of inference rules within a theory such as higher-order logic, term rewriting using a set of behaviour-preserving axioms which form a complete axiomatization of a particular formalism or model, and equivalence checking using the *labelled transition system* operational semantics of a particular process algebra. The first of these techniques is illustrated in Chapters 5 and 6, where the HOL higher-order logic formalism is discussed in detail. The remaining two techniques are demonstrated in Chapters 7 and 8, where the XCircal language and the Circal system are presented.

We use the word *validation* to embrace both simulation and verification. While the two approaches are quite distinct, they do have some features in common such as the requirement for an underlying model and the way in which they may be used in an integrated design and validation methodology. In this chapter we introduce both verification and simulation, and discuss features they have in common.

Note that verification refers to *behavioural* verification. In integrated circuit terminology, the term is frequently used to refer to the geometrical correctness of circuit layout with concepts such as distances between polysilicon and metal lines established by *design rule checking*. This latter use of the term verification is not discussed further here.

Simulation: Underlying Concepts

Simulation is the most commonly used approach to the problem of demonstrating design correctness. It is a dynamic process in which a model of a design is *exercised on test data* in a way which hopefully mimics the actions of the design when it is subsequently fabricated. Simulators traditionally use models that are particular to a given level of abstraction and thus to a particular form of description. For example, a commonly used simulator for VLSI is based on a switch primitive. This uses a switch-level model as found in the MOSSIM simulator of Bryant (1986) and the simulators found in many commercial design systems which were derived from it. Because of this restriction to a particular level of representation, the design process will entail the use of a number of simulators, one for each descriptive level.

The dynamic approach to validation provided by simulation can be illustrated by considering Fig. 4.1. In it a model of a design is pictured as a box with a number of input and output ports. Patterns of *test data* or *stimulus patterns* are applied to the device model via its input ports, and the simulation algorithm attempts to emulate or *simulate* the behaviour of the actual device and produce the appropriate patterns or sequences of output data.

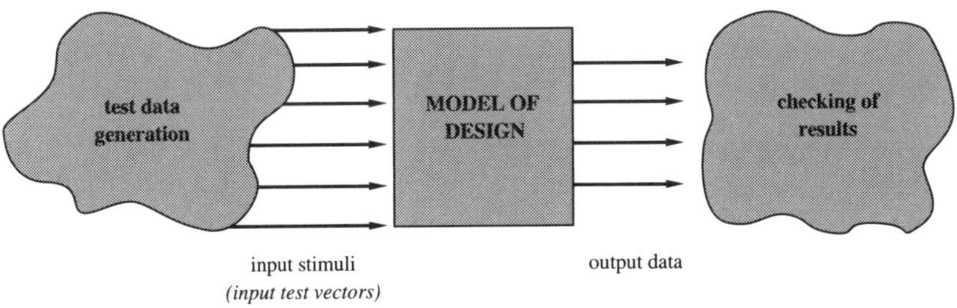

Figure 4.1 Example of simulation.

For simulation to establish a high degree of confidence in the correctness of a design requires the exhaustive application of stimulus patterns, known as *test vectors.* For each test vector used as input, the output must be observed and checked to see whether the expected values result.

In practice only a representative set of test vectors will be applied when a simulator is run on a particular design example. The reason for this is that most hardware is so complex that a *complete* test vector set would require a vast number of possible inputs to be exercised on the design representations. For most usefully sized hardware, total and exhaustive simulation entails running the simulator on a powerful, fast computer for periods as long as weeks or months. This is obviously not a practical possibility in most design exercises, and so only a representative subset of test vectors is used in practice. This creates its own problems: how do we know that our representative set covers all the significant scenarios which we wish to analyse, and even if we go for an exhaustive test set how can we guarantee that all cases have been covered? There are methods for automatically generating tests for certain types of faults (Breuer, 1972), and this test pattern generation satisfies some of the preceeding problems. There are also ways of utilizing simulation techniques, some of which are illustrated later in this chapter, which reduce the need for conducting monolithic simulation.

The difficulties encountered with simulation, in particular the problem that simulation can be used to detect design errors but cannot be used to guarantee their total absence, may lead to the conclusion that formal verification is a superior validation technique. A more accurate view is that some areas are supported by simulation and not by verification. In addition, verification tools and techniques are still in their infancy, while hardware simulation has been developing for 20 years or so and has reached a high degree of maturity and sophistication.

Areas where simulation makes a direct contribution in the design process and verification tools do not include providing designers with rapid feedback about the consequences of design decisions. Design engineers frequently work in a 'bread-board' style where they make design choices and apply particular stimulus patterns to the resulting design to see whether a particular aspect of it functions as required. If it does not, then they can do a quick redesign followed by a further simulation experiment. In addition, one of the particular uses of simulation in the future will be to validate design specifications. As formal verification techniques come into practical use this role of simulation will increase in importance; designers will aim for a full understanding of the intended specification of a design before verifying that a design implementation meets its specification. Thus even when powerful verification tools become available, such as those that are being developed from the approaches presented in this book, the experimental nature of simulation as a design aid is such that in an ideal design environment simulation and verification tools and techniques should both be available.

Formal Verification: Underlying Concepts

Verification is not usually thought of as an experimental procedure in the same way that simulation is. Again it uses a modelling formalism in which to capture design behaviour, but in this case mathematical techniques are used to *prove* that a design satisfies various properties. In fact the use of mathematical proof techniques to establish the correctness of a design has led to the term *formal verification* being used to denote this approach to design validation. The verification technique of most use to VLSI designers is proving that a design satisfies a specification of its intended behaviour, although simulation techniques could also be used for this purpose.

The ability to verify that a design realizes the specification of its intended behaviour is vitally important to a designer, who wants absolute assurance that a design is correct before fabrication proceeds. A design is then said to be *verified* when the implementation is shown to satisfy the specification for all possible inputs using formal mathematical techniques, not just a representative subset as in the case of simulation. This use of formal verification techniques establishes design correctness with respect to the specification: if the specification incorrectly describes the required behaviour, then the implementation and the verification proof will be worthless. The use of simulation to validate a specification, as discussed above, tackles this problem. Similarly, an inaccurate description of the behaviour of the design components used in the implementation, or inadequacies in the model itself, may also render the verification invalid. The degree of confidence inspired by formal verification, as with simulation, relates closely to the power of the underlying modelling formalism and the ease and accuracy in which descriptions can be specified using it.

Returning to what we mean by formal verification, we can consider the example pictured in Fig. 4.2. Both the specification of the hardware device to be implemented and a description of its intended design are produced using the language of the particular modelling formalism. The description of the design will be constructed from the description of its components in the constructive manner outlined in Chapter 2. As discussed previously, this entails *composing*

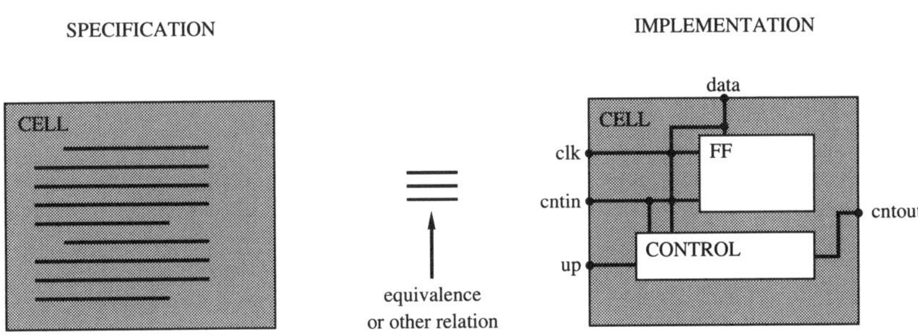

Figure 4.2 Formal verification.

component descriptions followed by the *abstraction* of internal details. Following this descriptive phase a mathematical proof would then be performed to establish whether a relationship exists between the two descriptions that make up the design step, the specification and the implementation. This may be an equivalence, or it may be some other form of satisfaction relation such that the design can be shown to *satisfy* the specification.

Verification is particularly effective in showing the functional correctness of an implementation in terms of smaller components in which its implementation is constructed. Most of the successful prototype hardware verification systems currently developed have been of this form. Examples include those of Gordon, 1988; Boyer and Moore, 1972; Barrow, 1986; and Bailey *et al.*, 1991. Other properties which do not fit into the specification versus implementation class may also be formally verified. These include particular issues such as the verification of timing properties in either temporal logic (Moszkowski, 1983; Clarke *et al.*, 1986) or a process algebra formalism (Milne, 1991).

A fundamental requirement for formal verification is that the modelling formalism directly supports mathematical reasoning. The two verification frameworks considered in detail in later chapters are verification systems based on higher-order logic and process algebra respectively. Higher-order logic allows proof to be conducted using the laws of the logic, while the operational semantics and axioms of the Circal process algebra, which provide a formal basis for the XCircal language, allow proofs to be performed on models described in XCircal.

Verification Versus Simulation

Verification may be contrasted with simulation by considering how a simple component is analysed to establish whether or not it behaves correctly when wired up to other components in all possible surrounding environments or contexts. A context is a design with some internal part of it removed; it is a circuit with some part missing.

When a simulator is used the desired output patterns for some given patterns of input stimuli are established from the specification, possibly by hand if a heterarchic or 'flat' simulator is being used, or by simulating the specification itself a hierarchical or multilevel simulator is used. This input pattern is then exercised by the simulator and the output checked to match the previously obtained projected output. If they match, the simulation process continues by selecting further input stimuli. If they fail to match, the design does not meet the specification and the process halts.

The main deficiency of simulation is revealed at this point, since the number of possible input patterns to be considered is vast for even a small number of input ports. It is not generally feasible to exercise a design under all possible input patterns, and so simulation cannot be used to ensure that a design will behave correctly when placed in any context. Like other forms of testing, simulation can be used to show the presence of errors but can never demonstrate their complete absence.

Returning to our notion of verification, if a proof can be constructed to ensure that the constructed design and the specification behave the same, that is they have the same behaviour, then we will have ensured that the design meets the specification under *all* input patterns. As with simulation, verification requires the use of a model in which to represent both the behaviour of a device and its specification. A correctness proof then establishes whether the two representations are equivalent (under some definition of equivalence) or not.

4.2 HARDWARE SIMULATION

Simulators are universally used to exhibit design behaviour: they are used by designers to experiment on a design, and to experiment on design choices before fabrication. All simulators use an underlying model, however primitive, to represent the structure and behaviour of designs, and the widely different formalisms used give us a range of simulators which can be used to validate different behavioural properties.

Simulators generate a software representation of a design using the underlying model, and exercise this representation using an algorithm which captures dynamic behavioural properties through time. The simulator applies a set of *input stimuli* to the representation, which then evolves in a way that hopefully corresponds to the behaviour of the actual circuit which would result from fabricating the design. The designer will observe the patterns of values at certain internal *nodes* and the outputs of the structural representation, and will attempt to interpret these patterns as desirable or undesirable, corresponding to a correct or incorrect design respectively.

After a design has been produced, a designer will wish to have some assurance that it satisfies his or her requirements before it is fabricated. Various types of simulators are available to the designer, but they are all used to analyse a design in an experimental way which mimics the actions of the device itself.

Circuit simulators such as SPICE (Nagel, 1975) allow the electrical properties of any design to be modelled accurately and in great detail, but this is an expensive and time-consuming process. The amount of detail needed to represent a design at this circuit level, and the computation needed to drive the simulation algorithms, make this approach infeasible for large MOS circuits. For many applications less accurate simulators which take a more abstract view of circuit behaviour are adequate for establishing whether certain functional and timing properties hold in a design.

Gate-level logic simulators involve describing a circuit in terms of interconnected model primitives which correspond to logic gates such as AND gates and inverters. These primitives generally capture logical and timing behaviour and use a number of discrete values to represent signal voltage levels. These simulators are generally based on an underlying Boolean model of gate networks which does not allow for a natural representation of the behaviour of MOS circuits.

The high-capacitance properties of MOS circuits and the use of bidirectional signals require the concept of *logic strengths* to be captured by the values in the model, with strengths dominating each other. The set of values used in a typical switch model is pictured in Fig. 4.3, where the ordering can be clearly seen. Essentially, when two values appear at a node the strong one overrides the weak one and two values that are different but of similar strength are replaced by an undefined value of the same strength. The lattice of values pictured in Fig. 4.3 can be read as having the higher values dominating the lower values.

Traditional gate-level models are unsuitable for modelling VLSI circuits at a fine level of detail, and a variety of switch-level models have been produced as a response to this situation, for example those mentioned in Bryant, 1984; Terman, 1983 and Hayes, 1986.

An interesting discussion on the underlying principles of logic simulation at the gate level is given by Hayes, 1986. The fundamental differences between representing a circuit as a network of logic gates and its implementation as a MOS design have resulted in the development of switch-level simulators for VLSI. These simulators represent a circuit at a transistor or switch level, with the model primitive being switches which are wired together via value-holding nodes.

Simulation Features

Simulators exercise a design by taking a representation or model of the design, applying stimuli to it, and then exhibiting the dynamic qualities of the design

		logical value		
		0	1	X
Strength	driven	DL	DH	DX
	weak	WL	WH	WX
	charged	CL	CH	CX

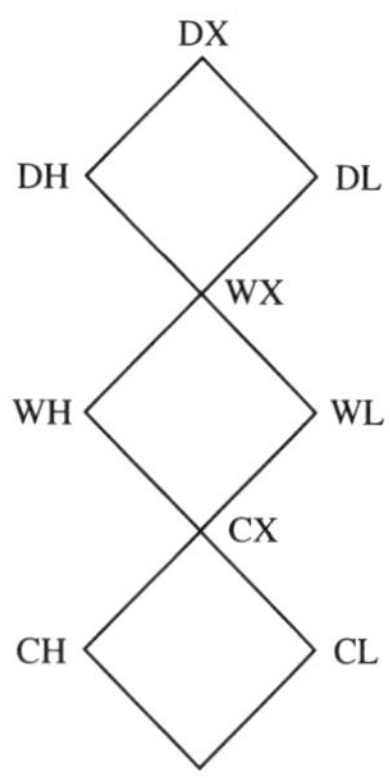

Figure 4.3 A multi-valued logic for switch-level simulation.

by the flow of information, such as sequences of 1s and 0s, through the representation. The outcome of the simulation in terms of the values output and the values retained within the circuit representation on the internal nodes should indicate whether the design functions correctly under a specific pattern of input stimuli. The stimulus patterns which a simulator applies represent the potential interaction with the environment in which the circuit may be used after it has been manufactured.

Simulators generally require all the components of a design to be reduced to a standard level of representation before the simulation can begin. Many commercial simulators available as part of a CAD package work at the switch level, one level below the gate level. Switch-level simulators require a complete design to be totally represented at the switch level, and any hierarchical or structuring information present when the design is created is lost as the design is flattened to this switch-level representation. Simulators known as hierarchical multilevel simulators allow simulations to be performed at different levels of design representation. There are considerable advantages to this, and multilevel simulation within the design process is mentioned later in this chapter.

The output generated by a simulator is used to analyse the behaviour of a device between the design and fabrication stages. This output must be interpreted carefully if the analysis is to be of any significance, and one of the problems of simulation is the large quantity of information which may be generated in a single simulation run.

The underlying concept found in all simulation systems is the ability to model circuits in a manner which allows test data, the input stimuli, to be *run* on the hardware description mirroring the way the actual device behaves. The model of a device can be thought of as a black box with named ports on the periphery. Before simulation proceeds, all input and output ports must have an initial value assigned to them; these are taken from a particular value set. A single pass of the simulator would apply a new set of stimuli to each of the input ports which are required to change. The simulation algorithm takes this input vector with one value per port, calculates the next state of the model, and produces the appropriate vector of output values. Figure 4.4 has design D with

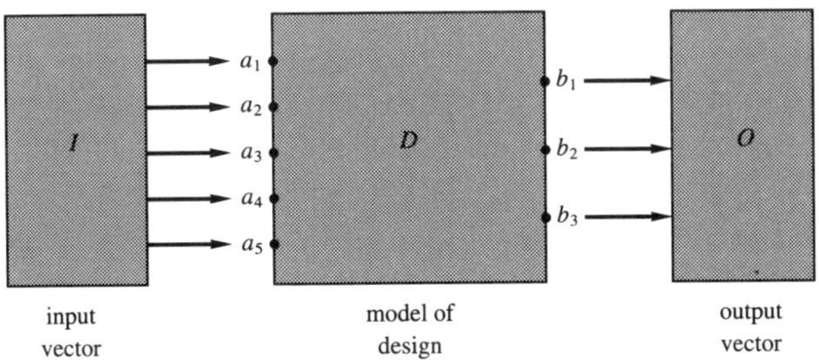

Figure 4.4 Applying simulation test patterns.

input ports a_1, a_2, a_3, a_4, a_5 and output ports b_1, b_2, b_3.

Some of the inputs may not be changed by a given input vector, and in this case it is only the inputs that do change which will cause the new output values to be generated. Not all output ports will have their value changed, however.

The design under analysis, pictured abstractly by the central box in Fig. 4.4, is not represented solely in terms of input and output ports. It will consist of a potentially very complex description in the modelling formalism, capturing the structure of the design in terms of primitive components connected by *nodes*. Before simulation proceeds, the internal nodes in the representation as well as the input and output ports must be given an initial value assignment such that the output is valid for the given internal and input values. These values constitute the *state* of the design description; when given a new input vector the description will evolve into a new state with a new output being generated, reflecting the actual behaviour of the real device.

The simulation process may be thought of as the exercising of a form of finite-state machine. A *simulation mapping* m takes a state vector $s \in S$ and an input vector $i \in I$ and produces a new state vector $s' \in S$ with output vector $o \in O$. Therefore

$$m \text{ has type } (S \times I) \rightarrow (S \times O)$$

This finite-state machine could be pictured by a state diagram with every arc labelled by an input/output pair. In a given state the arc indicates the output for a given input together with the next state. Such a finite-state machine is sometimes called a *Mealy machine.*

A simulation will only be of significance if the mapping function m calculates an input and a new state in a way which faithfully represents the behaviour of the physical device. The definition of m as a function or simulation algorithm is crucial to the whole simulation process; deciding on a modelling framework and defining m over the framework are the two main tasks awaiting the creator of a new simulator.

Switch-level Simulation

The underlying model used for switch-level simulation is a network of switches with nodes between them. The representation of a design in a switch-level model may be obtained in one of two ways.

1. A technique called *circuit extraction* is used to obtain a switch-level circuit representation from a mask or layout description. The MOSSIM (Bryant, 1984) and RSIM (Terman, 1983) simulators were developed for use in low-level design systems where designs were imagined to be produced graphically, say using a sticks design system (Williams, 1978).
2. Alternatively, a design language description of the design may be directly

translated into the switch-level representation. The CSA logic of Hayes (1982) can be thought of as a non-hierarchical design language which directly generates a switch-level representation. The Solo Design System (European Silicon Structures, 1990) is another example which automatically generates a switch-level representation of a design specified in the MODEL language presented in Chapter 2. The behavioural features of VHDL have also been chosen with an underlying simulation model in mind, though in this case a more general model involving the occurrence of events in a particular time-frame is used. In fact, all commercial computer-aided design vendors offer switch-level simulators based around the concepts outlined here, as part of their integrated-circuit design systems.

Whether a switch-level description is obtained by translating a language description of a design or is extracted from layout, it will have the following common features. Transistors are generally represented as switches; gates and larger components are represented by collections of switches; and the interconnecting signal lines are represented by nodes, possibly named nodes.

Switches connect input nodes to output nodes when on, and their behaviour is expressed as a change in output value when the gate node switches on. A switch is modelled dynamically, since an event on the gate causes an event on the output node; an event is a change in the value on a node. A complete device has its behaviour expressed by a composition of the individual switch functions, and its state is defined by the set of values allocated to the nodes.

This event-based switch model has input events or stimuli applied to it causing node values to change throughout the node network, with changes to the outputs possibly also occurring. A simple three-switch network is pictured in Fig. 4.5, where the n_i are nodes and s_i are switches.

The main task of a switch-level simulator is to calculate the new values at nodes throughout the network which result from applying input stimuli. Thus

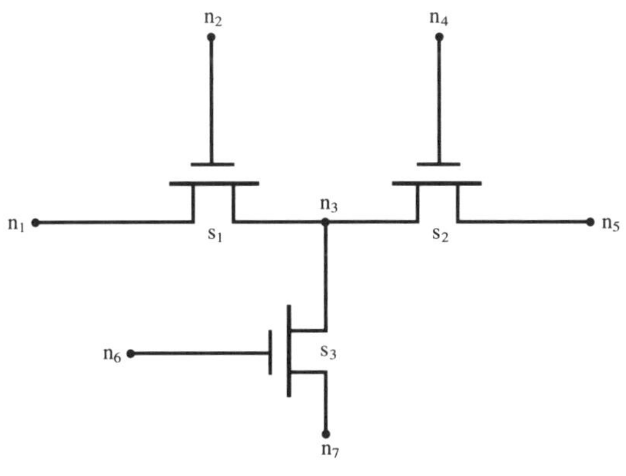

Figure 4.5 Example of a three-switch network.

a new state, a set of node values, is calculated from the current state and the input events. The algorithms used by switch-level simulators to calculate node values are inherently sophisticated, since they must attempt to model the complex interactions which occur due to the underlying electrical behaviour of MOS devices. Also complicating the issue is the practical problem of dealing with large circuits represented using a vast number of nodes. If a large value domain is used to aid the representation of physical properties such as resistance and capacitance in as realistic a manner as possible, then the complexity of node calculation may also increase; a typical value domain was pictured in Fig. 4.3. A simpler, coarser approximation of the physical behaviour often allows the resulting node values and output values to be calculated more easily. This illustrates the modelling dilemma where increased representational accuracy must be traded off against increased notational and manipulative complexity. This dilemma is faced in the design of both simulation and verification tools.

Stimuli Patterns

So far we have considered simulation in terms of a single simulation step. A simple input vector is given to an initialized switch-level model of a circuit and the simulation algorithm, the simulation function, causes an output vector and a new state to result.

The designer is interested in giving a *pattern* of input stimuli to an internal device representation and observing the output patterns which the simulator produces. Simulation is then considered to be a series of Mealey machine steps rather than just one. One of the most common user interfaces to a simulator is in terms of waveforms represented graphically, and a set of input waveforms represents sequences of changes to the input ports through time. An event-driven simulator will take these waveforms and treat them as patterns of input stimuli, and for every point in time will then calculate a new state and an output vector. This new state is then used with the input vector at the next time instance to calculate a further state and output vector, and so on. Figure 4.6 illustrates the sequence of state and output vectors which result from applying a sequence or pattern of input stimuli.

In Fig. 4.7 a typical set of waveforms is represented, with `r` and `s` denoting input ports and `q` and $\bar{\texttt{q}}$ denoting output ports. Input stimuli are only accepted at discrete time instants, and we assume that the assignment of values to nodes stabilizes before a further simulation step is made.

Continuously changing time is commonly represented by the values occurring at discrete sampling points in time, as in Fig. 4.7. Drawing a line vertically through the waveforms in Fig. 4.7 at every timing point gives the current input and output vectors. The output vector will generally relate to, or be caused by, a previous input vector and not the current one; that is because of propagation delays. The diagram in Fig. 4.6 assumes that the output for a given simulation step will appear before the next simulation step is made. However, this Mealey

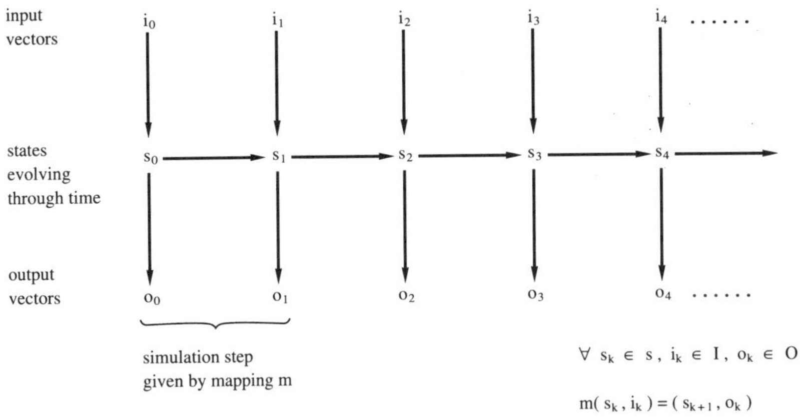

Figure 4.6 Sequence of state and output vectors.

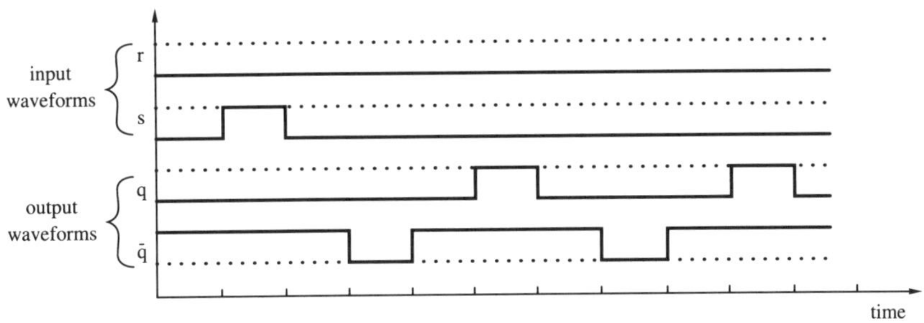

Figure 4.7 Simulation of spike causing oscillation in flip-flop.

machine view of the simulation process is simpler than what actually happens in commercial simulators.

Simulation Within the Design Cycle

Simulators are universally used for analysing integrated circuit behaviour, with the majority of simulators requiring the design process to have progressed to a detailed, low-level of design before simulation. This level of design may be the gate level, but more usually it is at the transistor level as with switch-level simulation. Any structural information that was present as a design evolved is lost, and a completely *flat* design representation is used by the simulator. The switch-level simulators of the previous section illustrate this, while a hierarchical design expressed in a specification language such as VHDL will lose this hierarchy when it is represented as a network of switches and nodes.

While this approach to simulation does allow accurate analysis of the behaviour of an integrated circuit, it also requires that the circuit is completely designed before this analysis can take place. If we imagine that a design is produced interactively in a number of steps, both top-down and bottom-up, then design errors could have been introduced at every step. If an error had been introduced at an initial top-down step, then this error would not manifest itself until the design had been completed at the transistor level and a simulation performed. The design effort following the point where the error was introduced is usually wasted; all design steps following the one which introduced the error have to be retraced. It is also helpful to a designer to have analytical feedback as early as possible during the design process. For these reasons it is therefore important to be able to perform simulation and also formal verification *during* the design cycle, rather than wait until a design is complete.

If a design is created using a top-down design methodology, there are various design levels: from the architectural level down to the transistor level. At every design step the opportunity exists to simulate the design and determine whether the projected device will behave as required. If the result of the simulation is satisfactory, the designer proceeds to the next level of design; if not, redesign at the current or higher levels is required. Since the design proceeds iteratively, with backtracking to correct design errors, the complete design process may be thought of as a cycle, passing between the design levels until analysis by simulation determines that the final design at the lowest level has been validated. A top-down design is illustrated in Fig. 4.8.

The main levels of design which may require to be simulated are as follows:

- **Software level** Software and the microcode of a proposed machine are developed using a model which allows both hardware and software to be represented. The machine is then simulated as a 'black box'. As a model is required to represent behaviour, hardware and software behaviour should be equally capable of representation. Designs may also be expressed by algorithms where very little structural information is available.
- **Architecture level** The initial architecture of the device will be represented and analysed by simulation.
- **Register-transfer level** A register-transfer level of design involving the control structure and data path should be capable of representation and simulation.
- **Logic level** The design will have reached the gate level, and functional behaviour will be determined in terms of gate behaviour.
- **Switch/transistor level** Electrical properties are approximated to allow MOS behaviour to be analysed, and detailed timing characteristics can also be obtained. Simulation at a lower transistor level will involve a circuit simulator such as SPICE, and is outwith the realms of a multilevel simulator.

Multilevel simulators differ from single-level simulators in their use of a behavioural description language such as VHDL. The interface to this simulator will be in terms of a description language which will allow the user to specify

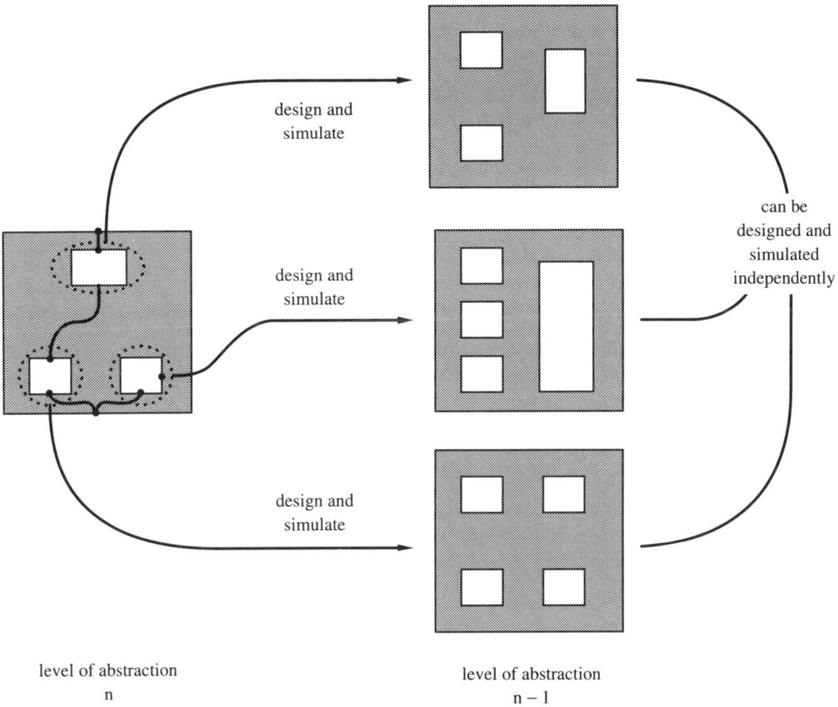

Figure 4.8 Example of a top-down design.

behavioural properties, as well as the structural properties of components, to a given level of abstraction. The language will allow components to be described, with a description at one level becoming the specification to be validated by simulation at the next lower level of design. The ability to express behaviour in an appropriate design language is therefore of paramount importance to a multilevel simulator.

Specification and Simulation

At the highest level of design the language will be used to describe the overall behaviour of the complete system by writing a specification of the system and then simulating it. This allows the relationship of input and output stimuli to be established for the desired behaviour specified by the designer.

The *black box* is then implemented at the next lower level of design, with the structure of the design being expressed as an interconnection of component parts or as parts having a richer and more detailed behaviour. Each of the parts must have its behaviour specified by the designer, and this behaviour is used by the simulator to simulate the implementation using the same stimuli as applied to the higher-level specification simulation. For a representative set of input stimuli, if there is a match between the output of the two simulation runs at the different levels of abstraction, we have established design correctness across that design step. If the results differ, then the design does not fully implement the specification and a redesign is necessary.

This validation of a single design step using a multilevel simulator is pictured in Fig. 4.9. Multilevel simulation will proceed hand-in-hand with the design process, and every design step will be validated by a simulation. Eventually a level of design is reached where system-provided basic building blocks are used exclusively to represent the design; their behaviour is obtained from the system library, and is used to validate this final design step. Behaviour is therefore introduced in two distinct ways. The designer expressed the design and its implementation at different levels of abstraction, and the system introduced the behaviour of primitive components at the lowest level of design. Primitive components can be at a gate or transistor level of representation, and their behaviour, while expressed using the same behaviour language as used by

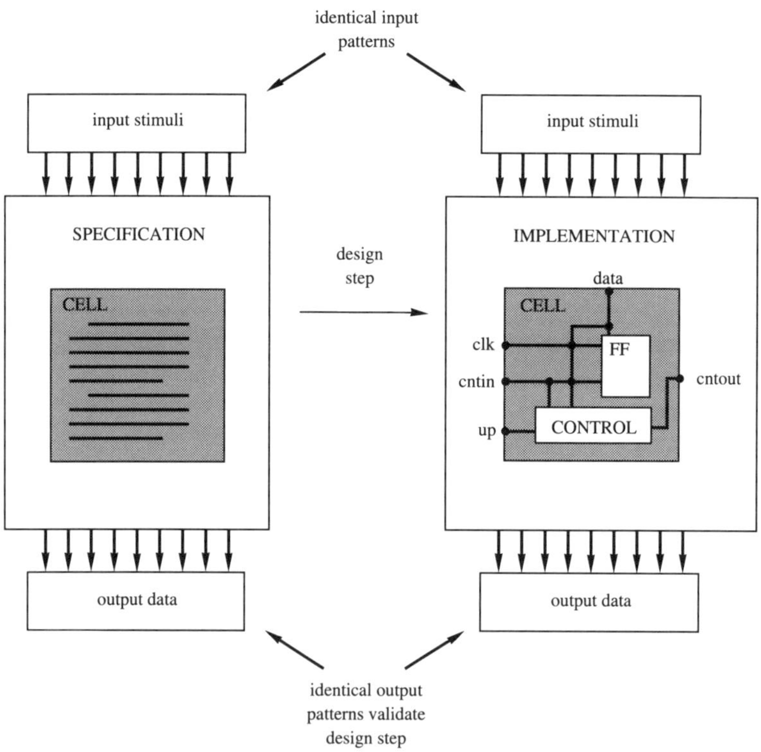

Figure 4.9 Validation using a multilevel simulator.

the designer, will be obtained by experimentation on the layout which corresponds to these components, possibly using a circuit simulator such as SPICE (Nagel, 1975).

This approach not only allows design errors to be discovered close to where they are introduced in the design cycle, it also partitions the simulation task. Rather than simulate a complete design it allows parts of a design to be simulated independently and the 'divide-and-conquer' philosophy is again used to structure the design and validation tasks.

If a design step can be validated as correct, then the components which make up the implementation are taken as the specifications for the next level of design. They must then be implemented and the implementation validated. The design and simulation of the components can be performed independently, so structuring the design and validation task and allowing different design groups to tackle their independent tasks concurrently with greatly improved design productivity. As the behaviour of a component which implements a correct design step exists, this behaviour together with structural or physical design attributes such as port orientation or width is all the information required to implement the component at the next lowest level of design.

When a circuit is simulated at the architectural level, for instance, every single event at this level of behavioural abstraction may represent a large number of equivalent switch-level events. The initial simulations conducted during the top-down design process will be used to validate the high-level design, and this will occur several times faster than a more detailed logic or switch-level simulation. This finer level of simulation will be held back until the design has evolved further. This is a further convincing argument for developing a multilevel simulator as part of a design system rather than relying on a single, low-level simulator.

To simulate a design at various levels of abstraction requires the use of a single description language which permits the behaviour of a design to be expressed at different levels of abstraction. The design language will have language features which allow behaviour to be naturally and accurately described. The VHDL language permits behaviour to be expressed for the reasons explained here, in contrast to purely structural languages such as MODEL.

Multilevel simulation captures the dynamic properties of behaviour using more than just the behavioural descriptions created in the design language. A *simulation algorithm* takes these descriptions and exercises them with input stimuli to mimic the behaviour of the device represented by the design. This dynamic property of behaviour is captured both by the language and the algorithm which implements or *animates* the behavioural descriptions. The introduction of behavioural features into a design language should therefore not be considered in isolation from the development of the simulator itself, which is in fact the strategy followed in the development of VHDL.

4.3 FORMAL VERIFICATION

Earlier in this chapter verification was defined as the process by which the correctness of a hardware component is established by formal mathematical proof techniques. This requires the presence of a modelling formalism which not only supports the descriptive process but also supports the task of verification. Two classes of properties require verification and both should be supported by the formalism; one involves verifying the *total* behaviour of the hardware device at some level of abstraction, while the other involves verifying that a particular *localized* property holds.

A total verification entails proving that a design is a faithful implementation of a specification, in other words that the design satisfies a specification of its intended behaviour. The second type of property requiring verification is more localized and concentrates on isolating a particular aspect of a design which needs to be formally verified. An example of this latter form of verification would be a proof which determines that a section of combinational logic always satisfies a minimum time bound, so allowing a given system clocking scheme to be used with impunity.

The requirements of total verification and the problems encountered when attempting to perform a rigorous simulation, as mentioned previously, lead to consideration of formal, mathematical techniques for determining design correctness. For localized properties requiring validation, simulation is the traditional, experimental technique adopted, although more rigorous formal verification techniques also have a central role to play at this level of validation. The consequences of being able to formally verify that a design meets its specification has such significance that we concentrate primarily on this form of verification using both the HOL and Circal formalisms. We also demonstrate how particular localized properties such as timing requirements may be described and verified in isolation from other behavioural or functional features. This use of formal verification techniques complements the more usual specification/implementation form of proof.

Specification and Implementation Equivalence

As mentioned above, one of the properties which we wish to establish formally is whether a design meets its specification. This property is of crucial importance to a designer who wishes to have an assurance that a design is correct before fabrication proceeds. A design could be modelled in its totality, completely representing every part of the design, and the resulting description might be notationally very complex. After abstracting away from certain internal details to be clarified later, a proof would be constructed to determine whether the complete design meets its specification.

This approach to establishing design correctness requires that the underlying modelling framework is used to describe both the implementation of the design and its intended, specified behaviour. Proof techniques which are developed from fundamental properties of the model are then used to establish the relationship between the two descriptions. This relationship may be complete in that the two descriptions have equivalent behaviour, as pictured in Fig. 4.2, or it may be sufficient to show that a weaker relationship holds.

In Chapters 5 and 6 we consider two of the most developed formal verification frameworks, those based on the HOL and the Circal formalisms. In each case we use a number of increasingly complex examples to illustrate the significant features of each approach, with verification using HOL being presented in Chapter 6 and verification within Circal being illustrated in Chapter 8. Before considering these approaches to hardware verification in detail we isolate features common to both of them. This commonality arises from a shared philosophy regarding hardware modelling and the verification process itself.

The Verification Process

The task of formally verifying that a constructed system correctly implements its specification, as pictured in Fig. 4.2, requires the following three steps:

1. A specification, independent of implementation details, is given in the description language of the formalism, the HOL or XCircal language for instance. This describes the intended behaviour of the complete system at a given level of abstraction.
2. The implementation has its behaviour constructed at a lower, more detailed level of abstraction than the specification. This behaviour is produced *constructively* from component descriptions using the appropriate composition construct, either the logical conjunction operation in HOL or the XCircal composition operator. Abstraction is then used to internalize parts of the constructed behaviour and produce a more abstract description at the same level of representation, or abstraction, as that of the specification. The externally visible *structure* of the design implementation will then match that of the design specification. This approach, across adjacent levels of abstraction, attacks the descriptive complexity problem to some extent since the implementation components will be of a lower level of abstraction than the specification. These components can then be separately verified by a subsequent verification cycle as illustrated in Fig. 4.10.
3. A proof is then constructed to establish whether the implemented design and its specification have the same behaviour, that is, that the design meets its specification. Equivalence between behavioural expressions is a property which requires to be made explicit to allow a proof to be performed. The distinct notions of equivalence used by HOL and XCircal are given in later chapters.

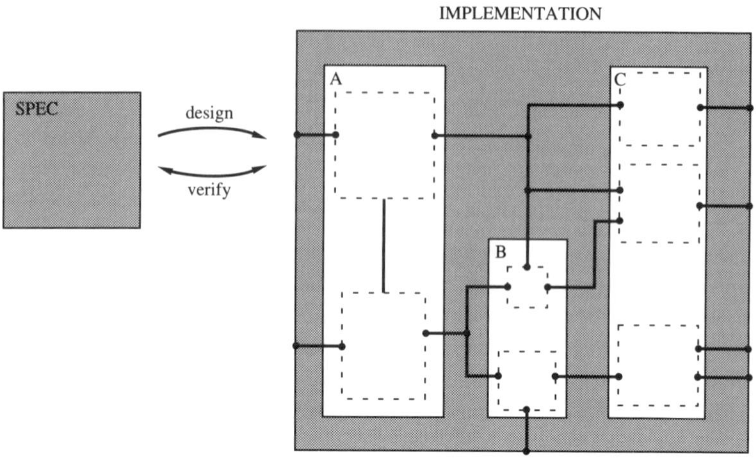

Figure 4.10 Design and verification.

4.4 VALIDATION AND DESIGN

In Chapter 1 we briefly introduced the concept of a *design step*, a self-contained part of the complete design process, and it is useful at this stage to consider how validation fits into the design process. We identify two approaches; validation after the design is completed or during the design process itself.

Post-design Validation

Validation tools and techniques are usually applied after much of the design has been completed. Simulators are frequently used to examine complete designs to investigate the presence, and hopefully the absence, of design errors. This post-design approach has two consequences; large, monolithic simulations have to be conducted, and if errors are found, a costly redesign effort is required. In fact the complexity of simulating completed VLSI designs is such that specialist simulation techniques and specialist simulation hardware have been introduced by necessity as designs have been scaled up from SSI through MSI to VLSI.

As an example of specialist simulation techniques mentioned previously, switch-level models have been introduced to capture VLSI behaviour in a tractable yet accurate way. Simulators based on such models, such as MOSSIM (Bryant, 1984), aim to mimic VLSI properties without the level of detail of SPICE (Nagel, 1975) which renders large-scale simulation infeasible.

Specialist computer hardware may also be produced to run particular simulation algorithms on particular behavioural models at exceptionally high speeds. This aids the design analysis process in that a large class of previously infeasible designs may now be investigated, but the target is always moving; new and even larger complete designs still remain beyond the scope of this specialist hardware. Examples of machines constructed as *simulation engines* are those produced by ZYCAD and the IBM Yorktown Simulation Engine (Pfister, 1982; Denneau, 1982).

Problems also arise in the analysis of a complete design in its totality when we are required to analyse the outcome of the validation. In the case of simulation, vast amounts of output information result from the application of the test patterns to the design model using the simulation algorithm. This information must then be interpreted to discover whether the design functions correctly, given the test data. If errors are caused by components deep inside the design, it may prove difficult to associate detectable erroneous output with the component modules which introduce it. Similarly, the result of a verification proof such as the equivalence in Fig. 4.2 may simply be of the form 'false'. This then gives the designer no information as to *why* the design fails to match the specification, or *which part* of the design caused the mismatch with the specification.

One of the uses of validation, in addition to determining whether a complete design is correct or not, is as a designer's aid. Validation tools and techniques can be used throughout the design process to analyse partially completed designs to give feedback about the consequences of a given design decision. This permits an iterative design and validation methodology, which is an improvement on the monolithic validation approach pictured in Fig. 4.2. This integrated design and validation technique capitalizes on any hierarchical structure present in the design. The correctness of the completed design can then be established by constructing increasingly larger design modules from previously validated components. This bottom-up approach to design and validation then partitions both the design and the validation tasks. Similarly, a top-down design methodology can also be used to partition the validation process by generating submodules which can then be validated independently. Such methodological approaches remove many of the problems associated with post-design validation.

Integrating Design and Validation

Another validation methodology was discussed in Sec. 4.2 as it relates to simulation; perhaps *the* best way of validating design is to perform the analysis as the design evolves. Working top-down from a high-level, abstract specification, the design procedure passes down step-wise through various representation levels until a level is reached which contains previously designed 'building blocks'. At every design step, validation is performed to establish that the design meets the specification. If it does, the design process proceeds with the design at one level becoming the specification to be implemented at the next lower level of design. If a design does not meet its specification a redesign is necessary, with the possibility existing that it may not be possible to produce a design to implement the given specification. In this case redesign must occur further up the design hierarchy.

Figure 4.10 shows a design in which the structure of the right-hand side, the implementation, is partitioned in a hierarchical way. The equivalence proof used to formally verify the partially completed design then entails showing that the behaviour which results from the interaction of the three major black-box modules A, B and C of the implementation satisfies that described by the specification. If the behaviour of the implementation is equivalent to that of the specification, then we can pass on to the next stage where each of these modules is independently designed and their implementations are verified. If the initial implementation is not equivalent to the specification, then at least one of the A, B or C modules must have its behaviour redescribed before repeating the validation step and progressing to the next level, the design and verification of the individual modules.

Integrating design and verification is a goal that is worth striving for, and is a central theme of this book. Its advantage is that verification and design proceed hand-in-hand, with erroneous design decisions being discovered as soon as they are made rather than waiting until the complete design has been produced, with the attendant high redesign costs of post-design verification. This hierarchical verification also helps keep the inherent notational complexity involved in describing VLSI devices under some sort of control, with separate parts of a design being designed and validated independently of the others. Figure 4.11 illustrates how verification and design can be performed using this hierarchical methodology.

While the example in Fig. 4.11 illustrates the use of formal verification in this integrated design and validation scenario, the validation step can equally well be performed using simulation as discussed in Sec. 4.2.

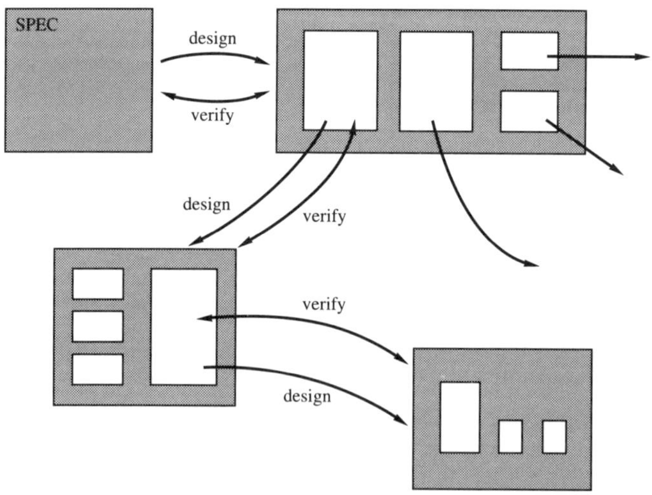

Figure 4.11 Hierarchical methodology.

Specification in the Validation Process

To obtain a high degree of confidence in the correctness of a design when it is eventually fabricated, a designer can check each step of the design process accurately using the various alternative validation techniques. Common to all such analytical techniques, including simulation and verification as well as specialist tools and techniques such as timing analysers (Hitchcock, 1982), is the ability to *specify* the properties requiring validation. In Chapter 1 we emphasized the importance of specification from a design and description perspective; here we can consider its role in the validation process.

Properties requiring validation must be *specified.* These properties can range from the complete intended behaviour which we wish an implementation to satisfy, as in the top-down hierarchical design and validation strategy described in the previous section, to the description of a particular feature which we require of a design, such as the arrival time of signals at given ports.

In a level-by-level design and validation methodology as proposed above, the specification which we require an implementation to achieve may be *partial.* In this case only certain properties of the intended design are of interest and require validation, and it is only this *partial specification* which the validation process must show to be correctly implemented by the lower-level design.

Whether a specification is total or partial, at each level of design the specification details the intended behavioural properties required. The components which implement this specification are described, and the behaviour of the implementation at this level of description is then obtained; by conjunction and existential quantification in HOL (Chapter 5) and by the composition and abstraction operators in Circal (Chapter 7), for example. In both cases the behaviour of the implementation is obtained by construction then abstraction. The design at the lower level of abstraction is a correct implementation of the specification at the higher level, if the behaviour of the implementation satisfies the specified properties.

As mentioned previously, even after a design step such as that in Fig. 4.9 has been validated we do not have a complete guarantee that the design will work correctly when physically realized. We know that if simulation techniques have been adopted it is possible for some particular design flaw to have slipped through because of the incompleteness of simulation. Also, the fabrication process itself may have introduced functional errors which have escaped post-fabrication testing. Finally, even if fabrication errors have not been introduced and formal verification techniques have been used to avoid the problems inherent in simulation, the correctness of the design is only as good as the specification. If the specification is incorrect and captures features which we do not really wish to hold, then a successful validation exercise only shows that the design satisfies the incorrect specification—a worthless result.

Specification has a pivotal role to play in an integrated design and validation methodology. There is therefore a pressing need to have confidence in the descriptive accuracy of the individual specifications used. This can be achieved by hierarchically constructing a specification using a composition operator, in the same way that design descriptions are created, or by simulating the specification itself, or by a combination of the two approaches.

4.5 BEHAVIOURAL DESCRIPTION LANGUAGES AND DESIGN VALIDATION

As stated above, design validation is the most significant reason for requiring a design language to have behavioural description capabilities. Simulation is the almost universal approach to this task at present, and will continue to be so for some time; this is evidenced by the creation of VHDL, where behavioural language features centre around an implied situation model. Verification by formal mathematical proof is a preferable alternative because it can guarantee that a circuit performs correctly under *all* patterns of inputs and internal states. This could only otherwise be done by exhaustive simulation, an impractical technique because of the vast numbers of possible inputs and states that must be checked.

Whether validation is performed by simulation or formal mathematical proof, very similar arguments apply to the need for languages to describe circuit behaviour. The language may differ in detail, depending on which validation technique is used, but the reasons for requiring a behavioural language are similar.

Even current simulation techniques require a formal description of behaviour, although this is usually done as part of the simulator program code rather than in a description language. For example, a switch-level simulator as discussed earlier in this chapter must have encoded in it some notion of the behaviour of various primitives such as pass transistors, pull-ups, etc. In order for such a simulator to simulate the behaviour of a complete circuit it must build up the behaviour from the behaviour of primitives, the latter being expressed in a rigorous way that the simulator 'understands'. While present simulators do not generally use a linguistic representation of this low-level switch behaviour, such an approach would have at least one decided advantage: the task of modifying the behaviour of primitives (e.g. for a change of manufacturing process) would become a simple task, not involving the modification of program code.

A second important role for behavioural description languages in design validation is their use at a much higher level of representation, for example with an event-based simulator such as those produced for VHDL. Consider how designs evolve at present, where the intended behaviour of a complete system is normally only specified informally. When it comes to validating the attempted implementation, the simulator output must be compared with this informal specification of the required behaviour. If the intended behaviour of the system is specified formally in such a way that it can be simulated, then the task of comparing implementation with specification becomes easier and more accurate, which is crucial since confidence in the validation process is necessary if the results are to have any significance.

So far the value of being able to describe behaviour formally at a high level of abstraction (system level) and a low level (e.g. switch level, circuit level) has been demonstrated, but it remains to be shown that this ability is necessary at *all* levels of abstraction. We will do this by considering a simple design and validation example and, in the remainder of the book, extend the principle to larger designs.

An exercise in Integrated Design and Validation

Our outline example is the bidirectional eight-bit counter pictured in Fig. 4.12. At the highest level it is a box with two inputs, a clock `clk` and direction control up, and eight outputs for the stored value (`data(0), . . . , data(7)`). If `up` is set the counter should increment its stored value on every rising edge of the clock; otherwise it should decrement on every rising edge of the clock.

The design proceeds down through three levels of abstraction until primitive components, in this case gates, are reached (Fig. 4.13(c)). These components may exist in a library, having been designed previously with a leaf cell editor. A conventional approach, taken by switch-level simulators, would make use of a simulator which is only able to model the behaviour of fully designed primitive components. Thus the designer is unable to simulate the design until he reaches the lowest level of design, where all hierarchical design information has been lost. This means that if his first decision, to build the counter from eight identical cells (Fig. 4.13(a)), was incorrect, then all the subsequent effort of designing the cells and the flip-flops was wasted. Extending this principle to the problems facing the designer of a large chip demonstrates the unsatisfactory nature of monolithic simulation. In such a design there may be many levels of hierarchy, and the amount of effort required to carry out the design down to the gate level or lower may be measured in person-years. Thus a mistake made at a high level in the hierarchy could be very costly.

A related problem of monolithic simulation is that, on discovering an error, the designer may not be able to ascertain immediately where it was made. The only information obtained by the simulation is whether or not the system performs its intended function. This problem can be overcome by 'bottom-up' simulation. In our example the designer would simulate first the flip-flop and

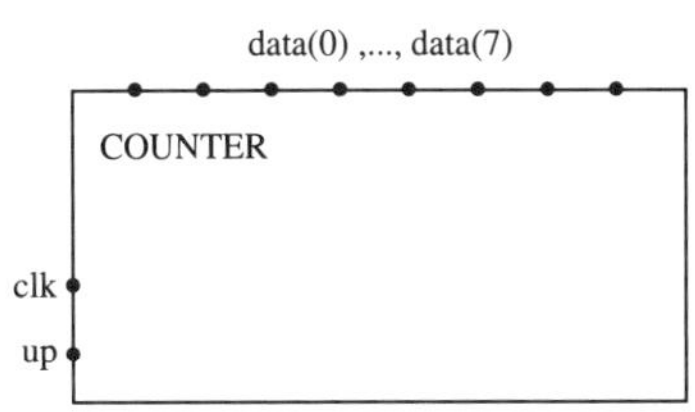

Figure 4.12 Counter: top-level representation.

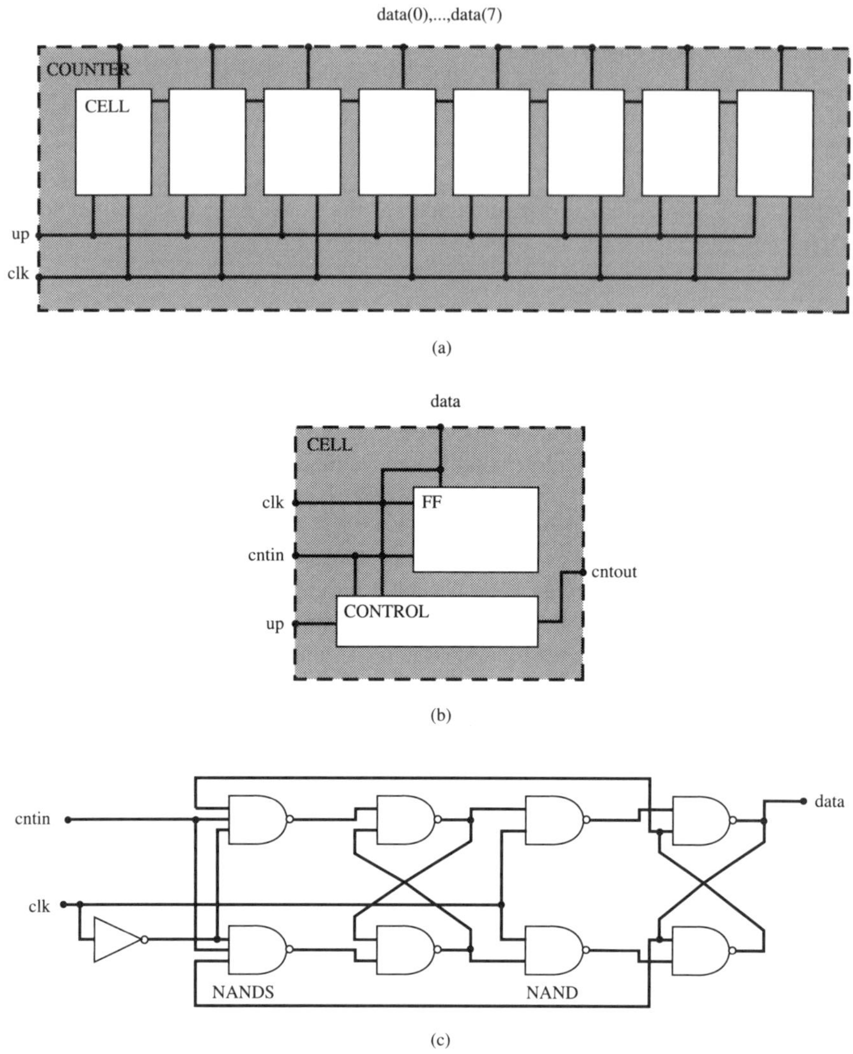

Figure 4.13 Implementation of counter at different levels of design hierarchy. (a) Second level. (b) Third level. (c) Lowest level.

the control gates to establish whether they perform as required, then the cell, then the whole counter. Thus the incorrectly designed part or erroneous design decision could be isolated.

An entirely preferable approach to the design and validation technique presented above, where validation follows the design, would be one where mistakes could be discovered as soon as they were made and where a designer could even experiment with different high-level design choices, validating each of them without having to carry the design right through to the level of primitive components. Such an integrated design and validation cycle could be achieved with the use of a behavioural description language such as VHDL and a simulator which accepts such a language as input, and such a system will now be described.

The designer begins by specifying the desired behaviour of the system using the design language. The circuit is then partitioned into a number of smaller blocks, the eight cells of Fig. 4.13(a) in our example, and the behaviour of each of these is also specified in the language. Then the top-level description of the system is simulated, the system described as the composition of smaller components is simulated, and the results of the two simulations are compared. If they do not agree, then a mistake has been made, either in the partitioning or in the behavioural specification of one of the components. Thus in our example if the behaviour of the cell were incorrectly specified there would now be no need to go on and design an incorrect cell; the mistake would be detected as soon as it was made.

The design and validation process continues in a similar way at the next level down in the hierarchy, now treating each smaller component as a complete system. This procedure is repeated at every level in the hierarchy until the lowest level of primitive components is reached. In our example the next step would be to describe the behaviour of the flip-flop and the control gates and simulate them, comparing the results with those obtained by simulating the cell. A pictorial representation of the integrated design and validation process, using three levels of hierarchy, is shown in Fig. 4.14.

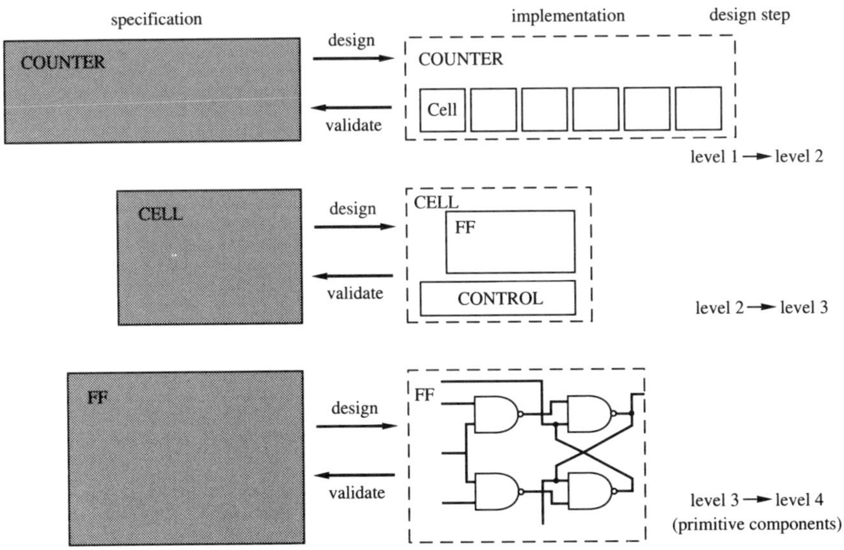

Figure 4.14 Integrated design and validation.

We have mainly discussed *simulation* as the validation tool because of its prevalence over the more formal, mathematical methods. The design and validation process described above could also readily be applied to formal verification methods such as those discussed in the subsequent chapters.

This design approach illustrates not only the need to be able to describe *behaviour* at all levels of abstraction but also the need for a formal way of representing hierarchical *structure*, as presented in Chapter 2.

CHAPTER

FIVE

MODELLING HARDWARE IN HIGHER-ORDER LOGIC

Rather than create a new formalism in which to describe and analyse hardware behaviour such as the Circal process algebra and the associated XCircal hardware description language, an alternative approach is to use an existing descriptive framework. Higher-order logic is a type theory developed as a foundation of mathematics (Hatcher, 1982), which has recently been shown to be a powerful language in which to describe hardware (Hanna and Daeche, 1985; Gordon and Melham, 1993). The significance of this approach to hardware modelling is due not just to the descriptive qualities of the language of higher-order logic, but also to its ability to support formal reasoning using the *inference rules* of the model. In this chapter we present both the descriptive features of higher-order logic and its use for formal hardware verification.

The formulation of higher-order logic which is used to illustrate this approach is HOL, a language due to Gordon (see Gordon and Melham, 1993). The principal concept underlying higher-order logic in general, and HOL in particular, is the use of a *predicate* to represent the behaviour of a hardware component. Predicates are functions which return the result `true` or `false`. A predicate `Px` represents the fact that `x` has property `P`; that is, `x` satisfies property `P` is true. Similarly a predicate `R(x,y)` with two arguments can be used to indicate that some relationship `R` exists between `x` and `y`; that is, `x` and `y` satisfy property `R`. More generally, a predicate could take any fixed number of arguments, as in $R(x_1, x_2, \ldots, x_n)$.

Higher-order logic uses the language, or notation, of predicate calculus (Hatcher, 1982). As well as using predicates as the descriptive primitive, the *logical operators* $\neg$, $\wedge$, $\vee$, $\supset$ and $=$ are used to construct descriptions from them. These symbols denote the usual logical operations of negation, conjunction (and-ing), disjunction (or-ing), implication and equality.

The *conditional statement* 'if c is true then t_1 else t_2' is described using a HOL term of the form $(c \Rightarrow t_1/t_2)$. *Function composition* is denoted by $f \circ g$ where the functions f and g are applied such that $f \circ g(x) = f(g(x))$.

Two forms of variable quantification are used; the *universal quantifier* ∀ and the *existential quantifier* ∃. The universal quantifier is used to capture the fact that a property holds for *every* variable it is applied to; ∀x.Px means that property or predicate P holds for every value of x. The existential quantifier captures the fact that a predicate holds for just *some*, but at least one, of the variables it is applied to; ∃x.Px means that property P holds for some values of variable x. Note the use of the abbreviations ∀xy.P(x,y) for ∀x.∀y.P(x,y) and ∃xy.P(x,y) for ∃x.∃ y.P(x,y).

Higher-order logic differs from first-order logic, such as the propositional calculus (Hatcher, 1982) in the ability of its predicates to take functions and predicates as arguments and to return them as results. That is, variables can range over functions and predicates as well as the usual data types. Of particular importance to modelling hardware behaviour is the use of predicates whose arguments are *functions over time*. In HOL the continuous time axis is approximated by a series of discrete steps leading from one point in time to another. Predicates are then used to define the relationship which must exist between the current and past values on the ports of a device using functions which map from integer points in time to port values.

In higher-order logic every logic term has a *type*; it is a *typed logic*. Primitive types include the natural numbers *num*, the Boolean values *bool* and strings such as 'i' and 'string'. *Type operators* are used to construct types from simpler types; for example the mapping function → taking natural numbers to Booleans is denoted by num → bool. Type information is usually not specified explicitly but is derived from the type of the primitive constructs from which HOL terms are constructed using the logical operators, functions and quantifiers presented above.

5.1 DESCRIBING BEHAVIOUR IN HOL

In HOL, hardware components have their behaviour described by predicates which capture the relationship between values which appear on their *external ports*. The component called CELL in Fig. 5.1 has external ports a, b, c and d through which it interacts with other components.

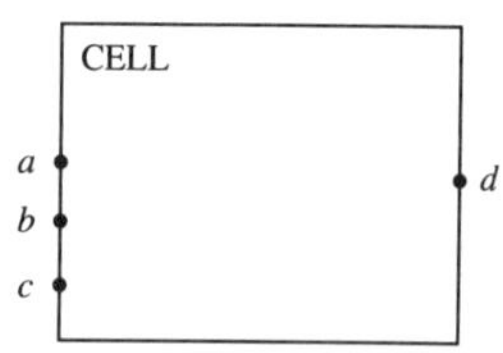

Figure 5.1 CELL structure.

The behaviour of CELL is given by a predicate, also called CELL, which has four arguments a,b,c, and d. CELL(a,b,c,d) is *true* only when the combination of values assigned to the variables is exactly those which we intend to appear on the respective ports of the component.

For example, a very simple two-port component called INV may always have the Boolean values on its ports as inverses of each other. For the component pictured in Fig. 5.2, its behaviour may be specified in HOL by the predicate INV, where

$$\mathtt{INV(a,b)} = \mathtt{a} = \neg\,\mathtt{b}$$

INV has type: $(\mathtt{bool} \times \mathtt{bool}) \rightarrow \mathtt{bool}$

and the predicate is true if and only if a and b are logical inverses. This is the case when the values (0,1) and (1,0) appear on the two ports of the INV component of Fig. 5.2.

Components usually have a behaviour that depends on time, with different values appearing on ports with different relationships between them at different points in time. This behaviour, which differs from the *time-independent* behaviour of the above INV component, can be described by predicates whose arguments are functions from discrete time, given as a natural number, to some data value.

As an example of this consider a component whose output value is identical to its input but appears some period of time later. If we assume that this delay consists of one unit of our natural number measurement of time then this delay component DEL can be defined by:

$$\vdash_{def} \mathtt{DEL(a,b)} = \forall\, \mathtt{t.b(t+1)} = \mathtt{a(t)}$$

In this example a and b are functions which correspond to the ports also named a and b, with the assumption that a is an input port and b is an output port. These functions map from natural numbers which denote points in time to values, such as Boolean values if DEL represents the behaviour of a unit delay register cell. The *definition* of behaviour DEL(a,b) using the equality operator = is such that this *relation* holds only if for all values of t (that is, at all points in time) the value of b at time t+1 equals the value of a at time t. Hence the value on port b equals that on port a one time unit later.

The 'turnstyle' symbol $\vdash$ is used in higher-order logic to indicate a fact that is true. In this case we have a definition, indicated by $\vdash_{def}$, binding the predicate identifier DEL to the predicate itself.

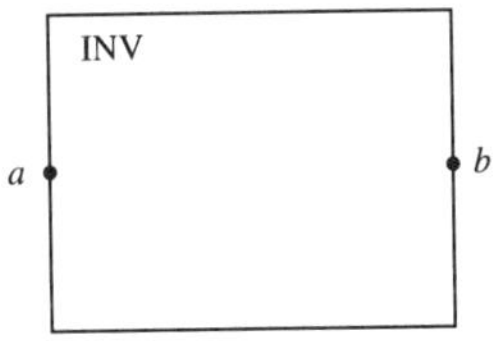

Figure 5.2 Inverter structure.

The functions which map from time to values can be thought of as *signals*. The specify a relationship between *sequences* of input and output values at successive moments of time. Hanna and Daeche (1985) also adopt the use of functions over time to specify signals, but their approach concentrates on modelling at a lower level of abstraction where signals are used to represent voltage-through-time waveforms.

5.2 DESCRIBING STRUCTURE IN HOL

Figure 5.3 shows three components D_1, D_2 and D_3 joined together with the *external ports* named `a,b,c` and `d` and *internal lines* `p` and `q`. The external ports indicate how the constructed device interfaces to the environment, the surrounding components, while the *internal lines* are dedicated as communication links joining the internal ports of D_1, D_2 and D_3 together.

The three component devices, each of which is pictured in Fig. 5.3 before being connected together to form the new device, has its behaviour specified by a predicate. D_1`(a,b,p)` is the predicate which corresponds to component D_1, and this predicate is such that D_1`(a,b,p)` is true only for the appropriate assignment of values to the three variables `a,b`, and `p`. Similarly, predicates D_2`(p,d,c,q)` and D_3`(q,b,d)` correspond to components D_2 and D_3 respectively.

The structural convention adopted is that similarly named ports belonging to components join together to form the new constructed hardware. This convention is similar to that used by hardware description languages such as VHDL and MODEL, discussed in earlier chapters. Taking the three components in Fig. 5.3 we can see that the `p,q` and `d` ports connect to form the structure in Fig. 5.4. Two questions now arise: how do we represent the interconnection of the components, and how do we designate the `p` and `q` lines to be internal and the `d` line external in the HOL language?

As a predicate specifies the behaviour of a single component, the behaviour of the constructed device is the logical expression which captures the effect of all component predicates holding, or being true at the same time. This is obtained in

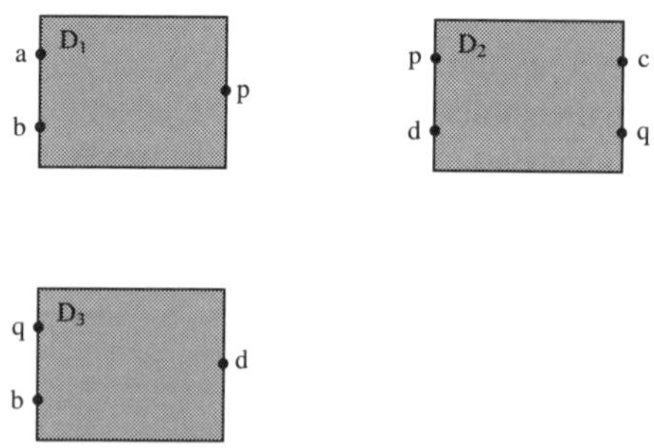

Figure 5.3 The three components.

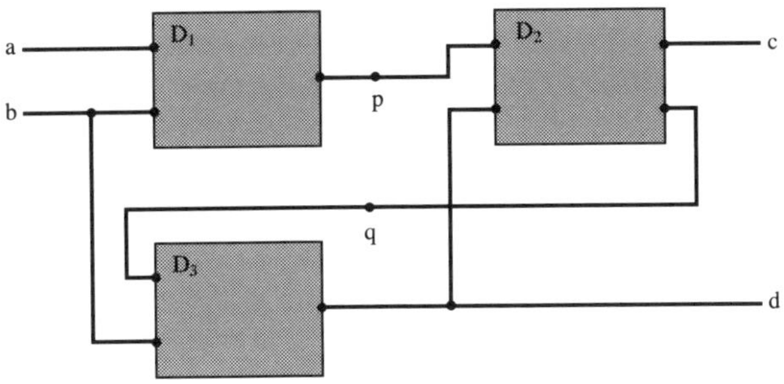

Figure 5.4 Joining three components.

logic by taking the conjunction of the component predicates with common variable names representing connected ports. The resulting HOL term is then

$$D_1(a,b,p) \wedge D_2(p,d,c,q) \wedge D_3(q,b,d)$$

We now wish to designate p and q as internal lines such that the behaviour of the system constructed out of components D_1, D_2 and D_3 only involves the values which appear on ports a,b,c and d. The particular assignment of values to variables a,b,c and d will denote the appropriate behaviour if the above conjunction of predicates is true for *some* values of p and q. This property is represented using the existential quantifier such that a,b,c and d are possible values on the external ports of the constructed system if and only if the following HOL term holds:

$$\exists p,q \,.\, D_1(a,b,p) \wedge D_2(p,d,c,q) \wedge D_3(q,b,d)$$

A new predicate D can now be defined as the behaviour of the system constructed from inter-connected components D_1,D_2 and D_3:

$$\vdash_{def} D(a,b,c,d) = \exists p,q \,.\, D_1(a,b,p) \wedge D_2(p,d,c,q) \wedge D_3(q,b,d)$$

As mentioned above, a correspondence can be seen between this approach to describing the structure of constructed systems in HOL and that adopted by VHDL. A significant difference is that constructed HOL terms such as that immediately above also give us a description of the *constructed behaviour* in the logic. This ability to express structure and behaviour using a single term in the modelling formalism is a property also held by the XCircal language; the XCircal composition operator $*$ corresponds to HOL conjunction, while the abstraction operator corresponds to the existential quantifier in HOL. Process calculi such as Circal, CCS (Milner, 1989) and CSP (Hoare, 1985) are consistent with HOL in that similarly named component ports join together, a convention that is becoming more and more of a standard as can be seen by its adoption in the VHDL language.

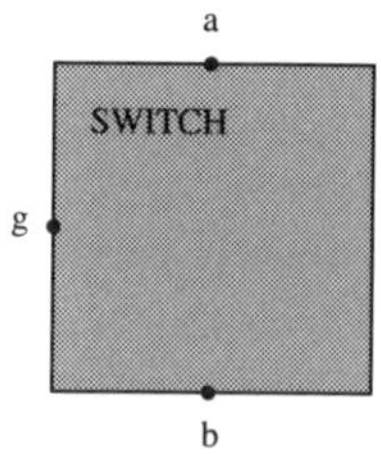

Figure 5.5 A simple switch.

5.3 CONSTRUCTING DESCRIPTIONS

The following example shows various features of higher-order logic description.

Switch

A simple switch, such as that used in the switch-level model of Chapter 4, can be described using the logical *implication* operator. A three-port switch component with gate `g` and input/output ports `a` and `b`, pictured in Fig. 5.5, may have its behaviour defined by the predicate

$$\vdash_{def} \texttt{SWITCH(g,a,b)} = (\texttt{g} \supset (\texttt{a} = \texttt{b}))$$

The `SWITCH` predicate holds only if whenever `g` is true then `a` and `b` are equal. The symbol '⊃' is read as *implies*, and the above predicate can be read as '`g` is true implies `a = b`'.

The following assignment of Boolean values to variables `g`, `a` and `b` explains this defined behaviour:

`SWITCH(T,F,F)` holds because `T⊃(F=F)` is true
`SWITCH(F,T,F)` holds because `F⊃(T=F)` is true
`SWITCH(T,T,F)` does *not* hold since `T⊃(T=F)` is false

The truth table shown as Table 5.1 indicates the two cases where predicate `SWITCH` is false.

Table 5.1

g	a	b	SWITCH(g,a,b)
T	F	F	T
T	T	T	T
T	T	F	F
T	F	T	F
F	F	F	T
F	T	T	T
F	T	F	T
F	F	T	T

This simple switch component may be used as a simple, delay-less model of a *bidirectional* transistor. The use of a predicate to describe the relationship between the variables `a` and `b` allows this potential bidirectionality, such that `a` or `b` may be used both for input and for output. Use of a function generating an output value from an input value would restrict the component to be unidirectional.

CMOS Inverter

This example illustrates how HOL may be used to describe the behaviour of transistor-level hardware.

A CMOS inverter which is constructed out of an n-type transistor, a p-type transistor, power, and ground is pictured in Fig. 5.6. The four components each have their behaviour described by a predicate.

The power source `VDD` is such that its single port `v` is always true:

$$\vdash_{def} \texttt{VDD(v) = (v = T)}$$

Ground is similar in that its single port `e` is always false:

$$\vdash_{def} \texttt{GND(e) = (e = F)}$$

The n-type transistor is modelled as a simple switch which is on connecting ports `a` and `b` when the gate port `g` is high (true):

$$\vdash_{def} \texttt{N(g,a,b) = (g} \supset \texttt{(a = b))}$$

Similarly, a p-type transistor connects its input and output ports `a` and `b` when the gate is off:

$$\vdash_{def} \texttt{P(g,a,b) = (} \neg \texttt{g} \supset \texttt{(a = b))}$$

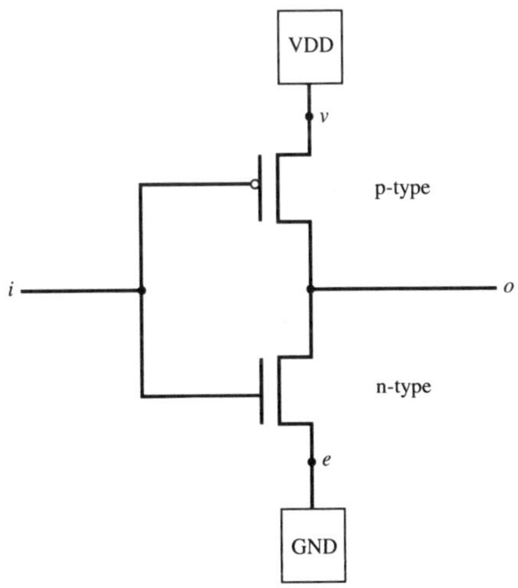

Figure 5.6 CMOS inverter.

The inverter is then modelled by instantiating the component predicates with the appropriate port variables such that they interconnect as in Fig. 5.6, taking the conjunction of the resulting predicates and abstracting out the internal lines `v` and `e` using the existential quantifier. The inverter predicate `INV` is then defined by:

$$\vdash_{def} \texttt{INV(i,o)} = \exists\, \texttt{v,e.VDD(v)} \wedge \texttt{P(i,v,o)} \wedge \texttt{N(i,o,e)} \wedge \texttt{GND(e)}$$

OR Gate

While the switch component was defined without a propagation delay, a specification of a component which implements the logical **OR** function with a single time unit delay may be defined by the following predicate:

$$\vdash_{def} \texttt{OR}(i_1, i_2, o) = \forall t\ .\ o(t+1) = (i_1(t) \vee i_2(t))$$

The output on port `o` will be the logical `OR` of the values on the input ports i_1 and i_2 at the previous time instant. The `OR` predicate then defines a simple, directional input/output relationship through time.

Full-adder

A full-adder circuit which is constructed out of two half-adder components and an **OR** gate as pictured in Fig. 5.7 may be used to illustrate how HOL is used to describe an existing design.

This construction of a full-adder has been used previously to illustrate structural VHDL language features. HOL uses similar conventions for describing structure and so it is not surprising that the behaviour of the full-adder can be given in an analogous fashion. Certain internal communication lines will be isolated from the outside environment, and so the behaviour given by the following predicate only concerns itself with the relationship between values on the external ports, represented by variables `a,b,cin,sum` and `cout`.

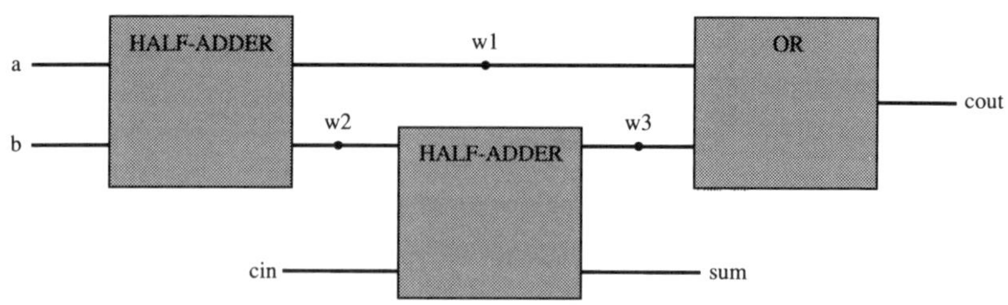

Figure 5.7 Full-adder.

```
⊢def FULL-ADDER(a,b,cin,cout,sum) = ∃ w1,w2,w3.
                                      HALF-ADDER (a,b,w1,w2) ∧
                                      HALF-ADDER(w2,cin,w3,sum) ∧
                                      OR(w1,w3,cout)
```

This *structural* definition of the FULL-ADDER predicate is a construction using smaller components, described in this case by the predicates HALF-ADDER and OR. But this definition is also *behavioural* since it is the conjunction of previously defined component predicates, that is, it is the logical conjunction of behavioural descriptions. FULL-ADDER is then a *constructed* predicate which fully describes the behaviour of the whole device in terms of the behaviour of its component parts.

The component predicates, such as OR(w1,w3,cout), are *instances* of the OR predicate defined above with variables w1,w3 and cout replacing the *generic* variables i_1, i_2 and o. As with the VHDL language, it is the particular choice of port name which indicates structure. Unlike VHDL, the corresponding variable names are also used to indicate behaviour, a common feature of both the HOL and XCircal languages.

Ripple-carry Adder

As with the VHDL example pictured previously in Fig. 2.15, a number of full-adder components can be chained together to produce a device which adds binary words of a certain length. An n-bit adder has its component structure represented in Fig. 5.8. Here the n-bit vector input and output ports have individual bit ports, e.g. x(0), x(1), x(2), etc.

The single-bit full-adder defined previously can now be instantiated n times with appropriately named variables to establish the behaviour of this structure. A *primitive recursive definition* can be used to define predicate ADD_n. This definition involves the functions a,b and out corresponding to the input ports a and b and the output port out, each of which communicates n-bit vectors. These

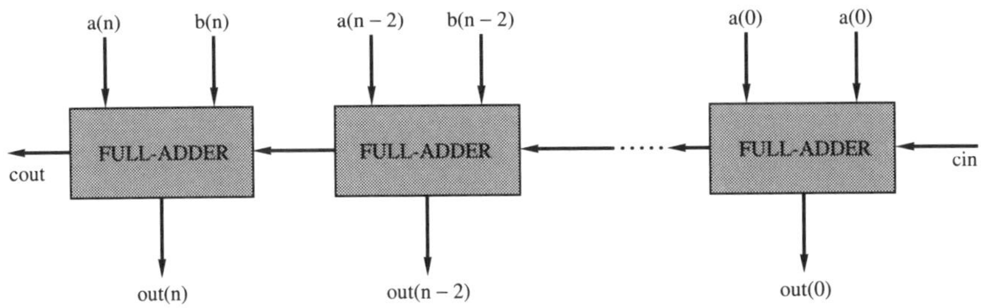

Figure 5.8 Ripple-carry adder.

functions map from the integers which represent bit position to Booleans, the value of the particular bit. For example, `x(0)` represents the first bit of input `x` while `x(i)` represents the `i+1`-th bit.

ADD_n is defined recursively as follows:

```
⊢def ADDn(n)(a,b,cin,cout,sum) = (n=0) ⇒ (cout = cin) |
                                  ∃c . ADDn(n−1)(a,b,cin,c,sum) ∧
                                  FULL-ADDER (a(n−1),b(n−1),c,cout,sum(n−1))
```

The recursive definition uses an integer to capture the *size* of the structure being modelled. The base case has integer variable `n` equal to `0` and this corresponds to a *null* adder performing no addition, with `cin` and `cout` wired together. Because it is a null adder the other signals no longer exist, hence they take no values.

The main part of the definition constructs the predicate ADD_n, representing the behaviour of an `n`-component structure, from the single-bit adder predicate called `FULL-ADDER` and a recursive call or instantiation of ADD_n with size variable `n−1`. The variable `c` represents the carry line which connects a single full-adder instance to the remaining chain of cells, and as this is an internal line it is abstracted out of the constructed predicate using the existential quantifier ∃.

Notice that the size of the vectors `a`, `b` and `sum` is the same as the argument immediately following the identifier ADD_n. In the above, reference to `a`, `b` and `sum` as arguments to ADD_n means that they are of width `n`, while in ADD_n`(n−1)` they are of width `n−1`. The `a(n−1)`, `b(n−1)` and `sum(n−1)` ports of the `FULL-ADDER` component give the additional external signals such that both the identifier and the body of the definition use `n`-bit wide buses.

Verification

In the next chapter we illustrate the use of HOL for performing hardware verification proofs. Frequently what is proved is that a *specification* of an intended design is actually satisfied by the description of its *implementation*. One such correctness proof is where we show that an `n`-bit adder as described above (the implementation) correctly performs addition (the specification).

Multiplier

This example illustrates how the desired behaviour of a multiplier may be specified. The specification is constructed from a number of higher-order functions which return *temporal predicates* as their result. These predicates capture the required timing properties which the specification and any design which is produced to implement it should satisfy. Predicates such as these form the basis of yet another model of hardware behaviour called *temporal logic*, details of which can be found in Halpern (1983) and Moszkowski (1983).

The multiplier takes an unspecified amount of time to produce a result; it raises a signal on its `done` port when the multiplication is completed and the result is available. The two input ports, the output port and the `done` completion signal port, are pictured in Fig. 5.9.

The following define temporal predicates which are used in the specification of the multiplier behaviour:

$$\vdash_{def} \mathtt{STABLE}(t_1,t_2)(f) = \forall t\ .\ t_1 \leqslant t \wedge t \leqslant t_2 \supset (f(t)=f(t_1))$$

$$\vdash_{def} \mathtt{NEXT}(t_1,t_2)(f) = t_1 < t_2 \wedge f(t_2) \wedge (\forall t\ .\ t_1 \leqslant t \wedge t \leqslant t_2 \supset \neg f(t))$$

`STABLE` is a higher-order function which takes a function as an argument and returns a temporal predicate as its result, allowing us to define a *class* of related temporal predicates using just one definition. The resulting predicate `STABLE` is true when function `f`, the argument, is constant in the time period between integers t_1 and t_2.

`NEXT` is also a predicate defining higher-order function which returns a predicate as a result. The definition consists of three parts, all of which must hold; $t_1 < t_2$ states that an interval of time ranges from time t_1 to time t_2; $f(t_2)$ states that property `f` must hold at the end of the time interval, at time t_2; the remaining predicate states that `f` is false throughout the time interval. Hence `f` only becomes true at time t_2 at the end of the interval. It is true if time t_2 is the first point in time at which $f(t_2)$ becomes true after time t_1.

The definition of the behaviour of the multiplier uses these two predicates. It is defined as follows:

$$\begin{aligned}\vdash_{def} \mathtt{MULT}(i_1,i_2,o,done) = (&done(t_1) \wedge \\ &\mathtt{NEXT}(t_1,t_2)(done) \wedge \\ &\mathtt{STABLE}(t_1,t_2)(i_1) \wedge \\ &\mathtt{STABLE}(t_1,t_2)(i_2)) \\ &\supset (o(t_2) = i_1(t_1) \times i_2(t_2))\end{aligned}$$

The behaviour of `MULT`, as specified above, is such that the signal `done` is high at time t_1, given by $done(t_1)$, and the next time it is high is at time t_2; `NEXT` gives this. Furthermore the inputs i_2 and i_2 are stable during the period between t_1 and t_2; `STABLE` gives this. If these properties hold then the output at the end of the interval, at time t_2, should equal the result of multiplying the two input values at the start of the interval, at time t_1.

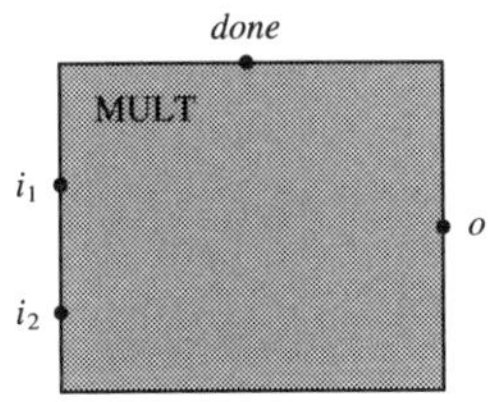

Figure 5.9 Multiplier.

This specification example shows how a description of the intended behaviour of a component may be constructed out of predicates in a rigorous and structured way. This ability to *construct* specifications aids their production and also provides some assurance that the specification is what is intended. The need to acquire confidence in a specification is crucial if we are to use it as the basis of a design which we may formally verify as a correct implementation of the specification; if the specification is flawed then the verification proof is worthless and we can have no confidence in the implementation.

In practice simulation has an important role to play in allowing a designer to experiment with a specification to see if it in fact is the one required. Coupled with a rigorous, structured approach to constructing the specification, this is the most reliable approach to generating the required specification. While HOL does support the construction of specifications, it does not readily support the direct simulation of HOL expressions.

The predicates STABLE and NEXT may not appear to convey their intended meaning at first reading. Similarly, the specification of MULT may not appear altogether obvious. This is a feature of assertional formalisms such as higher-order logic, although practice allows one to gain confidence that this approach does result in the creation of accurate models of hardware behaviour. Many hardware designers are more familiar with a finite-state machine type of model, and this state/event form of description is adopted by the XCircal language presented in detail in later chapters.

5.4 MODELLING IN HIGHER-ORDER LOGIC

Higher-order logic differs from the hardware description languages of Chapter 2 in that it is a descriptive formalism rather than just a descriptive language. Furthermore, an existing logical framework is used as the basis of the model rather than requiring the creation of a new one. The second feature may at first seem to be a disadvantage for descriptive reasons, in that the constructs available for description may not be the natural and appropriate ones which could be made available with a specially created description language. The examples shown previously, although fairly simple, indicate that this is in fact not the case and higher-order logics such as HOL utilize the logical constructs such as the conjunction operator and quantification to allow hardware structure and behaviour to be rigorously described. Significantly, the operators used to describe the structural interconnection of the sub-components of a circuit, by construction and abstraction, have a well-defined behavioural meaning allowing the behaviour of larger components to be established from the behaviour of the component parts.

The use of an existing logical framework gives access to the rules of that logic, so allowing hardware to be formally verified by reasoning within that formalism. This verification aspect makes the model different from both simulation-based hardware description languages such as VHDL and simulation-oriented switch-level models. In Chapter 4 we discussed the relative merits of verification and simulation and reached the conclusion that *both* are required in the design process. As mentioned previously, simulation has an experimental role to play in establishing the adequacy of a specification.

One drawback of using higher-order logic as the descriptive medium in the design process is its inability to drive a simulator directly. The reason for this is that in a logic framework such as HOL, description is in terms of predicates which assert that a given relationship exists between the values on the ports of the device at given points in time. This assertional form of behaviour description is inherently static and does not lend itself to direct simulation. In contrast, the event- and state-based Circal model is inherently dynamic, with events causing the *state* of a component to evolve, so leading directly to event-driven simulation.

This chapter explained how higher-order logic can be used to describe both structural and behavioural aspects of hardware. To summarize this approach briefly, predicates are defined to describe the behaviour of devices in terms of relations on inputs and outputs. At the lowest levels of specification, simple relationships, such as the behaviour of a logic gate, can be expressed directly in terms of basic logical and arithmetic functions and relations, for example $\neg$, $\wedge$, $\vee$, $\Rightarrow$, $=$, $+$, $<$, $\leqslant$. At higher levels, the behaviour of a composite device is defined hierarchically in terms of the behaviours of its components. Behaviour composition and internal signal hiding ('black-boxing') are expressed by logical conjunction and existential quantification respectively.

For simple combinatorial devices in situations where delay is not important, inputs and outputs can be represented by *time-independent* values. For example, the inputs and output of a simple logic gate can be represented by Boolean variables as shown below in the definition of `INV`, an inverter with no delay:

$$\vdash_{def} \texttt{INV (in,out)} = (\texttt{out} = \neg\ \texttt{in})$$

In the case of sequential circuits and other situations where delay needs to be modelled, inputs and outputs can be represented by functions from discrete time to sampled values. The definition of `INV-DEL` describes an inverter with a fixed propagation delay of 5 time units. In this definition `in` and `out` are now signal functions from discrete time to Boolean values:

$$\vdash_{def} \texttt{INV-DEL (in,out)} = \forall \texttt{t}.\quad \texttt{out (t+5)} = \neg\ \texttt{in(t)}$$

An important difference from many other hardware description languages is that the higher-order logic formalism is not predisposed towards a particular technology or design style, a property shared with XCircal. There are no built-in circuit models, or even a definitive way to use this formalism to describe hardware. In the following chapter we describe various models of hardware devices which are acceptable in certain well-understood situations. In some situations, a simple Boolean logic relation is an acceptable model of the physical device, in other situations a more detailed model may be required. A judicious choice between a simple model and a more detailed model depends on an understanding of the context and purpose of the model. Furthermore, it is always important to understand that even the most detailed model of hardware is still only an approximation of physical reality.

CHAPTER

SIX

HARDWARE VERIFICATION USING HIGHER-ORDER LOGIC

JEFFREY J. JOYCE

The preceding chapter explained how higher-order logic can be used to describe both structural and behavioural aspects of hardware. We now describe how the *axioms* and *inference rules* of higher-order logic can be used to prove hardware correct by establishing a formal relationship between structural and behavioural specifications. We begin by briefly discussing the difference between *formal proof* and *proof sketches*. Although the concrete result of formal verification is a formal proof, our discussion is limited to an outline of the overall strategy used to construct the formal proof. We describe several verification examples, in particular, correctness proofs for a 1-bit full-adder, an n-bit ripple-carry adder and a three-function ALU (arithmetic logic unit). Finally, we consider a much larger example: the formal specification and verification of a very simple eight-instruction microprocessor.

6.1 FORMAL PROOFS AND PROOF SKETCHES

A *formal proof* in higher-order logic is constructed from the axioms and inference rules of higher-order logic. In the HOL formulation of higher-order logic (Gordon, 1988), each line in a formal proof has the form $\Gamma \vdash t$ where Γ is a set of assumptions and t is a conclusion. A sequence of such lines is a proof if every line is either an axiom or can be obtained from a previous line by a rule of inference.

This style of proof where each line involves both a set of assumptions and a conclusion is called *natural deduction*. It is often more 'natural' than other (e.g. Hilbert-style) systems, because it reflects how we intuitively prove propositions of the form 'If X then Y' by assuming X and using this to prove Y. For each line $\Gamma \vdash t$, the conclusion t is a true proposition if all of the assumptions in Γ are true. If there are no assumptions, then the proposition is a theorem.

The HOL formulation of higher-order logic has five axioms and eight primitive inference rules. For example, when an implication $t1 \Rightarrow t2$ and its antecedent $t1$ appear on previous lines of a proof, the consequent $t2$ can follow on a later line inheriting assumptions from these two previous lines. This rule, called *modus ponens*, can be written as:

$$\frac{\Gamma 1 \vdash t1 \Rightarrow t2,\ \Gamma 2 \vdash t1}{\Gamma 1 \cup \Gamma 2 \vdash t2}$$

Another example is the rule for discharging an assumption. This rule (or something similar) is an essential feature of the natural deduction proof style; it is often used in the final steps of a proof to eliminate earlier assumptions. It can be written as

$$\frac{\Gamma \vdash t2}{\Gamma - \{t1\} \vdash t1 \Rightarrow t2}$$

The main advantage of a formal proof is that every single step has a precise justification which can be mechanically checked. The main disadvantage is that the formal proof of a non-trivial theorem typically involves a large number of steps. Even the relatively simple examples described in this section ultimately depend on thousands of primitive inference steps. However, the complexity of doing large formal proofs can be overcome with mechanical assistance from a computer both to check that each proof step is correct and to generate large portions of the proof automatically.

This section is about formal proofs of correctness for hardware, using the axioms and inference rules of higher-order logic. The purpose of this discussion is to describe the nature of these proofs with several example proofs of correctness. Because it is both impractical and not very helpful to reproduce every single line in a formal proof of correctness, we instead present *proof sketches* which outline the underlying strategies of the formal proofs.

The main simplification in our proof sketches is that most of the steps in the formal proof are left out: only a few intermediate steps are given to outline the proof strategy. We also make implicit use of natural deduction techniques: for instance, we describe direct manipulations ‘inside’ a theorem corresponding to a sequence of natural deduction steps in the formal proof. Another technique used in our proof sketches is to show that a propostion is logically equivalent to another proposition which has a trivial proof: typically, definitions and lemmas are used to reduce the desired propostion to a tautology or direct consequence of the assumptions.

The use of these techniques in our proof sketches correspond to formal deductions based on the axioms and inference rules of higher-order logic. These proof sketches are presented as summaries of formal proofs which have been generated with mechanical assistance from the HOL proof generating system (Gordon and Melham, 1993).

6.2. 1-BIT FULL-ADDER PROOF OF CORRECTNESS

The implementation of a 1-bit full-adder in terms of an OR gate and two half-adders is given by:

```
⊢def FULL-ADDER (a,b,cin,cout,sum)=
    ∃ w1 w2 w3.
       HALF-ADDER (a,b,w1,w2) ∧
       HALF-ADDER (w2,cin,w3,sum) ∧
       OR (w1,w3,cout)
```

Behavioural models for the OR gate and the half-adder are shown below. Here we are using a time-independent model where wires are represented by Boolean variables:

```
⊢def OR (a,b,out) = (out = (a ∨ b))

⊢def HALF-ADDER (a,b,cout,sum) =
       (cout = (a ∧ b)) ∧ (sum = ((a ∧ ¬ b) ∨ (¬ a ∧ b)))
```

The correctness of the 1-bit full-adder is stated in terms of a simple arithmetic relationship which holds between its inputs and outputs. This simple relationship states that, when the Boolean values `T` and `F` are interpreted as the numbers `1` and `0` respectively, the sum of the three inputs is equal to the value of the carry-out multiplied by two, plus the value of the sum output. This relationship is expressed formally by the equation

```
((Val a) + (Val b) + (Val cin)) = ((2 × (Val cout)) + (Val sum))
```

where `Val` is defined as a function which maps `T` and `F` to the numbers `1` and `0` respectively:

```
⊢def Val b = (b ⇒ 1 | 0)
```

To prove that this relationship holds between the inputs and outputs of a 1-bit full-adder, we start by deriving equations for the two outputs. For any two Boolean-valued terms `t1` and `t2`, the equation `t1 = t2` gives `t1 ⇒ t2`. Hence, the definition of `FULL-ADDER` gives:

```
⊢thm FULL-ADDER (a,b,cin,cout,sum) ⇒
    ∃ w1 w2 w3.
       HALF-ADDER (a,b,w1,w2) ∧
       HALF-ADDER (w2,cin,w3,sum) ∧
       OR (w1,w3,cout)
```

Here we are using the symbol $\Rightarrow$ for implication rather than the $>$ symbol used in the last chapter.

Expanding with the definitions of `HALF-ADDER` and `OR`, we obtain:

$$
\begin{array}{l}
\vdash_{thm} \texttt{FULL-ADDER (a,b,cin,cout,sum)} \Rightarrow \\
\quad \exists\, \texttt{w1 w2 w3}. \\
\qquad (\texttt{w1} = (\texttt{a} \wedge \texttt{b})) \wedge \\
\qquad (\texttt{w2} = ((\texttt{a} \wedge \neg \texttt{b}) \vee (\neg \texttt{a} \wedge \texttt{b}))) \wedge \\
\qquad (\texttt{w3} = (\texttt{w2} \wedge \texttt{cin})) \wedge \\
\qquad (\texttt{sum} = ((\texttt{w2} \wedge \neg \texttt{cin}) \vee (\neg \texttt{w2} \wedge \texttt{cin}))) \wedge \\
\qquad (\texttt{cout} = (\texttt{w1} \vee \texttt{w3}))
\end{array}
$$

The above theorem describes equations for the three existentially-quantified variables `w1, w2` and `w3` (which represent internal wires of the full-adder), along with equations for the two outputs, `sum` and `cout`. Using natural deduction techniques, we can directly manipulate these equations to eliminate all occurrences of `w1, w2` and `w3` in the equations for `sum` and `cout`. This symbolically models the effect of inputs propagating to outputs through internal gates and wires of the physical device. The resulting equations for sum and cout only involve the input variables `a, b` and `cin`.

$$
\begin{array}{l}
\vdash_{thm} \texttt{FULL-ADDER (a,b,cin,cout,sum)} \Rightarrow \\
\quad (\texttt{sum} = ((((\texttt{a} \wedge \neg \texttt{b}) \vee (\neg \texttt{a} \wedge \texttt{b})) \wedge \neg \texttt{cin}) \vee \\
\qquad\qquad (\neg((\texttt{a} \wedge \neg \texttt{b}) \vee (\neg \texttt{a} \wedge \texttt{b})) \wedge \texttt{cin}))) \wedge \\
\quad (\texttt{cout} = ((\texttt{a} \wedge \texttt{b}) \vee (((\texttt{a} \wedge \neg \texttt{b}) \vee (\neg \texttt{a} \wedge \texttt{b})) \wedge \texttt{cin})))
\end{array}
$$

The above theorem can be used to determine output values for any combination of input values. From this theorem, we can derive the following set of facts giving output values for each of the eight possible input combinations:

$$
\begin{array}{l}
\vdash_{thm} \texttt{FULL-ADDER (T,T,T,cout,sum)} \Rightarrow ((\texttt{cout} = \texttt{T}) \wedge (\texttt{sum} = \texttt{T})) \\
\vdash_{thm} \texttt{FULL-ADDER (T,T,F,cout,sum)} \Rightarrow ((\texttt{cout} = \texttt{T}) \wedge (\texttt{sum} = \texttt{F})) \\
\vdash_{thm} \texttt{FULL-ADDER (T,F,T,cout,sum)} \Rightarrow ((\texttt{cout} = \texttt{T}) \wedge (\texttt{sum} = \texttt{F})) \\
\vdash_{thm} \texttt{FULL-ADDER (T,F,F,cout,sum)} \Rightarrow ((\texttt{cout} = \texttt{F}) \wedge (\texttt{sum} = \texttt{T})) \\
\vdash_{thm} \texttt{FULL-ADDER (F,T,T,cout,sum)} \Rightarrow ((\texttt{cout} = \texttt{T}) \wedge (\texttt{sum} = \texttt{F})) \\
\vdash_{thm} \texttt{FULL-ADDER (F,T,F,cout,sum)} \Rightarrow ((\texttt{cout} = \texttt{F}) \wedge (\texttt{sum} = \texttt{T})) \\
\vdash_{thm} \texttt{FULL-ADDER (F,F,T,cout,sum)} \Rightarrow ((\texttt{cout} = \texttt{F}) \wedge (\texttt{sum} = \texttt{T})) \\
\vdash_{thm} \texttt{FULL-ADDER (F,F,F,cout,sum)} \Rightarrow ((\texttt{cout} = \texttt{F}) \wedge (\texttt{sum} = \texttt{F}))
\end{array}
$$

The formal verification of the 1-bit full-adder is completed by using the above set of facts to show that its behavioural specification is satisfied for any combination of input values. We recall that the behaviour specification of the 1-bit full-adder is expressed by an arithmetic equation relating outputs to inputs. The following theorem is derived from these eight facts by case analysis on the three Boolean inputs. This final proof step also uses the definition of `Val` and simple laws of arithmetic and Boolean logic:

```
⊢thm ∀ a b cin cout sum.
        FULL-ADDER (a,b,cin,cout,sum) ⇒
        (((Val a) + (Val b) + (Val cin)) = ((2 × (Val cout)) + (Val sum)))
```

This theorem states that any set of Boolean variables which satisfies the predicate `FULL-ADDER` also satisfies the arithmetic equation relating outputs to inputs. This illustrates the general form used to express correctness where the constraints imposed by a structural specification are shown to *imply* the behavioural specification.

This analysis is somewhat similar to the traditional approach of using Boolean algebra to establish the correctness of a simple design. In our case we prove theorems to establish correctness while the Boolean algebra approach entails using a truth table. This relationship only holds for simple examples, however. We usually wish to deal with timing issues in designs, and data types other than Booleans; hence the need for more powerful descriptive and analytic formalisms.

6.3. n-BIT RIPPLE-CARRY ADDER PROOF OF CORRECTNESS

The structure of the `n`-bit ripple-carry adder is given as the iteration, or repetition, of `n` 1-bit full-adders with the carry-out from each stage (except for the `n`th stage) connected to the carry-in of the next stage. A primitive recursive definition is used to specify the iteration of 1-bit full-adders. This defines a predicate `ADDn`, which expresses constraints on the outputs of the `n`-bit adder in terms of its inputs:

```
⊢def ADDn n (a,b,cin,cout,sum) =
     (n = 0) ⇒ (cout = cin) |
       ∃ c.
         ADDn (n−1) (a,b,cin,c,sum) ∧
         FULL-ADDER(a(n−1),b(n−1),c,cout,sum(n−1))
```

These inputs and outputs consist of single wires, represented by Boolean variables, as well as `n`-bit buses. An `n`-bit bus is represented by a function mapping bit positions to Boolean values. For example, the binary value 011 is represented by the function `f` where `f(0)` is `T`, `f(1)` is `T` and `f(2)` is `F`.

The correctness of the `n`-bit adder is also expressed in terms of an arithmetic equation. In this case, the `n`-bit input and output buses are interpreted as the unsigned binary representation of a number. Primitive recursion is used to define the function `Valn` which returns the value of the first `n` bits of a bus:

$\vdash_{def}$ `Val n b = ((n = 0) ⇒ 0 | ((2^(n−1) × (Val (b (n−1)))) + (Valn (n−1) b)))`

The correctness of the n-bit adder is expressed in terms of the following equation:

```
((Valn n a) + (Valn n b) + (Val cin)) =
    ((2^n × (Val cout)) + (Valn n sum))
```

This equation is derived from the structural specification of the n-bit adder by mathematical induction on n. Using the inductive proof strategy, it is sufficient to show that the equation holds for the basis step, when n is zero, and for the inductive step, n + 1, given the inductive hypothesis that the equation holds for n.

Basis Step

The basis step is a matter of proving that the assertion

```
ADDn 0 (a,b,cin,cout,sum) ⇒
(((Valn 0 a) + (Valn 0 b) + (Val cin)) =
((2^0 × (Val cout)) + (Valn 0 sum)))
```

is a theorem. Our strategy for achieving this goal is to show that it is logically equivalent to another theorem which has a trivial proof. Firstly, the definition of ADDn implies that a 0-bit adder is simply a wire connecting carry-in to carry-out. This fact is expressed by the lemma

$\vdash_{thm}$ `ADDn 0 (a,b,cin,cout,sum) = (cout = cin)`

which is used to simplify the antecedent of the above assertion. Secondly, the definition of Valn shows that the value of a 0-bit bus is zero. Hence, the terms (Valn 0 a), (Valn 0 b), and (Valn 0 sum) can be replaced by 0. After these replacements, we have

```
(cout = cin) ⇒ ((0 + 0 + (Val cin)) = ((2^0 × (Val cout)) + 0))
```

This new assertion is logically equivalent to the original assertion because each step in this simplification sequence involves the substitution of one term by a logically equivalent term. Therefore, it is sufficient to prove that this new assertion is a theorem, which can be done using natural deduction techniques by assuming the antecedent and proving the consequent. The antecedent is used to replace the single instance of cin in the consequent by the term cout. Arithmetic laws about exponentiation, multiplication and addition are then used to further simplify the consequent. The result is an equation of the form t = t which is a theorem (by the rule of reflexivity). This completes the basis step of the inductive proof.

Admittedly, a correctness proof for a 0-bit adder has little significance on its own; hence, the above proof sketch may seem out of touch with real problems in VLSI CAD design. It may also seem ridiculous to attach a value to a bus, the 0-bit bus, which does not even exist. However, as the basis step in a mathematical induction, this result leads to a correctness proof for ripple-carry adders of all sizes.

Inductive Step

As the following lemma suggests:

$$\vdash_{thm} \texttt{ADDn (n+1) (a,b,cin,cout,sum)} = \\ \exists \texttt{c.ADDn n (a,b,cin,c,sum)} \wedge \\ \texttt{FULL-ADDER (a n, b n,c,cout,sum n)}$$

the inductive step corresponds to the implementation of an n+1-bit adder from an n-bit adder and a 1-bit full-adder. This lemma also shows that the carry-out from the n-bit adder is connected to the carry-in of the 1-bit full-adder by an internal wire c.

The strategy for proving the inductive step centres upon two essential items of information: the inductive hypothesis which describes an arithmetic relationship between inputs and outputs of the n-bit adder,

$$((\text{Valn n a}) + (\text{Valn n b}) + (\text{Val cin})) = \\ ((2^n \times (\text{Val c})) + (\text{Valn n sum}))$$

and the correctness theorem for the 1-bit full-adder which describes an arithmetic relationship betwen the inputs and outputs of the 1-bit full-adder,

$$((\text{Val (a n)}) + (\text{Val (b n)}) + (\text{Val c})) = \\ ((2 \times (\text{Val cout})) + (\text{Val (sum n)}))$$

These two equations are used to establish the inductive step of the proof. Because the 1-bit full-adder is used at the nth bit position, both sides of the arithmetic equation relating inputs of the full-adder to its outputs are multiplied by 2^n. The result

$$(2^n \times ((\text{Val (a n)}) + (\text{Val (b n)}) + (\text{Val c}))) = \\ (2^n \times ((2 \times (\text{Val cout})) + (\text{Val (sum n)})))$$

is combined with the first equation using the arithmetic law

$$\vdash_{thm} \forall \text{n m p q. } (n = m) \wedge (p = q) \Rightarrow ((n + p) = (m + q))$$

to yield

$$((2^n \times ((\text{Val(a n)}) + (\text{Val(b n)}) + (\text{Val c}))) + \\ ((\text{Valn n a}) + (\text{Valn n b}) + (\text{Val cin}))) =$$

$$((2^n \times ((2 \times (\text{Val cout})) + (\text{Val (sum n)}))) + ((2^n \times (\text{Val c})) + (\text{Valn n sum})))$$

The inductive step of the proof is completed by using various arithmetic laws to simplify and re-arrange terms of the above equation. The term $(2^n \times (\text{Val c}))$ is then subtracted from both sides of the equation. Finally, the equation is simplified by the lemma

$$\vdash_{thm} \forall \text{b. } ((2^n \times (\text{Val (b n)})) + (\text{Valn n b})) = \text{Valn (n+1) b}$$

which can be derived from the definition of `Valn`. The result

$$((\text{Valn (n+1) a}) + (\text{Valn (n+1) b}) + (\text{Val cin})) = ((2^{n+1} \times (\text{Val cout})) + (\text{Valn (n+1) sum}))$$

shows that the arithmetic relationship between inputs and outputs holds for the `n+1`-bit adder establishing the inductive step of the correctness proof.

Having achieved both the bias and the inductive steps, the rule of mathematical induction allows us to conclude that the equation relating outputs to inputs of an `n`-bit adder holds for all `n`:

$$\begin{aligned}&\vdash_{thm} \forall \text{n a b cin cout sum.}\\ &\qquad \text{ADDn n (a,b,cin,cout,sum)} \Rightarrow\\ &\qquad (((\text{Valn n a}) + (\text{Valn n b}) + (\text{Val cin})) =\\ &\qquad\ ((2^n \times (\text{Val cout})) + (\text{Valn n sum})))\end{aligned}$$

6.4. AN ALTERNATIVE STATEMENT OF CORRECTNESS

The above correctness theorem can be used to derive additional theorems which express the behaviour of the `n`-bit adder in slightly different ways. For example, it is often useful to describe the function of an adder in terms of modulo arithmetic ignoring the value of the carry-out wire. This form of correctness statement is obtained by applying the modulus function (for the quotient 2^n) to both sides of the equation in the above theorem. The lemma

$$\vdash_{thm} \forall \text{n q b. } (((2^n \times \text{q}) + (\text{Valn n b})) \text{ MOD } 2^n) = \text{Valn n b}$$

is then used to simplify the right-hand side of the resulting equation. This yields the following correctness theorem:

$$\begin{aligned}&\vdash_{thm} \forall \text{n a b cin cout sum.}\\ &\qquad \text{ADDn n (a,b,cin,cout,sum)} \Rightarrow\\ &\qquad ((((\text{Valn n a}) + (\text{Valn n b}) + (\text{Val cin})) \text{ MOD } 2^n) = (\text{Valn n sum}))\end{aligned}$$

This second form of correctness is stated in terms of an equation for the value of the output bus when interpreted as an unsigned binary number. Yet another way to express the behaviour of the n-bit adder is an equation for the n-bit output bus itself instead of its interpreted value. To express behaviour in this form we need both a function which generates the n-bit binary representation of a number as well as a convention which ensures a unique representation for every n-bit bus.

The function BinRep generates the binary representation of a number using the modulus function. Since buses are represented by functions from bit positions to Boolean values, BinRep is a higher-order function which returns a function (denoted by λ-expression (Hatcher, 1982)):

$$\vdash_{def} \texttt{BinRep n} = \lambda\ \texttt{p.}\ \neg(((\texttt{n} - (\texttt{n MOD } 2^{\texttt{p}}))\ \texttt{MOD } 2^{\texttt{p}+1}) = 0)$$

The function Wordn truncates the binary representation of number after the nth bit by forcing all bits at positions greater than n to a fixed arbitrary Boolean value denoted by the constant ARB:

$$\vdash_{def} \texttt{Wordn n m} = \lambda\ \texttt{p. p} < \texttt{n} \Rightarrow (\texttt{BinRep m p}) \mid \texttt{ARB}$$

The convention of forcing all bits at positions greater than n to a fixed arbitrary value ensures that every n-bit bus has a unique representation. This convention is also followed in the definition of the predicate BusWidth, which is used to declare the width of an n-bit bus:

$$\vdash_{def} \texttt{BusWidth n b} = \forall\ \texttt{p. n} \leqslant \texttt{p} \Rightarrow (\texttt{b p} = \texttt{ARB})$$

These definitions result in two useful lemmas:

$$\vdash_{thm} \forall\ \texttt{n m. Wordn n (m MOD } 2^{n}) = \texttt{Wordn n m}$$
$$\vdash_{thm} \forall\ \texttt{n b. BusWidth n b} \Rightarrow (\texttt{Wordn n (Valn n b)} = \texttt{b})$$

To obtain a statement of correctness in terms of an equation for the n-bit output bus, the function-denoting term (Wordn n) is applied to both sides of the equation in the previous correctness statement. The left and right hand sides of the resulting equation are then simplified using the above lemmas, leading to the following result:

```
⊢thm ∀ n a b cin cout sum.
        ADDn n (a,b,cin,cout,sum) ∧
        BusWidth n sum ⇒
        (Wordn n ((Valn n a) + (Valn n b) + (Val cin)) = sum)
```

To summarize, the structural specification of the n-bit adder exploits hierarchy and iteration to define a system of simultaneous constraints. These constraints result in a complex Boolean relation on the individual input and output bits of the n-bit adder. From this complex low-level relation, we can derive a relatively simple arithmetic relationship using functions such as Valn and Wordn to relate low-level representations of data to higher algebraic levels. This illustrates an important strategy in hardware verification where complexity is controlled by relating behaviour to increasingly abstract levels.

6.5. A SIMPLE THREE-FUNCTION ARITHMETIC LOGIC UNIT

The n-bit adder can be combined with other n-bit structures to implement a very simple three-function arithmetic logic unit (ALU). Figure 6.1 shows the top-level structure of the ALU consisting of an n-bit parallel inverter, a hard-wired constant, an n-bit adder and multiplexing logic controlled by a 2-bit function code (f0, f1). The signal f0 also serves as the carry-in value for the n-bit adder. For example, when f0 and f1 are both low the multiplexing logic selects a and b as inputs to the adder to compute the n-bit sum of these two signal values. To increment input b, the hard-wired constant 1 is selected as the other input to the adder and the carry-in is set low. The difference a–b in twos complement arithmetic is obtained by routing input b through the parallel inverter into the adder with the carry-in set high.

This top-level structure is formally specified opposite. In addition to specifying the n-bit components of the ALU, the widths of internal buses are specified using the predicate BusWidth. The carry-out signal is hidden internally by existential quantification and so does not appear in Fig. 6.1; similarly, the internal wires b_1, b_2, b_3 and b_4 appear unlabelled.

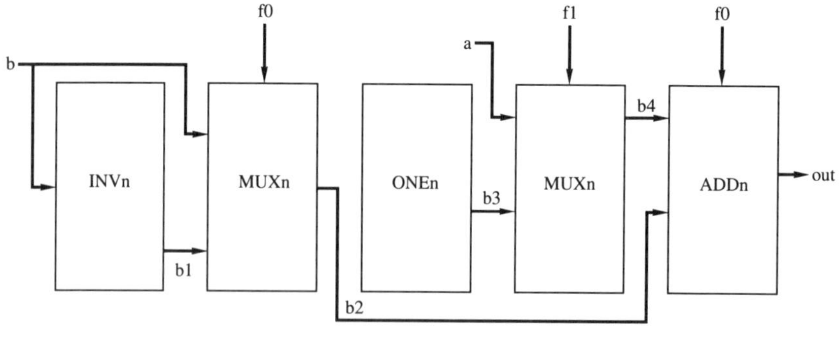

Figure 6.1 Top-level structure of the three-function ALU.

```
⊢def ALUn n (f0,f1,a,b,out) =
      ∃ b1 b2 b3 b4 cout.
        Vn n (b,b1) ∧
        MUXn n (f0,b,b1,b2) ∧
        ONEn n b3 ∧
        MUXn n (f1,a,b3,b4) ∧
        ADDn n (b2,b4,f0,cout,out) ∧
        BusWidth n b1 ∧
        BusWidth n b2 ∧
        BusWidth n b3 ∧
        BusWidth n b4
```

Theorems expressing correctness results for the n-bit parallel inverter, multiplexing logic and hard-wired constant are shown below. The function Notn is also defined to describe the result of applying logical negation to each bit in an n-bit bus.

```
⊢def Notn n b = λp. p < n ⇒ ¬(b p) | ARB
⊢thm ∀ n in out. INVn n (in,out) ∧ BusWidth n out ⇒ (out = Notn n in)
⊢thm ∀ n out. ONEn n out ∧ BusWidth n out ⇒ (out = Wordn n 1)
⊢thm ∀ n cntl a b out.
       MUXn n (cntl,a,b,out) ∧
       BusWidth n a ∧ BusWidth n b ∧ Buswidth n out ⇒
                                  (out = (cntl ⇒ b | a))
```

These correctness results, along with the correctness theorem for the n-bit adder, can be used to prove a correctness statement for the ALU. The n-bit operations implemented by the ALU are expressed in terms of arithmetic functions using the functions Valn and Wordn to translate between natural numbers and their binary representations. Because subtraction in two's complement arithmetic differs from subtraction on the natural numbers, we cannot simply use '–' to specify this operation. Instead, we define a function Negn which returns the negative value of an n-bit word in two's complement representation. The subtraction operation is then defined in terms of addition and Negn:

```
⊢def Incn n b = Wordn n ((Valn n b) + 1)
⊢def Addn n (b1,b2) = Wordn n ((Valn n b1) + (Valn n b2))
⊢def Negn n b = Wordn n ((Valn n (Notn n b)) + 1)
⊢def Subn n (b1,b2) = Wordn n ((Valn n b1) + (Valn n (Negn n b2)))
```

The correctness of the ALU is expressed by the following theorem in terms of these n-bit operations. The ALU is designed to implement only three functions: incrementation, addition and subtraction. The remaining unused function code (T,T) results in the computation of an unspecified value denoted by the existentially quantified variable x.

```
⊢thm ∀ n f0 f1 a b out.
        ALUn n (f0,f1,a,b,out) ∧
        BusWidth n a ∧ BusWidth n b ∧ Buswidth n out
        ⇒
        ∃ x.out =
                (((f0,f1) = (F,T)) ⇒ Incn n b |
                 ((f0,f1) = (F,F)) ⇒ Addn n (a,b) |
                 ((f0,f1) = (T,F)) ⇒ Subn n (a,b) | x)
```

The strategy used to prove this theorem considers each of the three valid function codes. In each case, the function code determines how inputs are propagated through the internal logic of the ALU to the output bus. To illustrate this strategy, we consider the case of subtraction which has the function code (T, F). In this case, it is necessary to prove that the equation

```
out = Subn n (a,b)
```

is a consequence of the ALU specification for the function code (T, F). We can do this by showing that this equation is logically equivalent to another equation which follows directly from the ALU specification for this function code.

Expanding with the definitions of Subn and Negn, the new goal is:

```
out = Wordn n ((Valn n a)
        + (Valn n (Wordn n ((Valn n (Notn n b)) + 1))))
```

In the above equation, the value 1 is added to inverted bits of b to form the two's complement negation of b. This contrasts with the implementation of substraction in the ALU where the value 1 is added to the sum of the n-bit adder inputs by setting the carry-in of the n-bit adder high. Our proof strategy is to transform the above goal into an equation which more closely reflects how subtraction is actually implemented in the ALU. This new goal will follow directly from the structural specification of the ALU and correctness results for the ALU components.

We first use the lemma

```
⊢thm ∀ n p q.
        (Valn n (Wordn n (p+q))) =
        (((Valn n (Wordn n p)) + (Valn n (Wordn n q))) MOD 2^n)
```

to expand the above equation for `out` into

```
out =
  Wordn n ((Valn n a) +
      (((Valn n (Wordn n (Valn n (Notn n b)))) + (Valn n (Wordn n 1)))
      MOD 2^n))
```

and then simplify with the lemmas

```
⊢thm ∀ n b. Wordn n (Valn n (Notn n b)) = Notn n b
⊢thm ∀ n p q. Wordn n (p + (q MOD 2^n)) = Wordn n (p+q)
```

to obtain the new goal:

```
out = Wordn n ((Valn n a)
        + (Valn n (Notn n b)) + (Valn n (Wordn n 1)))
```

The special case where `n` is 0 can be reduced to an equation of the form `t = t` since all 0-bit buses are represented by a unique function. Otherwise, we can assume that `n` is greater than 0, in which case the term `(Valn n (Wordn n 1))` simplifies to the value 1:

```
out = Wordn n ((Valn n a) + (Valn n (Notn n b)) + 1)
```

The above goal follows directly from the structural specification of the ALU and correctness results for the ALU components. To show this, we first derive equations for the internal buses and output bus of the ALU. These equations have already been simplified for the case where `(f0, f1)` is equal to `(T, F)`:

```
⊢thm ALUn n (T,F,a,b,out) ∧
    BusWidth n a ∧ BusWidth n b ∧ Buswidth n out
    ⇒
    ∃ b1 b2 b3 b4.
     (b1 = Notn n b) ∧
     (b2 = b1) ∧
     (b3 = Wordn n 1) ∧
     (b4 = a) ∧
     (out = Wordn ((Valn n b2) + (Valn n b4) + (Val T)))
```

Using natural deduction techniques, we can directly manipulate these equations to eliminate all occurrences of `b1`, `b2`, `b3` and `b4` in the equation for `out` to obtain:

```
⊢thm ALUn n (T,F,a,b,out) ∧
   BusWidth n a ∧ BusWidth n b ∧ Buswidth n out
   ⇒
   (out = Wordn n ((Valn n (Notn n b)) + (Valn n a) + (Val T)))
```

By the definition of `Val`, the term `(Val T)` simplifies the value 1. Finally, a simple re-ordering of terms results in a theorem satisfying the current goal. This completes the subtraction case in the ALU correctness proof.

6.6. A SIMPLE EIGHT-INSTRUCTION MICROPROCESSOR

Figure 6.2 shows the *register-transfer-level* architecture of a very simple microprocessor. The top-level view of this architecture is separated into a control unit and a data path. The microcoded control unit consists of a ROM (read-only memory) for storing microcode, a microinstruction decoder, and the microcode program counter unit which consists of a register for the address of the current microinstruction and logic for computing the address of the next microinstruction. The data path consists of a system bus interconnecting registers, memory, and various functional elements such as the ALU. The data path is controlled by signals from the control unit which, in turn, receives feedback from the data path.

The *programming level model*, also called the *external architecture*, of this microprocessor hides most of these implementation details. In the programming-level model, the externally visible state of the microprocessor consists of the memory MEM, program counter PC, and accumulator ACC. The operation of the microprocessor is defined by the semantics of the instruction set described informally by the table in Fig. 6.3. This simple instruction set precludes the possibility of illegal operations, and events such as arithmetic overflow or interrupts cannot be detected.

The word size of the microprocessor is not fixed at a specific value; instead it is given by a parameter `n` which specifies the width of the address field in an instruction. For instance, `n` could be 13 resulting in a word size of 16 since 3 additional bits are needed for the instruction opcode.

Implementation Description

This simple microprocessor has been designed to illustrate the use of higher-order logic to reason about hardware at a larger scale than the two preceding examples. We shift our focus away from the details of implementing `n`-bit wide structures towards a model which is more suited to reasoning about sequences

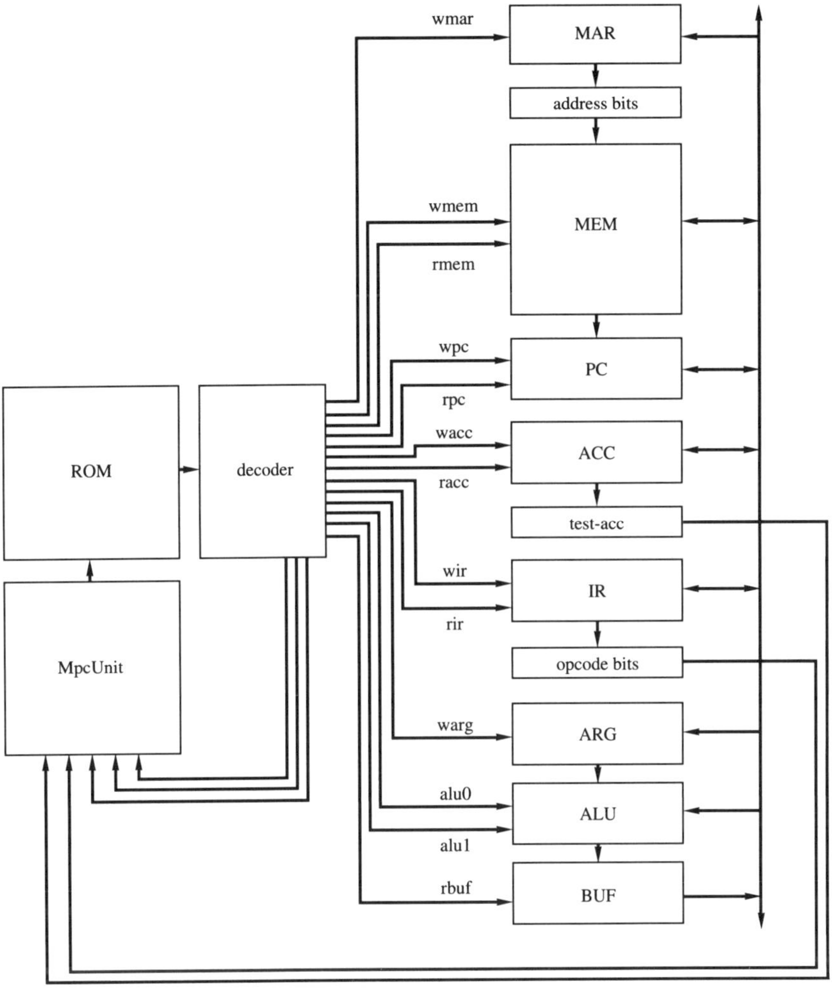

Figure 6.2 Register-transfer level architecture.

000—address—	JZR	jump if ACC = 0
001—address—	JMP	jump
010—address—	ADD	add contents to ACC
011—address—	SUB	subtract contents from ACC
100—address—	LD	load ACC
101—address—	ST	store ACC
110—address—	NOP	jump to next instruction
111—address—	NOP	jump to next instruction

Figure 6.3 Processor instruction set.

of data transfers in a microprocessor under the control of microcode. In this model, wires and buses are modelled as time-dependent signals; in particular, as functions of discrete time. Wires are represented by functions mapping discrete time to Boolean values, and `n`-bit buses are represented by functions mapping discrete time to numbers.

A possible problem with using numbers to represent sampled values of `n`-bit buses is that `n`-bit wide structures only provide finite representations of numbers. The register-transfer models presented here are carefully designed to limit the range of bus values within the set of values that could actually be represented in an `n`-bit wide structure. This is achieved by defining operations on bus values in terms of modulo arithmetic.

We begin by defining a behavioural model of the three-function ALU similar to the behavioural specification previously derived from an implementation of this component. The main difference from before is that the inputs and outputs of the ALU in this new model are time-dependent signals (although delay is not modelled in the ALU itself) that that the ALU operates on numbers instead of `n`-bit values. To accommodate this latter difference, the functions `Incn`, `Addn` and `Subn` are re-defined here as operations on numbers

```
⊢def Incn n a = ((a + 1) MOD 2ⁿ)
⊢def Addn n (a,b) = ((a + b) MOD 2ⁿ)
⊢def Subn n (a,b) = ((a − b) MOD 2ⁿ)
⊢def ALUn n (f0,f1,a,b,out) =
        ∀ t. ∃ x.
            out t =
                (((f0 t,f1, t) = (F,T)) ⇒ Incn n (b t) |
                 ((f0 t,f1 t) = (F,F)) ⇒ Addn n (a t,b t) |
                 ((f0 t, f1 t) = (T,F)) ⇒ Subn n (a t,b t) | x)
```

We continue with behavioural specifications for voltage sources and simple logic gates:

```
⊢def PWR out = ∀ t. out t = T
⊢def GND out = ∀ t. out t = F
⊢def AND (a,b,out) = ∀ t. out t = (a t ∧ b t)
⊢def OR (a,b,out) = ∀ t. out t = (a t ∨ b t)
```

The definition of `Bits` uses `MOD` in combination with natural number division, `DIV`, to describe the result of extracting a sub-field of `m` bits beginning at bit position `n` in a word: the modulus function masks out all but the `m` rightmost bits after 'shifting' right `n` bit positions using division by 2^n. The predicate `BITS` uses the function `Bits` to specify a behavioural model of wiring which connects its output to a sub-field of its input:

```
⊢def Bits (n,m) a = ((a DIV 2^n) MOD 2^m)
⊢def BITS (n,m) (in,out) = ∀ t. out t = Bits (n,m) (in t)
```

NORn defines a behavioural model for a chain of n NOR gates which, as the behavioural model suggests, tests whether its input is not equal to zero. Even though the size n is not used in the definition of NORn, it is included as a parameter to maintain a specification style consistent with the specification of other register-transfer level components.

```
⊢def NORn n (in,out) = ∀ t. out t = ¬(in t = 0)
```

Three hard-wired constants are required in the implementation of the next address logic in the control unit. Instead of three separate predicates, we define a single predicate, HWCn, parameterized by the word size n and the actual value c of the hard-wired constant.

```
⊢def HWCn n c out = ∀ t. out t = (c MOD 2^n)
```

The definitions of both MUXn and ADDn are similar to the behavioural specifications given earlier except that they now involve time-dependent signals. The behavioural model for the adder also assumes that the carry-in signal has been wired low.

```
⊢def MUXn n (cntl,a,b,out) = ∀ t. out t = (cntl t ⇒ b t | a t)
⊢def ADDn n (a,b,out) = ∀ t. out t = ADDn n (a t,b t)
```

All of the above specifications represent functional elements in the register-transfer architecture and do not model any form of delay. The only form of delay modelled at the register-transfer level corresponds to the clocking of sequential devices such as registers and memory. The simplest form of clocked sequential device used in the microprocessor is an n-bit register, or latch, which is updated every clock cycle. Here, a clock cycle corresponds to a single unit of time:

```
⊢def DELn n (in,out) = ∀ t. out (t+1) = in t
```

A more versatile type of register is modelled by the predicate REGn. This type of register can be selectively loaded and has a tri-state output gate for asserting the contents of the register onto a bus:

```
⊢def REGn n ((w,r,in,bus,out),(P)) =
     ∀ t.
        (out (t+1) = (w t ⇒ in t | out t)) ∧
           ⇒ r t ⇒ (bus t = out t))
```

The above specification of REGn is parametrized by a predicate P which represents an external, time-dependent condition on the environment. This is intended to reflect the fact that a register can only successfully assert its contents onto a bus provided no other device is also attempting to assert a value onto the bus. The predicate P does not correspond to any physical wire or bus in the microprocessor; rather it represents a *virtual* time-dependent signal associated with the behaviour of the register. To help distinguish between physical and virtual signals, the parameter list of REGn is divided into two sub-groups, (w,r,in,bus,out) and (P). This grouping is simply meant to improve the readability of these specifications and has no logical significance.

The memory for this simple microprocessor is assumed to be a synchronous device which completes read and write requests in single clock cycles. Its formal specification is similar to the register specification except that the internal memory state is represented by a function from addresses to the values stored at each address. The function Update is defined to model the effect of updating the memory state at a given address:

```
⊢def Update (mem,addr,data) = λ a. (a = addr) ⇒ data | (mem a)
⊢def MEMn n ((w,r,addr,bus),(P,mem)) =
      ∀ t.
      (mem (t+1) = (w t ⇒ Update (mem t,addr t,bus t) | mem t)) ∧
         (P t ⇒ r t ⇒ (bus t = mem t (addr t)))
```

As shown above, the output of the memory is controlled by a tri-state output gate. Like the register model, the memory behaviour is parametrized by an external, time-dependent condition on the environment. In addition to P, the memory specification is parametrized by another virtual signal, mem, corresponding to the internal memory state.

The predicate CheckCntls defines the external, time-dependent condition on the environment which governs use of the bus in the data path. This predicate simply checks that at most one of the 'read signal' values is true:

```
⊢def CheckCntls (rmem,rpc,racc,rir,rbuf,P) =
      ∀ t.
         P t =
          ((rmem t) ⇒ (¬(rpc t ∨ racc t ∨ rir t ∨ rbuf t)) |
           (rpc t) ⇒ (¬(racc t ∨ rir t ∨ rbuf t)) |
          (racc t) ⇒ (¬(rir t ∨ rbuf t)) |
           (rir t) ⇒ (¬(rbuf t)) | T)
```

At this point, the implementation of the data path can be formally specified in terms of these register-transfer level components and the predicate CheckCntls. The list of physical signals consist of control signals and feedback signals. For example, `zeroflag` is the output of test-acc and `opc` the output of opcode bits; both of these signals pass back to the control unit. The list of virtual signals consists of signals for the contents of every register as well as the internal state of memory. Notice that components dealing with instructions, such as the registers, are extended by '+3' to make them the same size as the data bus.

```
⊢def DataPath n (
      (wmar,wmem,rmem,wpc,rpc,wacc,racc,wir,rir,warg,
         alu0,alu1,rbuf,zeroflag,opc),
      (mar,mem,pc,acc,ir,arg,buf)) =
      ∃ P bus addr alu pwr gnd.
         CheckCntls (rmem,rpc,racc,rir,rbuf,P) ∧
         REGn (n+3) ((wmar,gnd,bus,bus,mar),P) ∧
         BITS (0,n) (mar,addr) ∧
         MEMn (n+3) ((wmem,rmem,addr,bus),(P,mem)) ∧
         REGn (n+3) ((wpc,rpc,bus,bus,pc),P) ∧
         REGn (n+3) ((wacc,racc,bus,bus,acc),P) ∧
         NORn (n+3) (acc,zeroflag) ∧
         REGn (n+3) ((wir,rir,bus,bus,ir),P) ∧
         BITS (n,3) (ir,opc) ∧
         REGn (n+3) ((warg,gnd,bus,bus,arg),P) ∧
         ALUn (n+3) (alu0,alu1,arg,bus,alu) ∧
         REGn (n+3) ((pwr,rbuf,alu,bus,buf),P) ∧
         PWR pwr ∧
         GND gnd
```

The signals which control the operation of the data path are generated by the control unit and determined ultimately by the contents of the microcode ROM. Every word stored in the 16-word by 19-bit ROM is a microinstruction organized into a 13-bit control word, a 2-bit test field and a 4-bit address field. The 13-bit control word of the current microinstruction generates the 13 control signal values. The test and address fields are used within the control unit to determine the address of the next microinstruction:

13-bit control word	2-bit test field	4-bit address field

The contents of the microcode ROM are specified as a function mapping addresses to microinstructions. Microinstructions are represented by `n`-tuples of Boolean values and numbers. The function Microcode is defined below with the help of the functions `Cntls` and `NextMpc`. These auxiliary functions allow the microcode specification to be expressed in a readable form instead of a pattern of Boolean values and numbers.

```
⊢def Cntls (tok1,tok2) =
       ((tok2 = 'wmar'),
        (tok2 = 'wmem'),
        (tok1 = 'rmem'),
        (tok2 = 'wpc'),
        (tok1 = 'rpc'),
        (tok2 = 'wacc'),
        (tok1 = 'racc'),
        (tok2 = 'wir'),
        (tok1 = 'rir'),
        (tok2 = 'warg'),
        (tok2 = 'sub'),
        (tok2 = 'inc'),
        (tok1 = 'rbuf'))


⊢def NextMpc (tok,addr) =
       ((tok = 'jop') ⇒ ((T,F),addr) |
        (tok = 'jnz') ⇒ ((F,T),addr) |
        (tok = 'jmp') ⇒ ((T,T),addr) |
                        ((F,F),addr))


⊢def Microcode n =
       ((n = 0)  ⇒ (Cntls ('rpc','wmar'), NextMpc ('inc',0)) |
        (n = 1)  ⇒ (Cntls ('rmem','wir'), NextMpc ('inc',0)) |
        (n = 2)  ⇒ (Cntls ('rir','wmar'), NextMpc ('jop',0)) |
        (n = 3)  ⇒ (Cntls ('none','none'), NextMpc ('jnz',10)) |
        (n = 4)  ⇒ (Cntls ('rir','wpc',), NextMpc ('jnp',0)) |
        (n = 5)  ⇒ (Cntls ('racc','warg'), NextMpc ('jmp',12)) |
        (n = 6)  ⇒ (Cntls ('racc','warg'), NextMpc ('jmp',13)) |
        (n = 7)  ⇒ (Cntls ('rmem','wacc'), NextMpc ('jmp',10)) |
        (n = 8)  ⇒ (Cntls ('racc', 'wmem'), NextMpc ('jmp',10)) |
        (n = 9)  ⇒ (Cntls ('none','none'), NextMpc ('inc',0)) |
        (n = 10) ⇒ (Cntls ('rpc','inc'), NextMpc ('inc',0)) |
        (n = 11) ⇒ (Cntls ('rbuf','wpc'), NextMpc ('jmp',0)) |
        (n = 12) ⇒ (Cntls ('rmem','add'), NextMpc ('jmp',14)) |
        (n = 13) ⇒ (Cntls ('rmem','sub'), NextMpc ('inc',0)) |
        (n = 14) ⇒ (Cntls ('rbuf','wacc'), NextMpc ('jmp',10)) |
                   (Cntls ('none','none'), NextMpc ('jmp',0)))
```

The above definitions illustrate how a simple microassembler can be expressed within higher-order logic. These definitions can be used to derive the 'assembled' form of the microcode specification shown below as a set of theorems.

```
⊢thm Microcode 0  = ((T,F,F,F,T,F,F,F,F,F,F,F,F),(F,F),0)
⊢thm Microcode 1  = ((F,F,T,F,F,F,F,T,F,F,F,F,F),(F,F),0)
⊢thm Microcode 2  = ((T,F,F,F,F,F,F,F,T,F,F,F,F),(T,F),0)
⊢thm Microcode 3  = ((F,F,F,F,F,F,F,F,F,F,F,F,F),(F,T),10)
⊢thm Microcode 4  = ((F,F,F,T,F,F,F,F,T,F,F,F,F),(T,T),0)
⊢thm Microcode 5  = ((F,F,F,F,F,F,T,F,F,T,F,F,F),(T,T),12)
⊢thm Microcode 6  = ((F,F,F,F,F,F,T,F,F,T,F,F,F),(T,T),13)
⊢thm Microcode 7  = ((F,F,T,F,F,T,F,F,F,F,F,F,F),(T,T),10)
⊢thm Microcode 8  = ((F,T,F,F,F,F,T,F,F,F,F,F,F),(T,T),10)
⊢thm Microcode 9  = ((F,F,F,F,F,F,F,F,F,F,F,F,F),(F,F),0)
⊢thm Microcode 10 = ((F,F,F,F,T,F,F,F,F,F,F,T,F),(F,F),0)
⊢thm Microcode 11 = ((F,F,F,T,F,F,F,F,F,F,F,F,T),(T,T),0)
⊢thm Microcode 12 = ((F,F,T,F,F,F,F,F,F,F,F,F,F),(T,T),14)
⊢thm Microcode 13 = ((F,F,T,F,F,F,F,F,F,T,F,F,F),(F,F),0)
⊢thm Microcode 14 = ((F,F,F,F,F,T,F,F,F,F,F,F,T),(T,T),10)
⊢thm Microcode 15 = ((F,F,F,F,F,F,F,F,F,F,F,F,F),(T,T),0)
```

The microcode ROM is simply a device which produces the microinstruction addressed by its 4-bit input:

```
⊢def ROM (addr,data) = ∀ t. data t = Microcode (addr t)
```

The output of the ROM is a microinstruction which needs to be separated into the control word, test and address fields. The wiring which separates the microinstruction into these fields is modelled by the predicate `Decoder`.

```
⊢def Decoder (
       rom,test0,test1,addr,
       wmar,wmem,rmem,wpc,rpc,wacc,racc,wir,rir,warg,
       alu0,alu1,rbuf) =
       ∀t.
          ((wmar t,wmem t,rmem t,wpc t,rpc t,wacc t,
            racc t,wir t,rir t,warg t,alu0 t,alu1 t,rbuf t),
           ((test0 t,test1 t),addr t)) =
          (rom t)
```

The above definition of `Decoder` is expressed in terms of an equation where the left-hand and right-hand sides of the equation are `n`-tuples. Two `n`-tuples are equal if and only if they have exactly the same number of elements, and matching elements of each `n`-tuple are equal both in type and in value. In the definition of `Decoder`, the right-hand side of the equation, `rom t`, denotes the current output of the ROM. The current output of the ROM is an `n`-tuple in the form used to represent microinstructions. The left-hand side of the equation consists of the individual output signal values organized into an `n`-tuple which exactly matches the representation of a microinstruction. Hence, the definition of `Decoder` effectively 'assigns' individual components of a microinstruction to the corresponding output signals.

The final component of the control unit is a block containing the next address logic together with the MPC register (implemented by an instance of DEL). As shown in Fig. 6.4, this block consists of 4-bit register-transfer-level components and a small amount of control logic implemented by a pair of logic gates.

```
⊢def MpcUnit (test0,test1,zeroflag,opc,addr,mpc) =
      ∃ w1 w2 zero one three b1 b2 b3 b4 b5.
        AND (test1,zeroflag,w1) ∧
        OR (test0,w1,w2) ∧
        MUXn 4 (test1,opc,addr,b1) ∧
        MUXn 4 (w2,mpc,b1,b2) ∧
        HWCn 4 0 zero ∧
        HWCn 4 3 three ∧
        MUXn 4 (test1,three,zero,b3) ∧
        HWCn 4 1 one ∧
        MUXn 4 (w2,one,b3,b4) ∧
        ADDn 4 (b2,b4,b5) ∧
        DELn 4 (b5,mpc)
```

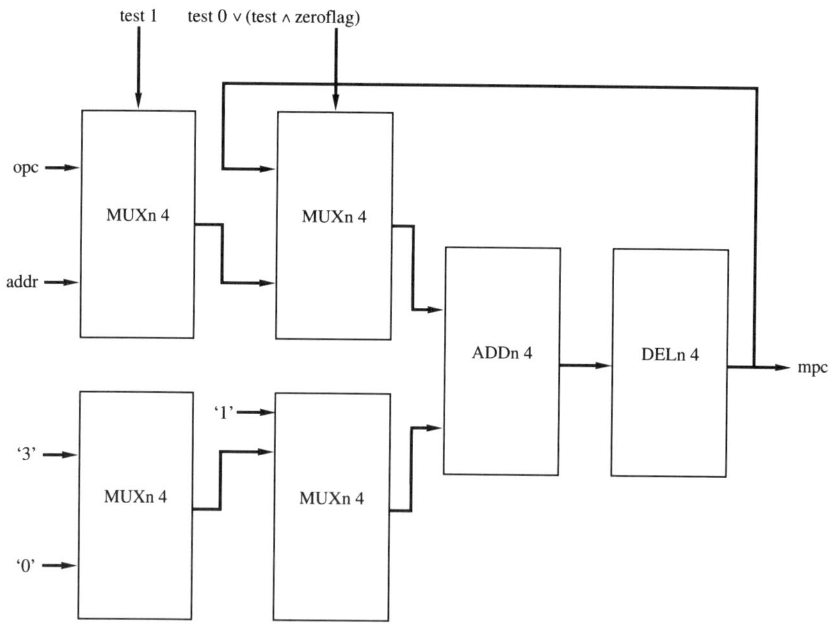

Figure 6.4 MPC unit implementation.

The control unit specification describes the assembly of these components. A shown below, the physical signals of the control unit consist of control and feedback signals to and from the data path. In addition to these physical signals, the address of the current microinstruction is externally available as a virtual signal.

```
⊢def CntlUnit (
      (zeroflag,opc,
       wmar,wmem,rmem,wpc,rpc,wacc,racc,wir,rir,
       warg,alu0,alu1,rbuf),
      (mpc)) =
      ∃ rom test0 test1 addr.
        ROM (mpc,rom) ∧
        Decoder (
          rom,test0,test1,addr,
          wmar,wmem,rmem,wpc,rpc,wacc,racc,wir,rir,
          warg,alu0,alu1,rbuf) ∧
        MpcUnit (test0,test1,zeroflag,opc,addr,mpc)
```

Finally, the top-level specification of the microprocessor implementation is obtained by combining specifications for the control unit and the data path. There are no physical inputs or outputs in the formal specification of the microprocessor at this highest level in the specification hierarchy. The parameter list at this level consists entirely of virtual signals corresponding to the internal state of the microprocessor:

```
⊢def Implementation n (mpc,mar,mem,pc,acc,ir,arg,buf) =
       ∃ zeroflag opc
         wmar wmem rmem wpc rpc wacc racc wir rir warg alu0 alu1 rbuf.
         CntlUnit (
           (zeroflag,opc,
            wmar,wmem,rmem,wpc,rpc,wacc,racc,wir,
            rir,warg,alu0,alu1,rbuf),
           (mpc)) ∧
         DataPath n (
           (wmar,wmem,rmem,wpc,rpc,wacc,racc,wir,
           rir,warg,alu0,alu1,rbuf,
            zeroflag,opc),
           (mar,mem,pc,acc,ir,arg,buf))
```

This completes the formal specification of the microprocessor implementation. Some features of the microprocessor such as a reset capability are not included in the formal specification. These features are excluded here partly to keep the dicussion simple, although there are also some methodological grounds for not modelling some of them. The main purpose of this model is to verify the operation of the register-transfer level architecture under the control of microcode. With this purpose in mind, it seems inappropriate to model a reset capability at the register-transfer level because it is really an implicit feature at this level in the same way that clock signals are not explicit in the register-transfer level specification. For similar reasons, we also assume that there is an external means of loading values into memory which is not formally modelled.

Behavioural Specification

The next step is to formally specify the intended behaviour of the microprocessor. This specification is a formalization of the programming level described earlier by Fig. 6.3.

The function `Inst` is defined to extract the current construction word from the memory state and value of the program counter. The functions `Opc` and `Addr` extract the opcode and address field of the current instruction word. So far, the formal parameters `mem`, `pc` and `acc` have been signals, i.e. functions of time. However, these formal parameters are signal values, i.e. memory states and numbers, in the following function definitions:

$\vdash_{def}$ `Inst n (mem,pc) = mem (pc MOD 2`^{n}`)`

$\vdash_{def}$ `Opc n (mem,pc) = Bits (n,3) (Inst n (mem,pc))`

$\vdash_{def}$ `Addr n (mem,pc) = Bits (0,n) (Inst n (mem,pc))`

The semantics of each instruction are specified as a function which returns a 3-tuple giving the next values of the memory state, program counter and accumulator. These values are computed from the current values of the memory state, program counter and accumulator. These functions are then combined to define a next-state function which uses the opcode of the current instruction to determine the next state of the microprocessor:

$\vdash_{def}$ `JZR n (mem,pc,acc) =`

`(mem,((acc = 0)` $\Rightarrow$ `(Inst n (mem,pc))` $\mid$ `(Incn (n+3) pc)),acc)`

$\vdash_{def}$ `JMP n (mem,pc,acc) = (mem,(Inst n (mem,pc)),acc)`

$\vdash_{def}$ `ADD n (mem,pc,acc) =`

`(mem,(Incn (n+3) pc),(Addn (n+3) (acc,mem (Addr n (mem,pc)))))`

$\vdash_{def}$ `SUB n (mem,pc,acc) =`

`(mem,(Incn (n+3) pc),(Subn (n+3) (acc,mem (Addr n (mem,pc)))))`

$\vdash_{def}$ `LD n (mem,pc,acc) = (mem,(Incn (n+3) pc),mem (Addr n (mem,pc)))`

$\vdash_{def}$ `ST n (mem,pc,acc) =`

`(Update (mem,Addr n (mem,pc),acc),(Incn (n+3) pc),acc)`

```
⊢def NOP n (mem,pc,acc) = (mem,(Incn (n+3) pc),acc)
⊢def NextState n (mem,pc,acc) =

        ((Opc n (mem,pc) = 0) ⇒ JZR n (mem,pc,acc) |
         (Opc n (mem,pc) = 1) ⇒ JMP n (mem,pc,acc) |
         (Opc n (mem,pc) = 2) ⇒ ADD n (mem,pc,acc) |
         (Opc n (mem,pc) = 3) ⇒ SUB n (mem,pc,acc) |
         (Opc n (mem,pc) = 4) ⇒ LD n (mem,pc,acc) |
         (Opc n (mem,pc) = 5) ⇒ ST n (mem,pc,acc) |
                                 NOP n (mem,pc,acc))
```

As shown above, `NextState` is defined in terms of a sequence of nested conditional expressions. The next state of the microprocessor is given for each of the eight possible opcodes including the two NOP opcodes, `6` and `7`, which are given by the 'default' case in this sequence.

Finally, we use the function `NextState` to define the predicate `Behaviour` which specifies the intended behaviour of the microprocessor as a relation on the time-dependent signals `mem`, `pc` and `acc`. This specification states that the sampled values of these signals from one time point to the next is determined by the function `NextState`:

```
⊢def Behaviour n (mem,pc,acc) =
      ∀ t. (mem (t+1),pc (t+1),acc (t+1)) = NextState n (mem t,pc
      t,acc t)
```

This specification hides not only structural details of the microprocessor implementation but also timing details about the number of microinstructions executed for each instruction. To be more precise, the behavioural specification describes the operation of the microprocessor in terms of an abstract scale of time where each instruction is uniformly executed in a single unit of time. This abstract time scale is different from the concrete time scale used to specify the behaviour of register-transfer level components. With respect to the underlying register-transfer level time scale, a single unit of abstract time is coarser and varies depending on the number of microinstructions executed for each programming level instruction. As explained in the next section, the formal verification of the microprocessor takes account of this difference by establishing a formal relationship between the concrete and abstract time scales.

Formal Verification

In general, the architecture of a microprocessor can be viewed as a hierarchy of interpretation levels. For instance, four distinct levels of interpretation are described by Anceau (1986) for the Intel I8505 microprocessor: instruction language, machine cycle language, timing state language, and clock phase lanage. Each intepretation level defines a virtual machine which is used to interpret higher levels.

The simple microprocessor described here has just two levels of interpretation, as shown in Fig. 6.5. The lowest level is the interpretation of individual microinstructions by the hardware. This level of interpretation defines a virtual machine for executing sequences of microinstructions. Higher up, programming-level instructions are interpreted by sequences of microinstructions. This second level of interpretation defines a virtual machine which corresponds to the programming-level model of the microprocessor.

This hierarchy of interpretation levels provides the basis for a strategy to verify the correctness of the simple microprocessor. The correctness proof is divided into three main steps:

1. Prove that each microinstruction is correctly interpreted by the hardware.
2. Prove that each programming level instruction is correctly implemented by the corresponding sequence of microinstructions.
3. Relate concrete time-scale behaviour to abstract time-scale behaviour.

The first two steps correspond to the two levels of interpretation shown in Fig. 6.5. This is followed by a third step in which correctness results from the first two steps are packaged into a single statement of correctness for the microprocessor based on a formally defined relationship between the concrete and abstract time scales.

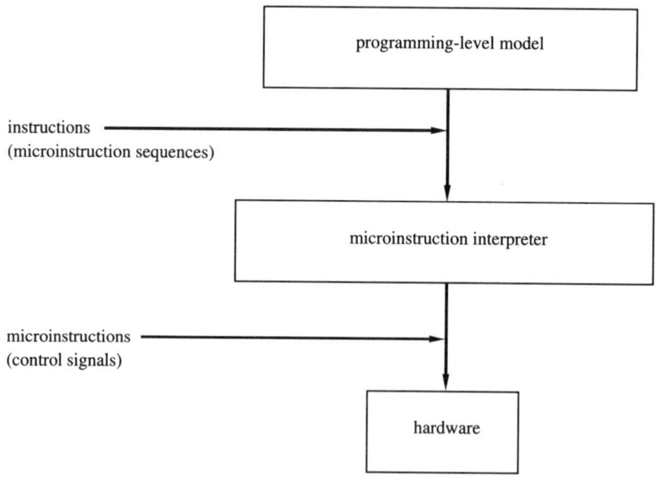

Figure 6.5 Hierarchy of interpretation levels.

Microinstruction Interpretation Correctness

The first main step in verifying the microprocessor is to establish that the 16 microinstructions (at locations 0 to 15 in the microcode ROM) are correctly interpreted by the hardware. To illustrate this process, we outline the steps taken to establish that microinstruction 0, i.e. the microinstruction at location 0, is correctly interpreted by the hardware.

The intended effect of microinstruction 0,

```
(Cntls ('rpc','wmar'),NextMpc ('inc',0))
```

is to transfer the contents of the program counter PC to the memory address register MAR and to increment the microcode program counter to 1 (the unused value of the address field is arbitrarily set to 0). Furthermore, the execution of this microinstruction leaves the internal state of the memory and the contents of the program counter PC and accumulator ACC unchanged. The effect of this microinstruction on the remaining components of the microprocessor's internal state, namely the ARG and BUF registers, is unimportant and can be ignored.

To derive a theorem which shows that microinstruction 0 does indeed have this effect, we use inference rules of higher-order logic to execute symbolically the interpretation of this microinstruction by the hardware. *Symbolic execution* is used here as a purely descriptive term for a proof technique; we emphasize that this technique is formal proof based on the inference rules of higher-order logic.

We start with the assumption that the microcode program counter is zero at time `t`. We then use the definitions of `ROM` and `Microcode` to derive the following equation for the current output of the ROM:

```
rom t = (Cntls ('rpc','wmar'),NextMpc ('inc',0))
```

The definitions of `Cntls` and `NextMpc` are then used to transform this equation into a form which explicitly shows the pattern of bits and value of the address field specified by this microinstruction:

```
rom t = ((T,F,F,F,T,F,F,F,F,F,F,F,F),(F,F),0)
```

The behavioural specification of the decoder is used to assign this bit pattern and the value of the address field to the control signals, test and address field signals. This results in a set of equations stating that all of the control signals are low (i.e. equal to `F`) except `wmar` and `rpc` which are high (i.e. equal to `T`), that the pair of test field signals are low and that the address field signal is equal to 0.

We have reached the point in the symbolic execution of microinstruction 0 where values for the control signals and the test and address field signals have been generated as outputs of the microinstruction decoder. We now consider the effect of these signal values on the next address logic in the control unit and on components of the data path.

The pair of test field values `(F, F)` causes the next address logic of the control unit to simply increment the current value of the microcode program counter from 0 to 1. This effect on the next address logic is easily derived from the specification of `MpcUnit` and behavioural models of its components:

```
mpc (t+1) = 1
```

The effect of the control signal values on the data path is derived in a similar manner from the specification of `DataPath` and behavioural models of its components. In particular, the value of every 'read signal' is false except for `rpc` satisfying the condition that only one bus device can asssert a value on to the bus of the data path. Hence, the value of the program counter is successfully read on to the bus. The control signal `wmar` then completes the data transfer by causing the value of the bus to be written into the memory address register:

```
mar (t+1) = pc t

mem (t+1) = mem t

 pc (t+1) = pc t

acc (t+1) = acct
```

The above equations are then combined in the following theorem, which states that microinstruction `0` is correctly interpreted by the hardware:

```
⊢thm ∀ n mpc mar mem pc acc ir arg buf.
        Implementation n (mpc,mar,mem,pc,acc,ir,arg,buf)
        ⇒
        ∀ t.
          (mpc t = 0) ⇒
          ((mpc (t+1) = 1) ∧
           (mar (t+1) = pc t) ∧
           (mem (t+1) = mem t) ∧
           (pc (t+1) = pc t) ∧
           (acc (t+1) = acc t))
```

A similar pattern of reasoning is used to derive correctness results for the remaining 15 microinstructions. Each of these theorems showing that the microinstruction satisfies a set of equations for the next state of the microprocessor at time `t+1` in terms of its state at time `t`.

Instruction Interpretation Correctness

The second main step of the verification procedure is the symbolic execution of programming-level instructions implemented by sequences of microinstructions. The results are used to show that the net effect of these execution sequences satisfies the semantics of the instruction set formally defined in the 'Behavioural specification' section on page 130.

For example, the sequence of microinstructions executed for an ADD instruction is located in the microcode ROM at locations 0, 1, 2, 5, 12, 14, 10 and 11. The reader can easily find this sequence by'stepping through' the microcode source (i.e. the definition of Microcode) assuming that the opcode for an ADD instruction causes a jump from microinstruction 2 to microinstruction 5.

To derive the net effect of this microinstruction sequence, we start with the assumption that the microcode program counter is zero at time `t` and that the opcode of the current instruction is two (i.e. the opcode for an ADD instruction). These two assumptions are formally expressed by:

```
mpc t = 0

Opc n (mem t,pc t) = 2
```

Each step in the symbolic simulation of the microcode corresponds to the execution of a single microinstruction. The effect of executing each microinstruction is given directly by one of the 16 theorems just mentioned. For instance, the theorem for microinstruction 0 is used to determine the internal state of the microprocessor at time `t+1`. Next, the theorem for microinstruction `1` is used to deetermine its state at time `t+2`.

By time `t+2`, the instruction addressed by the program counter PC has been read from memory and written into the instruction register IR. The three high-order bits of the instruction register form the opcode for the current instruction. In this case, we have assumed that the value of the opcode is 2. The theorem describing the effect of microinstruction 2 records the fact that the address of the next microinstruction is obtained by adding 3 to the value of the opcode; hence, the address of the next microinstruction is 5. This fact is shown below along with equations for the other relevant components of the microprocessor state at time `t+3`:

```
mpc(t+3) = 5

mar(t+3) = Inst (mem t,pc t)

mem(t+3) = mem t

pc(t+3)  = pc t

acc(t+3) = c t

ir(t+3)  = Inst (mem t,pc t)
```

This sequence continues with the symbolic execution of microinstructions 5, 12, 14, 10 and 11; eventually we obtain a set of equations for the state of the microprocessor at the end of this particular execution sequence, time `t+8`, in terms of its initial state at time `t`. At this point, we are only interested in the net effect on the microcode program counter, memory, program counter and accumulator. The contents of the remaining registers are no longer important and can be ignored.

```
mpc(t+8) = 0

mem(t+8) = mem t

pc(t+8)  = Incn (n+3) (pc t)

acc(t+8) = Addn (n+3) (acc t,Addr n (mem t,pc t))
```

The above set of equations describes the net effect of executing the microinstruction sequences for an ADD instruction. These equations are then used to show that the net effect of this execution sequence satisfies the semantics of an ADD instruction (as given by the definition of ADD in the 'Behavioural specification' section). This result is expressed by the following theorem:

```
⊢thm ∀ n mpc mar mem pc acc ir arg buf.
    Implementation n (mpc,mar,mem,pc,acc,ir,arg,buf)
    ⇒
    ∀t.
      (mpc t = 0) ∧
      (Opc n (mem t,pc t)) = 2)
      ⇒
      (mpc (t+8) = 0) ∧
      ((mem (t+8),pc (t+8),acc (t+8)) = ADD n (mem t,pc t,acc t))
```

There are eight further cases to consider: one case for the JZR instruction when the value of the accumulator is zero; another case for the JZR instruction when the accumulator is non-zero; and six more cases, one for each of the six remaining instructions. In each case, the net effect of the corresponding execution sequence is shown to satisfy the semantics of the instruction.

Top-level Correctness Statement

The final step in the verification procedure packages these individual results for the eight instructions of the microprocessor into a single statement of correctness based on a formally defined relationship between the concrete and abstract time scales.

The first step is to hide explicit references to differing lengths of microinstruction sequences for each instruction using the function MicroCycles. This function computes the length of the microinstruction sequence for the instruction addressed by the program counter.

```
⊢def MicroCycles n (mem,pc,acc) =
    let opc = Opc n (mem,pc) in
```

```
((opc = 0) ⇒ ((acc = 0) ⇒ 5 | 6) |
 (opc = 1) ⇒ 4 |
 (opc = 2) ⇒ 8 |
 (opc = 3) ⇒ 8 |
 (opc = 4) ⇒ 6 |
 (opc = 5) ⇒ 6 |
 (opc = 6) ⇒ 6 | 5)
```

Using this function definition, and the fact that the value of the 3-bit opcode ranges between 0 and 7, the following theorem can be derived to combine individual correctness results for each of the eight instructions of the microprocessor into a single statement of correctness:

```
⊢thm ∀ n mpc mar mem pc acc ir arg buf.
       Implementation n (mpc,mar,mem,pc,acc,ir,arg,buf)
       ⇒
       ∀ t.
         (mpc t = 0)
         ⇒
         let m = MicroCycles n (mem t,pc t,acc t) in
         ((mpc (t+m) = 0) ∧
          ((mem (t+m),pc (t+m),acc (t+m)) =
           NextState n (mem t,pc t,acc t)))
```

The next step is to define a formal relationship between the concrete time scale used to model the behaviour of components in the register-transfer level implementation and the abstract time scale used to specify the programming level model of the microprocessor.

If every programming-level instruction was implemented by the same number of microinstructions, then the relationship between the two time scales could be expressed very simply by arithmetic equation. However, this is not the case for our implementation of the microprocessor. For instance, the ADD instruction is implemented by a sequence of eight microinstructions as shown in Fig. 6.6

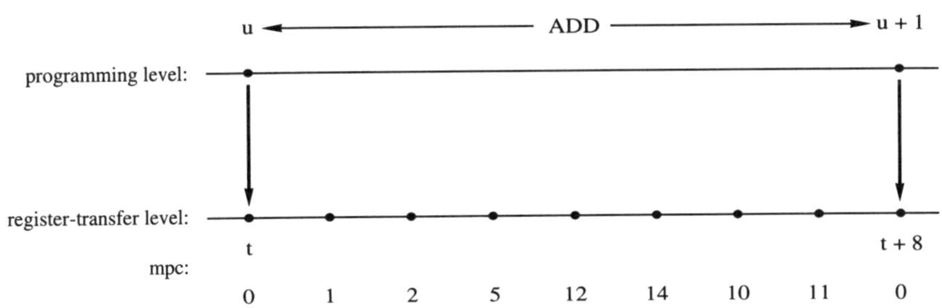

Figure 6.6 ADD microinstruction sequence.

whereas the JMP instruction is implemented by a sequence of four microinstructions as shown in Fig. 6.7. Therefore, we cannot use a simple arithmetic equation to define a formal relationship between the abstract and concrete time scales.

Instead, we define a primitive recursive function `TimeOfCycle` which computes the concrete time of every abstract time point using `MicroCycles` to determine the number of microinstructions executed between adjacent points on the abstract time scale. To compute the concrete time of `u`, we recursively compute the concrete time of `u-1` and then add the number given by `MicroCycles` for the length of the next microinstruction sequence to be executed.

```
⊢def TimeOfCycle n (mem,pc,acc) u =
      (u = 0) ⇒ 0 |
        (let t = (TimeOfCycle n (mem,pc,acc) (u-1)) in
         (t + (MicroCycles n (mem t,pc t,acc t))))
```

The function denoted by the term `(TimeOfCycle n (mem,pc,acc))` is a mapping from abstract time to concrete time; this function is represented by the downward arrows in Figs 6.6 and 6.7. For instance, in the ADD microinstruction sequence where `t` is the concrete time of `u`, the next point on the abstract time scale, `u+1`, is mapped to `t+8` on the concrete time scale. In the JMP microinstruction sequence, `u+1` is mapped to `t+4`.

Now that we have established a formal relationship between the abstract and concrete time scales, we can use this relationship to derive correctness results expressed in terms of the abstract time scale from results already obtained which are expressed in terms of the concrete time scale. In particular, we want to show that from one abstract time point to the next, the microprocessor executes a single programming level instruction.

We first need to show that every point on the abstract time scale corresponds to the start of a microinstruction sequence. It is sufficient to show that every abstract time point maps to a concrete time when the microcode program counter is zero since every microinstruction sequence begins at this location. It is necessary to assume that the microcode program counter initially has the value zero; that is, time begins when the microcode program counter is reset.

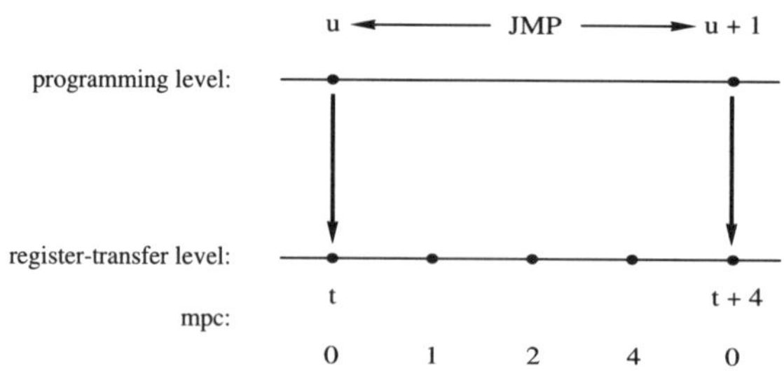

Figure 6.7 JMP microinstruction sequence.

The following theorem can be proved by mathematical induction on `u`:

```
⊢thm ∀ n mpc mar mem pc acc ir arg buf.
      Implementation n (mpc,mar,mem,pc,acc,ir,arg,buf) ∧
      (mpc 0 = 0)
      ⇒
      ∀ u. mpc (TimeOfCycle n (mem,pc,acc) u) = 0
```

We now use natural deduction reasoning to show that from one abstract time point to the next, the microprocessor executes a single programming level instruction. Consider any point `u` on the abstract time scale. Let `t` be equal to the concrete time of `u`:

```
t = TimeOfCycle n (mem,pc,acc) u
```

By the above theorem, we know that this corresponds to the start of a sequence of microinstructions implementing a programming level instruction:

```
mpc t = 0
```

By an earlier theorem, we know that the execution of this sequence is eventually completed `m` time units later where:

```
m = MicroCycles n (mem t,pc t,acc t)
```

Furthermore, this theorem also states that the net effect of this microinstruction sequence results in the state specified by the function `NextState`:

```
(mem (t+m),pc (t+m),acc (t+m)) =
NextState n (mem t,pc t,acc t)
```

By the definition of `TimeOfCycle`,

```
t+m = TimeOfCycle n (mem,pc,acc) (u+1)
```

which together with the preceding assertion implies that the externally visible state of the microprocessor at `u+1` on the abstract time scale is the state specified by the function `NextState`. Thus, we can obtain the following theorem:

```
⊢thm ∀ n mpc mar mem pc acc ir arg buf.
      Implementation n (mpc,mar,mem,pc,acc,ir,arg,buf) ∧
      (mpc 0 = 0)
      ⇒
      let f = TimeOfCycle n (mem,pc,acc) in
      ∀u.
        (mem (f (u+1)),pc (f (u+1)),acc (f (u+1))) =
        NextState n (mem (f u),pc (f u),acc (f u))
```

Next, we replace all terms of the form `(g (f x))` by logically equivalent terms of the form `((g o f) x)` where `g` is a signal and `o` is the infix operator for function composition:

```
⊢thm ∀ n mpc mar mem pc acc ir arg buf.
     Implementation n (mpc,mar,mem,pc,acc,ir,arg,buf) ∧
     (mpc 0 = 0)
     ⇒
     let f = TimeOfCycle n (mem,pc,acc) in
     ∀u.
       ((mem o f) (u+1),(pc o f) (u+1),(acc o f) (u+1)) =
       NextState n ((mem o f) u,(pc o f) u,(acc o f) u)
```

The terms `(mem o f)`, `(pc o f)` and `(acc o f)` denote programming-level signals corresponding to the register-transfer-level signals `mem`, `pc` and `acc`. These programming-level signals are obtained by sampling the register-transfer-level signals at each point on the abstract time scale.

The final step in the proof relates the implementation specification of the microprocessor given by the predicate `Implementation` to its behavioural specification given by the predicate `Behaviour`. In particular, we show that the constraints imposed by `Implementation` on the register-transfer-level signals of the implementation satisfy the constraints imposed by `Behaviour` on the corresponding programming-level signals.

The above theorem states that the relation

```
∀u.
  ((mem o f) (u+1),(pc o f) (u+1),(acc o f) (u+1)) =
  NextState n ((mem o f) u,(pc o f) u,(acc o f) u)
```

is implied by the predicate `Implementation` (and the assumption that the microcode program counter is reset at time 0). This is equivalent to the relation denoted by the term

```
Behaviour n (mem o f,pc o f,acc o f)
```

that is, the constraints imposed directly on the programming level signals by the predicate `Behaviour`. Hence, we obtain the top-level statement of correctness for the microprocessor:

```
⊢thm ∀ n mpc mar mem pc acc ir arg buf.
     Implementation n (mpc,mar,mem,pc,acc,ir,arg,buf) ∧
     (mpc 0 = 0)
     ⇒
     let f = TimeOfCycle n (mem,pc,acc) in
     Behaviour n (mem o f,pc o f,acc o f)
```

This theorem states that the predicate `Behaviour` is an abstract model of the underlying register-transfer implementation specified by the predicate `Implementation`. Therefore, true statements about the behaviour of the abstract model can be related to true statements about the behaviour of the implementation model. In particular, we have established a verified model of the implementation which allows us to reason about the execution of programs using the formally defined semantics of the instruction set.

Proof Summary

To summarize the strategy used to construct this proof of correctness, the complexity of the proof was reduced by first proving that each microinstruction is correctly interpreted by the hardware and then using these results to prove that programming-level instructions are correctly implemented by the corresponding microinstruction sequences.

In effect, this strategy amounts to the introduction of an intermediate level of specification between the register-transfer-level architecture and the programming level model of the microprocessor. This intermediate level consists of a finite-state machine whose state transitions correspond to the execution of individual microinstructions by the hardware. These state transitions are described by the 16 theorems derived in the first main step of the verification procedure.

This use of an intermediate level of specification may be described as a *structured* approach to formal verification. In this approach, intermediate levels of specification are used to clarify what forms of complexity are being reduced at each step in the proof. In the verification of the simple microprocessor, the finite-state machine is a major simplification of the underlying register-transfer-level architecture because it eliminates structural aspects of verification problems. The second main step of the verification procedure, the derivation of the programming-level model from the finite-state machine behaviour, considers the net effect of microinstruction sequences. The main simplification at this level is the contraction of behaviour over time into a single state transition for each programming level instruction.

The third main step of the proof formalizes the abstract notion of time used in the programming-level model of the microprocessor where each instruction is executed in a single unit of abstract time. This illustrates how formal logic can be used to support the informally developed concepts commonly used to describe the operation of a microprocessor.

Finally, we note that this very simple example avoids some of the more difficult aspects of specifying and verifying microprocessor systems. For instance, the register-transfer-level behaviour of a typical microprocessor is often much less regular than in our simple example: this can be due to WHILE loops in microcode which implement 'wait states' during handshaking interactions with external devices. However, many of these more difficult aspects of behaviour can also be handled in a sufficiently powerful formalism such as higher-order logic.

6.7. THE HOL PROOF GENERATING SYSTEM

As mentioned earlier, the proof sketches presented in this section are summaries of formal proofs in the HOL formulation of higher-order logic. Every step in these proofs has been mechanically checked by the HOL proof generating system. Furthermore, large portions of these proofs have been automatically generated by the HOL system.

The user interacts with the HOL system through a strongly typed, functional programming language called ML. Theorems are presented by ML data objects. Initially, the only theorems in the system are the axioms of the HOL logic. New theorems are generated from existing theorems by ML functions corresponding to the eight primitive inference rules. The type discipline of ML ensures that inference rules can only be applied to data objects representing previously generated theorems. This guarantees that the only way to obtain a theorem in the system is by the generation of a formal proof.

Primitive inference rules correspond to the smallest steps in a formal proof; to make large proofs feasible, ML functions can be programmed to apply sequences of primitive inference rules as single steps in a proof. A large number of these ML functions, called *derived inference rules*, are built into the HOL system. Some of these rules can potentially collapse hundreds (or even thousands) of primitive inferences into a single step. The user can also implement derived rules either to extend the built-in repertoire of general-purpose rules or to perform a specific sequence of inferences in a particular proof (e.g. symbolic simulation of a microinstruction in the microprocessor correctness proof). Because the implementation of derived inference rules, either built-in or user-defined, ultimately depends on the axioms and eight primitive inference rules, the security of theorem generation is not compromised by the implementation of a new rule.

The development of a formal proof as a linear sequence of proof lines is a bottom-up process, called *forward* proof, which starts with axioms and uses inference rule to eventually prove the desired theorem. When developing a proof in this manner, it is often difficult to tell whether or not a sequence of proof steps will ultimately be successful. In practice, proofs are usually developed in a top-down manner, called *goal-oriented* or *backwards* proof, starting with the conclusion of the desired theorem and reducing the problem of proving this theorem to simpler sub-goals. Some of the proof sketches described earlier in this section used a simple form of top-down reasoning by showing that a desired theorem is logically equivalent to another theorem which has a trivial proof. More generally, top-down reasoning reflects how we intuitively solve problems: 'I could prove X if I had a proof of Y and Z'. In this case, the goal X is reduced to the sub-goals Y and Z. Sub-goals are repeatedly reduced to one or more sub-sub-goals until they are all achieved by trivial inferences. Once all of the sub-goals have been achieved, the top-down development of the proof is used to guide the mechanical generation of a forward proof for the desired theorem. The HOL system supports the top-down development of proofs by providing semi-automatic mechanisms to reduce a goal to sub-goals. Furthermore, the system constructs a forward proof of the desired theorem as a side-effect of generating sub-goals.

A more detailed description of the HOL system may be found in a report by Gordon (1988), the system documentation (Cambridge SRI International, 1989) and in a new textbook by Gordon and Melham (1993). The HOL system is a descendant of the Edinburgh LCF system which is described in a book by Gordon *et al.* (1979). Many of the LCF system features re-used in the HOL system are also described in a book by Paulson (1987).

CHAPTER

SEVEN

A HARDWARE DESCRIPTION LANGUAGE DERIVED FROM PROCESS ALGEBRA

GEORGE A. McCASKILL

7.1. THE CIRCAL PROCESS ALGEBRA

Introduction

Circal (`CIR`cuit `cal`culus) is a mathematical framework in which to describe and analyse concurrent systems (Milne, 1985, 1991). Circal is used to reason about *processes* which have *state*, and which perform, or respond to, *actions*. As an introductory explanation of these terms, we model a change-dispensing machine using the *state diagram* of Fig. 7.1:

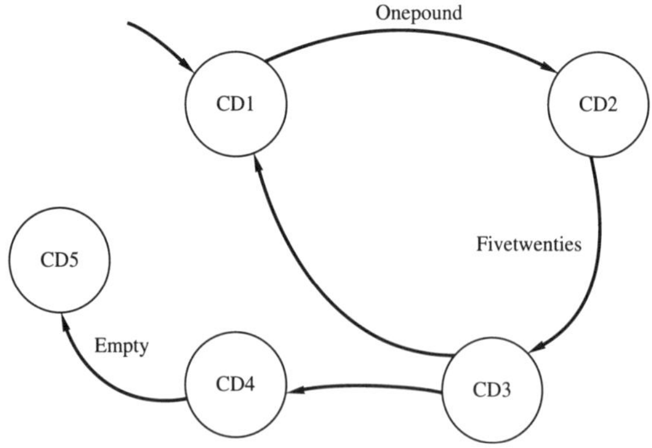

Figure 7.1 A change dispenser.

In a state diagram, we use circles to denote states, and labelled arrows to denote actions. An unlabelled arrow denotes an *empty transition*, while start states are indicated with a thicker arrow. Terminal states, if any, are those with no arrows leaving them.

In the change-dispenser example, the actions `OnePound`, `FiveTwenties` and `Empty` are abstractions of the following 'real' phenomena:

- `OnePound` A one-pound coin is pushed into the machine, and the machine keeps it. Note that this constitutes a two-sided 'agreement'; we use `OnePound` as an abstraction for the condition that the coin is both provided *and* accepted.
- `FiveTwenties` Five twenty-pence pieces are dispensed from the machine.
- `Empty` The machine illuminates its empty indicator.

The states `CD1`, `CD2`, `CD3`, `CD4` and `CD5` correspond to the following 'real' situations:

- `CD1` The machine has coins to dispense.
- `CD2` The machine has just accepted a pound coin.
- `CD3` The machine has just dispensed five twenty-pence coins, and must now determine whether it has any more twenty-pence coins left.
- `CD4` The machine has run out of twenty-pence coins, and so must now illuminate its empty indicator.
- `CD5` The empty indicator is now on, and the machine will participate in no further actions.

The transition from `CD3` to `CD1` and from `CD3 to CD4` are interesting in that they have no associated actions; this results from the fact that state `CD3` corresponds to an *internal* state of the machine where the availability of twenty-pence coins is checked, i.e. an external observer of the machine is not aware of this checking process until the `Empty` action is performed and coins are no longer accepted.

Now that we have a machine, we model a user as in Fig. 7.2.

The user continues to put pound coins into the machine until it is empty. Should the machine respond to a pound coin not by issuing five twenties, but by becoming empty, the user will become angry! We may be interested in asking the following types of questions: *what is the composite behaviour of the change dispenser and the user?*, or *will the user ever become angry*?

The composite behaviour of `CD1` and `U1` is very hard to determine just by placing the two diagrams side by side and trying to correlate the actions by eye. This is because we have two loci of control, and no obvious way to reconcile the many potential interactions between the processes; we need some *rules* to determine what happens when several processes interact. It is the role of process algebras, of which Circal is an example, to define the rules that enable us to answer these, and other more important questions. In particular, we will need

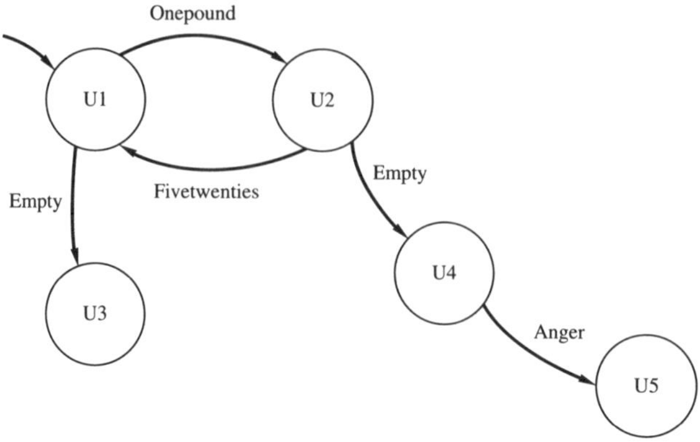

Figure 7.2 A change dispenser user.

to be able to determine whether two processes are *equivalent*.

With this short example, the following important issues have been raised:

- Actions are used to model arbitrary real world events.
- Processes are used to model sequences of actions (sometimes infinite sequences), often corresponding to a physical entity such as a machine.
- An action can model something which *happens to* a process, or is *initiated by* a process (it is unnecessary to make a distinction).
- An action may be shared between several processes, indicating a potential communication or interaction between them. In such a system of composed communicating processes, a shared action often has a *happens to* interpretation in one process and an *initiated by* interpretation in another.

Process Syntax

While pictures can serve well as representations of processes, as shown by Petri net diagrams (Peterson, 1981), another graphical notation, they are not too easy to manipulate, and become less appropriate as numbers of states become large. To describe and manipulate complex processes, we must define a language.

In this section we present the syntax of Circal processes; for each operator of the language we give its corresponding state diagram. Each Circal process has associated with it a set of atomic actions called a sort (a port-list to use the terminology of Chapter 2), which can be thought of as the set of labelled ports through which the process interacts with the environment. We call the set of all possible actions `Act`.

The Circal operators are as follows, where $\texttt{PROC}_L$ denotes the set of Circal processes of sort `L`, $\texttt{L} \subseteq \texttt{Act}$ and $\texttt{PROC} = \bigcup_{L \subseteq Act} \texttt{PROC}_L$:

- **Termination** / \ (pronounced 'delta') is a constant representating a process which can participate in no actions. It is used to denote a process which has

Figure 7.3 A deadlocked process.

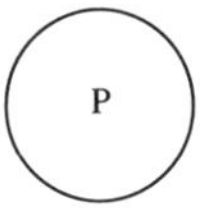

Figure 7.4 A terminated process.

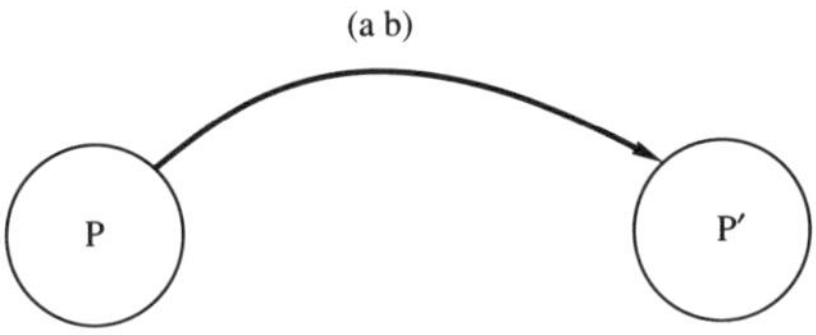

Figure 7.5 Action set with one element.

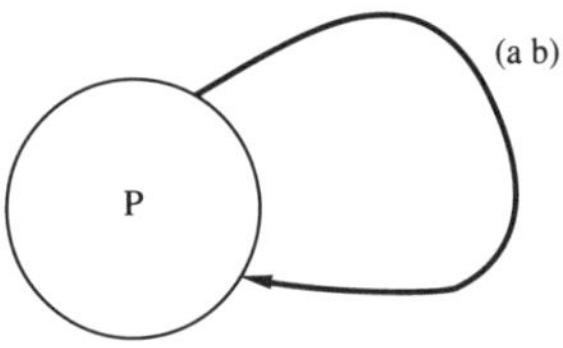

Figure 7.6 Recursive use of identifier.

terminated or which has deadlocked as shown in Fig. 7.3. / \ is characterized by the fact that no arrows ever leave it.

- **Definition (i)** We can associate an identifier, such as `P`, with any Circal process, using the definition operator ←. As an example, we could define `P` to be the **`Termination`** process by writing P ← / \. This corresponds to giving a name to the state as shown in Fig. 7.4.
- **Guarding** Given any process $P \in PROC_L$ and any action set $m \subseteq L$ $(m \neq 0)$, the term `m P` represents the process which can perform the action set `m` and evolve into the process `P` upon doing so. As an example, the term

$$P \leftarrow (a\ b)\ P'$$

represents the process which will participate in an action involving a synchronization via the `a` atomic action simultaneously with a synchronization via the `b` atomic action, and then evolve into `P′` as in Fig. 7.5. When an action set has only one element, parenthesis may be dropped (see Fig. 7.7).

The fact that the processes are guarded by action *sets* is a key feature of Circal, and greatly enriches the modelling potential of the algebra.

- **Definition (ii)** When giving a Circal process a name with the definition operator, we may recursively use the identifier being defined within the definition itself; for example $P \leftarrow (a\ b)\ P$ as in Fig. 7.6.

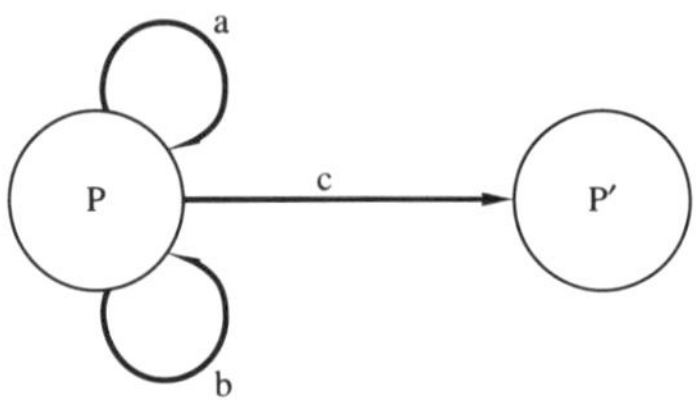

Figure 7.7 Choice of environment.

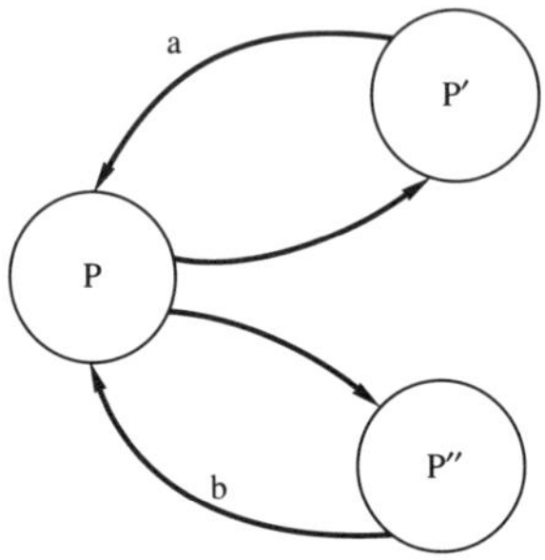

Figure 7.8 Non-deterministic choice.

- **Choice** Given processes P,Q ∈ PROC_L the term P + Q represents the process which can perform either the actions of the subterm P or the actions of the subterm Q, the choice of which being decided by the environment in which the term is executed. Figure 7.7 shows P ← a P + b P + c P′.
- **Nondeterminism** Given processes P,Q ∈ PROC_L, the term P & Q represents the process which can perform either the actions of the subterm P or the actions of the subterm Q, similar to the process P + Q. However, unlike the choice operator, the chosen computation path is decided autonomously by the process itself without any influence from its environment.
  P <- a P & b P is shown in Fig. 7.8.

  The empty transitions from P to P′ and from P to P″ enforce the inability of the environment to influence which path is chosen. An alternative graphical shorthand for this example is shown in Fig. 7.9.
- **Concurrent composition** Given processes P ∈ PROC_L and Q ∈ PROC_M, the term P⋆Q ∈ $\text{PROC}_{L\cup M}$ represents the process which can perform the actions of the subterms P and Q together. Any synchronizations which can be made between the two terms, due to some atomic action being common to the sorts

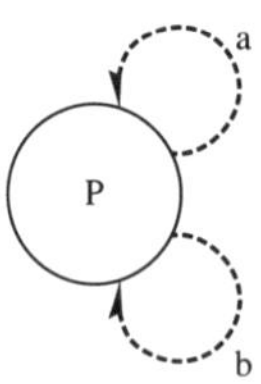

Figure 7.9 Alternative deterministic choice.

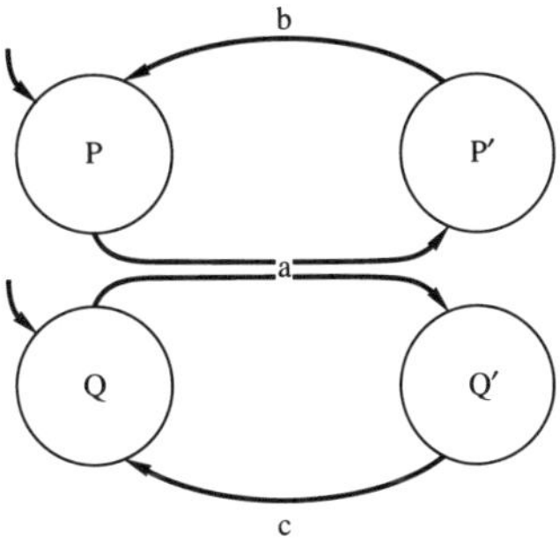

Figure 7.10 Process composition.

of both subterms, must be made. If this is not the case the actions of the subterms may occur asynchronously. As an example the composite process P + Q is defined as follows:

```
P ← a P′
P′ ← b P

Q ← a Q′
Q′ ← c Q

P⋆Q
```

and is represented as in Fig. 7.10.

Note that this diagram has two loci of control (indicated by the fact that there are two start state arrows). In the next section we discuss the rules which enable us to resolve the diagram into a new one where there is only a single locus of control.

- **Abstraction** Given some process $P \in PROC_L$ and some action $a \in L$, the term $P-a \in PROC_{L\setminus\{a\}}$ represents a process which is identical to P except where the action a has been abstracted away from the actions of P. As an example see the process P−a is defined as follows:

```
P ← a P′
P′ ← b P

P−a
```

and is represented as in Fig. 7.11.

- **Relabelling** Given some process $P \in PROC_L$ and some actions $a, b \in L$, the term P[b/a] is a new version of P such that wherever the action a occurs in

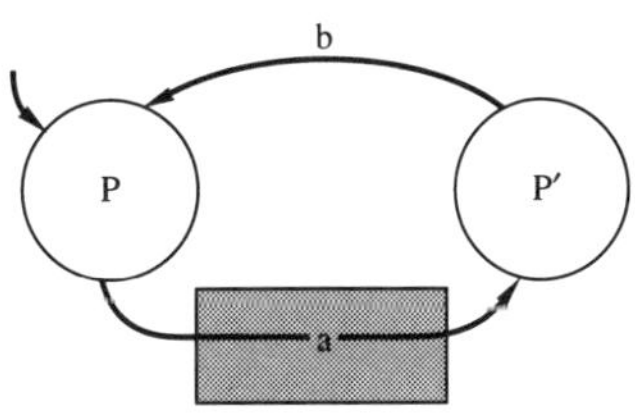

Figure 7.11 Abstraction.

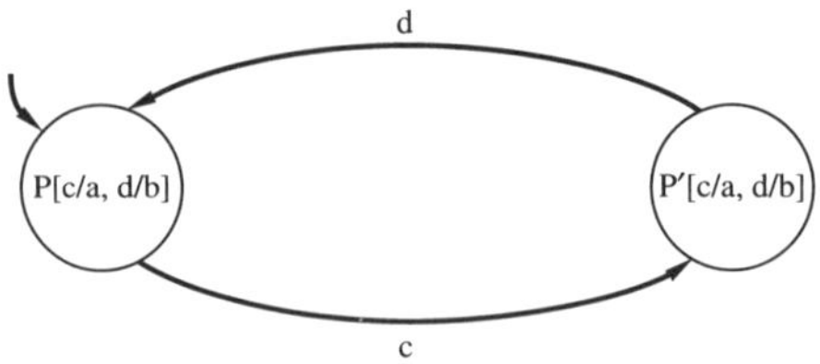

Figure 7.12 Relabelling.

`P` it is replaced with the action `b` (read `b` replaces `a`). As an example process `P[c/a, d/b]` is defined by

```
P ← a P′
P′ ← b P

P[c/a,d/b]
```

corresponds to Fig. 7.12.

The syntax of Circal processes can be summarized in the following BNF expression, where `P` is a process, `Da` is a process definition, `Act` is the set of possible actions, `m⊆Act`, `a, b ∈ Act` and `X` a process variable:

```
P ::= /\ | m P | P + P | P & P | X | P ★ P | P − m | P[a/b]
D ::= X ← P
```

7.2. PROCESS BEHAVIOUR

Behavioural Operators

For the **Deadlock**, **Choice**, **Nondeterminism**, **Guarding** and **Definition** operators, collectively known as the *behavioural* operators, we can see that their graphical interpretation as state transition systems is quite intuitive. For example /\ is a state from which there are no transitions and `Guarding` is represented by a transition from one state to another on a particular action set.

Formally, the semantics of these operators is given by the following *transition rules* (Moller, 1989):

$$P \rightarrow P; \qquad \text{(Idling)}$$

$$mP \xrightarrow{m} P; \qquad \text{(Guarding)}$$

$$\text{if } P \rightarrow P', \text{ then } P + Q \neg P' + Q \text{ and } Q + P \rightarrow Q + P'; \qquad \text{(Choice)}$$

$$\text{if } P \xrightarrow{m} P' \text{ for } m \neq \emptyset, \text{ then } P + Q \xrightarrow{m} P' \text{ and } Q + P \xrightarrow{m} P'; \qquad \text{(Choice)}$$

$$P \;\&\; Q \rightarrow P \text{ and } P \;\&\; Q \rightarrow Q \qquad \text{(Nondeterminism)}$$

The `Idling` rule simply means that all processes can make an empty transition to themselves. No rules are needed for **Termination**. For **Definition**, we add the rule:

$$\texttt{if } P \leftarrow Q \texttt{ and } Q \xrightarrow{m} Q' \texttt{ then } P \xrightarrow{m} Q' \qquad \texttt{(Definition)}$$

Structural Operators

The composition and abstraction operators, which together with relabelling are known as the *structural* operators, are not as intuitive; for instance, what is the precise meaning of the composite system P∗Q (see Fig. 7.13).

Formally, composition is defined by the following transition rule:

Given `P` of sort `M` and `Q` of sort `N`, `m` an action `P` can perform and `n` an action `Q` can perform, and $m \cap N = n \cap M$:

$$\texttt{if } P \xrightarrow{m} P' \texttt{ and } Q \xrightarrow{n} Q' \texttt{ then } P \star Q \; J\xrightarrow{m \cup n} P' \star Q' \qquad \texttt{(Composition)}$$

Here we are considering two processes, `P` and `Q`, which are to be composed. `P` can perform the action set `m` and evolve to `P′` and `Q` can perform `n` and evolve to `Q′`. The composition transition rule states that if the intersection of `m` and the sort of `Q` is equal to the intersection of `n` and the sort of `P`, i.e. $m \cap N = n \cap M$, then the composed system $P \star Q$ can evolve on the action set $m \cup n$ to $P' \star Q'$. One possibility is that the intersection of the sort of one process, say `M`, and an action, say `n`, of the other process `Q` is empty; in this case `P` evolves to `P′`, where `P′` is simply `P` (using the empty transition rule $P \rightarrow P$), while `Q` evolves to `Q′` on the independent `n` action.

If we apply this transition rule to our example `P⋆Q`, we get the result shown in Fig. 7.14.

Notice that the composition operator is used to form part of the new state-name (e.g. `P⋆Q`). An informal description of the composite behaviour of this example is: `P⋆Q` *can perform an* a *and then performs* b *and* c *in any order, including simultaneously, evolving back to the start state.*

For abstraction we have:

$$\texttt{If } P \xrightarrow{m} P' \texttt{ then } P - a \xrightarrow{m \setminus \{a\}} p' - a \qquad \texttt{(Abstraction)}$$

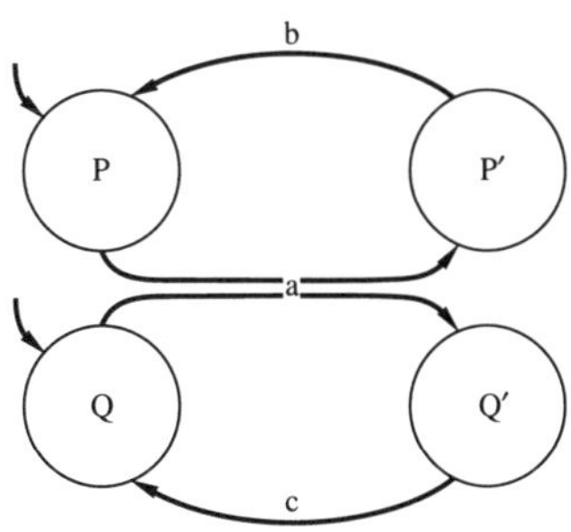

Figure 7.13 A composite system.

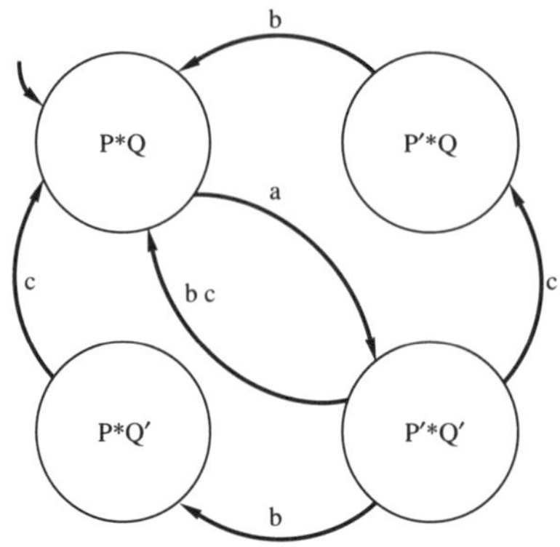

Figure 7.14 Result of applying composition rule.

Here we are considering a process P that evolves to P′ on the action set m. Should we wish to abstract the action a, then we give rise to a transition between two processes, where a no longer appears in the transition action set. If the action set m is equal to a, then we have created an empty transition, and hence, possible non-determinism.

Using these transition rules, and a notion of equivalence known as testing equivalence (De Nicola and Hennessy, 1984; Hennessey, 1988), which we describe in the next section, a set of complete and sound laws can be generated. Figure 7.15 shows the set of laws generated for a finite subset of Circal.

For further details on the derivation of the laws shown in Fig. 7.15 the reader is referred to Moller (1989). For a slightly different set of transition rules, and the treatment of recursion, the reader is referred to the thesis of Wenbo Mao (1992).

7.3. THE XCIRCAL HARDWARE DESCRIPTION LANGUAGE

Introduction

The Circal process algebra provides an ideal basis from which to build and reason about process models. The algebra's syntax, however, falls short of the kind of medium in which it is convenient to build large or complex process models. With no loss of formality, we can embed the algebra within the high-level language XTC (McCaskill, 1991), and extend the descriptive facilities available to the Circal user. We call the resulting hardware description language XCircal.

The hardware description language XCircal has many features derived from the programming language C (Kernighan and Ritchie, 1978), a very widely used

$(+_1)\ (x + y) + z = x + (y + z)$

$(+_+)\ x + y = y + x$

$(+_3)\ x + x = x$

$(+_4)\ x + /\backslash = x$

$(\&_1)\ (x \,\&\, y) \,\&\, z = x \,\&\, (y \,\&\, z)$

$(\&_2)\ x \,\&\, y = y \,\&\, x$

$(\&_3)\ x \,\&\, x = x$

$(+\,\&_1)\ mx + my = mx \,\&\, my$

$(+\,\&_2)\ x + (x \,\&\, y) = (x + y) \,\&\, (x + z)$

$(+\,\&_3)\ x \,\&\, (y + z) = (x \,\&\, y)\ (x \,\&\, z)$

$(\&)\ mx \,\&\, my = m(x \,\&\, y)$

$(x\,\&_4)\ x \,\&\, y \leqslant x + y$

$(\&\star_1)\ x\star\ (y \,\&\, z) = (x\star y) \,\&\, (x\star z)$

$(\&\star_2)\ (x \,\&\, y) \star z = (x\star z) \,\&\, (y\star z)$

$(+\star)$ for $x = \sum_{1\leqslant i\leqslant m} \lambda_{ix_i}$ of sort M, and $y = \sum_{1\leqslant j\leqslant n} \mu_j y_j$ of sort N,

$$x\star y = \sum_{\substack{1\leqslant i\leqslant m\\ \lambda_i\cap N=\emptyset}} \lambda_i(x_i\star y) + \sum_{\substack{1\leqslant j\leqslant n\\ M\cap\mu_j=\emptyset}} \mu_{j(x\star y_j)}$$

$$+ \sum_{\substack{1\leqslant i\leqslant m\\ 1\leqslant j\leqslant n\\ \lambda_i\cap N=M\cap\mu_j}} (\lambda_i\cup\mu_j)\ (x_i \star y_j)$$

$$(+-)\ \left(\sum_{1\leqslant i\leqslant n} \lambda_i x_i\right) - a \overset{\text{def}}{=} \begin{cases} (D{+}N) \,\&\, N, & \text{if } \exists i \text{ such that } \lambda_i = \{a\},\\ D & \text{Otherwise}, \end{cases}$$

where $D = \sum_{\substack{1\leqslant i\leqslant n\\ \{a\}\neq\lambda_i}} (\lambda_i\backslash\{a\})\ (x_i - a)$,

and $N = \&_{\substack{1\leqslant i\leqslant n\\ \{a\}\neq\lambda_i}}\ (x_i - a)$;

$(\&-)\ (\&_{1\leqslant i\leqslant n} x_i) - a = \&_{1\leqslant i\leqslant n}(x_i - a)$

Figure 7.15 The laws of Circal.

programming language. The principle features which ease the construction of process models are:

- **types** We predefine data-types for Circal action sets, `Event`, and Circal processes, `Process`. Arrays of these types may also be used.
- **functions** We can construct parametrized functions which build and then return a `Process`.
- **control structures** `FOR` loops and `IF` statements can be used in the construction of a `Process`.

We call the software implementation of the XCircal language the Circal system. The part of this system which is concerned with the implementation of the Circal laws and equivalence relations is known as the Circal kernel. The net result of *running* an XCircal program using the Circal system is the construction and manipulation of Circal processes. All high-level forms, such as functions and arrays, are defined as translations into the pure Circal calculus, allowing a formal treatment of the source language. Program 7.1 illustrates how Circal processes are declared and manipulated in XCircal:

Program 7.1

```
Event a, b, c             // declare 3 events
s=a b                     // make "s" a short hand for the set "a b"
                          // n.b., no need to "declare" s

Process P(s),Q(a b)       // declare 2 processes of the same sort

Process /\s(s)            // declare a deadlock "/\s" of sort "s"

Process C                 // declare a process "C" of unknown sort

P <- a P + (a b) Q        // define "P" to accept an "a" and evolve
                          // to "P", or accept "a" and "b" simultaneously
                          // and evolve to "Q"

Q <- (a 5) /\s            // define Q to accept 5 "a"s and then terminate.

C <- P*Q - b              // define "C" to be "P" composed with "Q" with the
                          // event "b" abstracted away

print (a P & Q)[c/a]      // print out the (non-deterministic choice of ("P"
                          // guarded by "a") and "Q") with "a" replaced by "c"
```

`Events` corresponding to single actions may be combined into `Events` corresponding to action sets in the following main ways (in each example we combine `a` and `b`):

- **sorts** `Process P(a b)`
- **guards** `P <- (a b) Q`
- **abstractions** `P - (a b)`
- **assignments** `s = a b`

The last form is often used to provide abbreviations for sorts used in more than one process definition. If the variable name `s` had not yet been used in the current scope, the XCircal compiler automatically infers that it is an `Event` variable.

Program 7.1 can be executed by the XCircal compiler, causing the following output to be generated:

```
(a P & Q)[c/a] == (c P[c/a] & Q[c/a])
P[c/a] == (c P[c/a] + (c b)Q[c/a])
Q[c/a] == c c c c c /\
```

The `print` statement causes a representation of the `Process (a P & Q)[c/a]` to be displayed, together with the recursive display of its sub-processes `P[c/a]` and `Q[c/a]`.

The declaration of an `Event` or `Process` causes the definition of a corresponding entity in the Circal kernel. The XCircal language follows normal C-language scoping rules, i.e. names of local variables may *hide* variables of the same name at an outer level. The Circal kernel requires a flat name-space, i.e. all `Process` and `Event` names must be unique. To achieve this, `Process` and `Event` variables defined in nested scopes are given a numeric suffix within the Circal kernel. These modified names manifest themselves when behaviours are `print`ed, as demonstrated in Program 7.2:

Program 7.2

```
Process P () {
  Event a, b
  Process p
  p <- (a b) p
  return p
}

print P()
print P()
```

Program 7.2 generates the following output:

```
p_2 <- (b_1 a_0) p_2
p_5 <- (b_4 a_3) p_5
```

If we wish an `Event` or `Process` to be reused on subsequent calls of a function, then we can use the `static` qualifier to achieve this. Program 7.3 demonstrates how we may modify Program 7.2 so that the `Events` are reused:

Program 7.3

```
Process P () {
  static Event a, b
  Process p
  p <- (a b) p
  return p
}

print P()
print P()
```

Program 7.3 generates the following output:

```
p_2 <- (b_1 a_0) p_2
p_3 <- (b_1 a_0) p_3
```

We now have enough notation with which to explore the semantic content and modelling potential of the Circal calculus.

Composition

The essence of Circal is its composition operator $*$. In Sec. 7.2 we explained composition with respect to the transition semantics, in this section we work through an example using the composition law (+$*$) of Fig. 7.15.

When we execute Program 7.4 the following output is generated by the print statement on line 14:

Program 7.4

```
1    Event a, b, c, d          // declare 4 atomic actions
2
3    Process P(a b c),
4            P'(a b c),
5            Q(a d),
6            Q'(a d)           // declare 4 processes
7
8    P  <- a P' + b P'         // define mutually recursive P and P'
9    P' <- a P + c P
10
11   Q <- a Q' + d Q'          // define Q
12   Q' <- a Q
13
14   print ~(P*Q)              // ~ causes the application of the circal
15                             // expansion law until a fix point is reached.
16
17   display ~(P*Q- b)         // demonstrate abstraction
```

```
P*Q == a (P'*Q') + d (P*Q') + (d b) (P'*Q') + b (P'*Q)
P'*Q' == a (P*Q) + c (P*Q')
P*Q' == a (P'*Q) + b (P'*Q')
P'*Q == a (P*Q') + d (P'*Q') + (d c) (P*Q') + c (P*Q)
```

Figure 7.16 depicits `P*Q` before and after the application of the composition

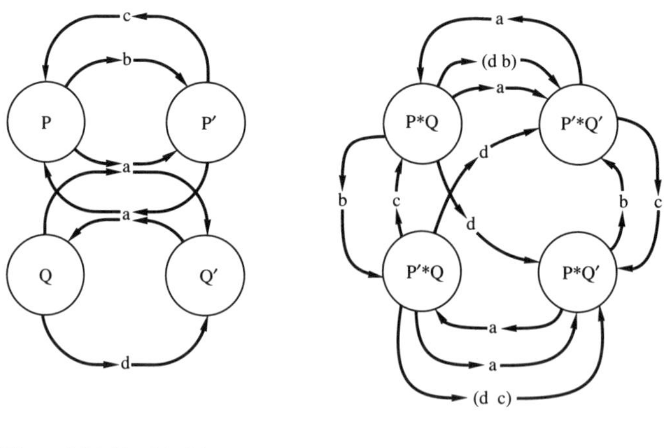

Figure 7.16 Graphical interpretation of expanded `P*Q`.

law. Note that the $*$ operator merely states that two processes are composed: it is the operator ~ that causes the definition of Circal composition (and abstraction) to be applied, allowing us to defer the expansion of behaviours until we actually need them.

Processes `P,P'` and `Q,Q'` share the action `a`, while `b` and `c` are private to `P,P'` and `d` to `Q,Q'`. The combined behaviour `P*Q` exercises every summand in the composition law, (+*) of Fig. 7.15, which we annotate here to reflect the current example:

let $a_1 = a,\ a_2 = b$ and $b_1 = a,\ b_2 = d$

$$P{\star}Q = \sum_{\substack{1\le i\le 2\\ a_i\cap\{a\ d\}=\emptyset}} a_i(P_i{\star}Q) + \sum_{\substack{1\le j\le 2\\ \{a\ b\ c\}\cap b_j=\emptyset}} b_j(P{\star}Q_j)$$

$$+ \sum_{\substack{1\le i\le 2\\ 1\le j\le 2\\ a_i\cap\{a\ d\}=\{a\ b\ c\}\cap b_j=\emptyset}} (a_i \cup b_j)(P_i{\star}Q_j)$$

$$+ \sum_{\substack{1\le i\le 2\\ 1\le j\le 2\\ a_i\cap\{a\ d\}=\{a\ b\ c\}\cap b_j\neq\emptyset}} (a_i \cup b_j)(P_i \star Q_j)$$

`P*Q` can evolve to `P'*Q'` on action `a` due to the last summand (synchronization), it goes to `P'*Q'` on action `(d b)` due to the third summand (simultaneous independent action), it goes to `P*Q'` on `d` due to the second summand (independent `Q` action), and finally `P'*Q` on `b` due to the first summand (independent `P` action). Applying the composition law up to recursion involves performing the above computation until all pairs of reachable state combinations have been expanded.

Line 17 of Program 7.4 exercises the Circal abstraction operator –, and also introduces an alternative method of viewing Circal behaviours, `display`. Line 17 generates the following output:

```
S0 == ((((d S1 + d S2) + a S1) + S3) & S3)
S1 == (c S2 + a S0)
S2 == ((a S3 + S1) & S1)
S3 == (((c S0 + (d c)S2) + d S1) + a S2)
```

Here `S0` is a shorthand for `((P*Q)-b)`, `S1` replaces `((P*Q')-b)`, etc.: renaming state identifiers does not alter the described behaviour, but it can make it much more readable because state names can grow very large. This example demonstrates that abstraction can introduce non-determinism into a behaviour, both explicitly by the `&` operator, and implicitly by having two reachable states guarded by the same action set, e.g. `S0` can evolve to either `S1` or `S2` on the action `d`. Before being able to derive a graphical version of this behaviour, we must substitute `S0`'s unguarded deterministic choice term `S3` with the term it

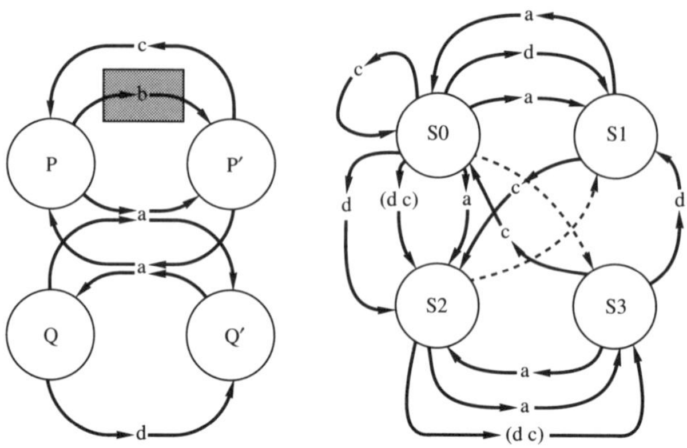

Figure 7.17 Graphical interpretation of expanded `P*Q-b`.

stands for, giving:

```
S0 == ((((d S1 + d S2) + a S1) + (((c S0 + (d c)S2) + d S1)
      + a S2)) & S3)
S1 == (c S2 + a S0)
S2 == ((a S3 + S1) & S1)
S3 == (((c S0 + (d c)S2) + d S1) + a S2)
```

This behaviour is represented in Fig. 7.17.

Replicated Structures

When modelling in XCircal, we quite often need to build replicated structures such as arrays of processes and simultaneous guards built from arrays of events, as in Program 7.5.

Program 7.5

```
Event a[10]
Process P[10]

Process ArrayCompose(Process P[]) {
  Process p
  p = P[0]
  for (i=1;i<sizeof P;i++) p = p*P[i]
  return p
}

Event ArrayCombine(Event e[]) {
  Event s
  s = e[0]
  for (i=1;i<sizeof e; i++) s = s e[i]
  return s
}

print (ArrayCompose P)
print (ArrayCombine a)
```

- Line 1 of Program 5 declares an array of 10 events indexed from 0 to 9 (following normal C language array conventions).
- Line 4 starts the definition of a function `ArrayCompose` whose purpose is to compose together all elements of the process array `P`. Following ANSI C function syntax, we can see that the function returns a result of type `Process` and requires a single process array parameter.
- Line 5 declares a local process, `p`, in which we will accumulate the result.
- Line 6 initializes `p` to be the first element of the process array parameter `P`.
- Line 7 uses a `FOR` loop to compose together the rest of the array. The size of the array is returned by the XCircal built-in function `sizeof`.
- Line 8 returns the resulting composition.
- Line 11 starts the definition of a similar function to `ArrayCompose`; this time we concatenate together an array of events into a single simultaneous event.
- Line 14 is the loop that accumulates, by concatenation, the current event `e[i]` onto `s`.

Program 7.5 generates the following output:

```
P[0]*P[1]*P[2]*P[3]*P[4]*P[5]*P[6]*P[7]*P[8]*P[9]
(a[9] a[8] a[7] a[6] a[5] a[4] a[3] a[2] a[1] a[0])
```

The simultaneous `a[i]` events when printed appear in an order arising from the Circal kernel's internal representation of simultaneous events. The functions `ArrayCompose` and `ArrayCombine` (which is also defined for `Bool` arrays) are pre-declared as the unary operator $*$, overloaded over `Process`, `Bool` and `Event` arrays, i.e. we can rewrite Program 7.5 as:

```
Event a[10]
Process P[10]

print (*P)
print (*a)
```

Program 7.6, which uses the array operators, shows the Circal description of a simplified version of a scheduler example, due to Milner (1989), as pictured in Fig. 7.18.

The goal is to construct a ring of stations c_n which perform the action a_n and then fire their adjacent station with a c_{n+1} action. We wish to verify that the combined network of stations fires the `a` actions in an ascending cyclic order (i.e. `Spec <- a[0] a[1] . . . a[n] Spec`). We can do this by composing the `c` stations together and abstracting away the `c` internal communication actions and the start action s, and finally comparing this behaviour with the specification.

Lines 1–5 of Program 7.6 define yet another replicating function, this time to build a process built out of successive guards taken from an array of events,

Program 7.6

```
Process ArrayGuard(Event c[], Process p) {
  n = sizeof c
  for (i=0;i<n;i++) p = c[n-i-1] p
  return p
}

int n = 5
Event s, c[n], a[n]

print "Running for n = " n "\n"
Process Start, C[n], /\(s), Sched, Spec

Start <- s /\

C[0] <- s a[0] c[1] C[0] + c[0] a[0] c[1] C[0]

for (i=1;i<(n-1);i++)
  C[i] <- c[i] a[i] c[i+1] C[i]

C[n-1] <- c[n-1] a[n-1] c[0] C[n-1]

Sched <- ~(Start*(*C) - (s (*c)))

Spec <- ArrayGuard(a, Spec)

print Spec
display Sched
print "Sched == Spec ? " (Sched == Spec) "\n"
```

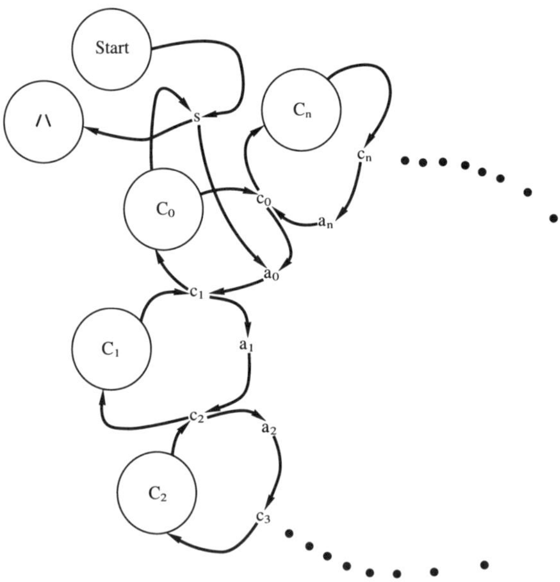

Figure 7.18 A simple scheduler.

and is called on line 23 to build the specification. Line 10 shows an example of string concatenation, and string–integer concatenation where the integer value `n` is made part of the string to be printed out. Line 27 calls the Circal kernel's equivalence checking procedure to compare the scheduler implementation `Sched` with its specification `Spec`. The following output is generated:

```
Running for n = 5
Spec <- a[0] a[1] a[2] a[3] a[4] Spec
S0 == S1
S1 == a[0] S2
S2 == S3
S3 == a[1] S4
S4 == S5
S5 == a[2] S6
S6 == S7
S7 == a[3] S8
S8 == S9
S9 == a[4] S10
S10 == S1
Sched == Spec ? true
```

The `display Sched` command of line 27 causes the lines `S0 == S1` to `S10 == S1` to be printed, corresponding to the behaviour of the implementation, which is indeed equivalent to the specification. The full scheduler example, which is emerging as a process algebra benchmark (Enders *et al.* 1991), has an extra action b_n which indicates that the station has completed its task, and which can arbitrarily interleave with the firing c action. In XCircal we can also specify that the station can finish its task simultaneously with the firing of the next station, e.g. line 18 of Program 7.6 becomes:

```
C[i] <- c[i] a[i] ( b[i] c[i+1] C[i] +
                    c[i+1] b[i] C[i] +
                   (c[i+1] b[i] C[i])
```

7.4. INSTANTIATING PROCESSES USING FUNCTIONS

Circal relabelling can become an error-prone and tedious operation when we have to deal with large numbers of actions. We have found it more reliable to make use of conventional function abstraction to achieve the instantiation of XCircal processes. Program 7.7 (which is illustrated in Fig. 7.19), introduces the modelling style we adopt for building repeatedly instantiated processes:

- Lines 3–9 contain the definition of a process which will instantiate a 'philosopher'.

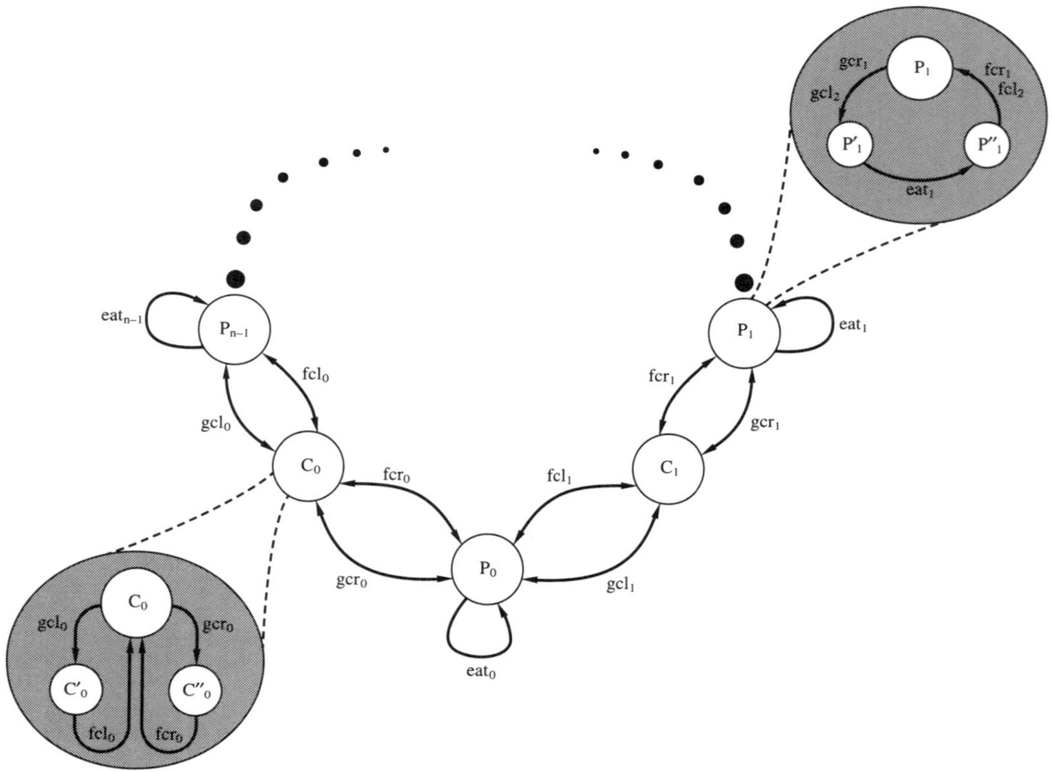

Figure 7.19 The dining philosophers.

Program 7.7

```
1   // Dining Philosophers
2
3   Process Phil(Event gcL, fcL, gcR, fcR, Eat) {
4     static Event gcl, fcl, gcr, fcr, eat
5     static Process Ph {
6       Ph <- (gcl gcr) eat (fcl fcr) Ph
7     }
8     return Ph[gcL/gcl, fcL/fcl, gcR/gcr, fcR/fcr, Eat/eat]
9   }
10
11  Process Chop (Event gcL, fcL, gcR, fcR) {
12    static Event gcl, fcl, gcr, fcr
13    static Process Ch {
14      Ch <- gcl fcl Ch + gcr fcr Ch
15    }
16    return Ch[gcL/gcl, fcL/fcl, gcR/gcr, fcR/fcr]
17  }
18
19  int n=5           // number of philosophers
20
21  int Inc(int i) {  // modulo n increment
22      return (i+1)%n
23  }
24
25  Process C[n], P[n]
26  Event gcl[n], gcr[n], fcl[n], fcr[n], eat[n]
27
28  for (i=0;i<n;i++)  // instantiate n philosophers
29      P[i] <- Phil(gcr[i], fcr[i], gcl[Inc(i)], fcl[Inc(i)], eat[i])
30
31  for (i=0;i<n;i++) // instantiate n chopsticks between them
32      C[i] <- Chop(gcl[i], fcl[i], gcr[i], fcr[i])
33
34  display ~((*C)*(*P))
```

- Line 3 shows that we are declaring a function called `Phil` which takes five `Event` parameters and which returns a `Process`.
- Line 4 declares five `static Event` variables which are local to the function `Phil`. The `static` specifier ensures that these events are only ever created once.
- Line 5 begins the definition of a local `static Process` called `Ph`. XCircal has the feature that a block which begins on the same line as a static variable declaration is only executed once, which is true of lines 5–7. Inside this block, `Ph` is defined (we discuss the intended interpretation of the behaviour later).
- Line 8 returns the process `Ph` with its local event variables relabelled with the formal parameters. This is the key to efficient instantiational because our local variables and definition are specified as `static` every call of `Phil` shares the same process `Ph`, but with a fresh relabelling.
- Lines 11–17 build a process instantiating function for chopsticks.
- Lines 21–23 define a function which is used to calculate array indexes using modulo `n` arithmetic.
- Lines 28–29 call the `Phil` function with appropriate event parameters.
- Lines 31–32 build the chopstick processes.
- Line 34 builds and displays the system of philosophers and chopsticks.

The dining philosophers is a classic problem in concurrency theory, due to Dijkstra (1972). The philosophers are seated at a large round table on which there is a large selection of Chinese food. Between each philosopher there is a chopstick. To eat food, a philosopher requires the use of both of his or her adjacent chopsticks. The problem is to work out schemes whereby the philosophers may cooperate in such a way that they all have a chance to eat, and none starve!

The XCircal model of Program 7.7 describes a philosopher as a process which waits for simultaneous access to the chopstick on his or her left and right (events `gl` and `gr`), then enters a state in which he or she eats, marked with the event `eat`, and then frees both chopsticks (events `fl` and `fr`).

Each chopstick is represented with a process which stipulates that it can either be taken by the philosopher on its left, and then freed, or taken by the philosopher on its right, and then freed.

The actual behaviour generated by line 32 is quite large, for example 352 states are needed for `n=5`, so we only show the first few states:

```
S0 == (gcr[3] gcl[4] S1 +
      (gcr[2] gcl[3] S2 +
      (gcr[1] gcl[2] S4 +
      (gcr[4] gcl[0] S7 +
      (gcr[0] gcl[1]) S10 +
      (gcr[3] gcr[1] gcl[4] gcl[2]) S3 +
      (gcr[4] gcr[1] gcl[2] gcl[0]) S5 +
      (gcr[4] gcr[2] gcl[3] gcl[0]) S6 +
      (gcr[2] gcr[0] gcl[3] gcl[1]) S8 +
      (grc[3] gcr[0] gcl[4] gcl[1]) S9

S1 == eat[3] S13 +
      (gcr[1] gcl[2]) S3 +
      (gcr[0] gcl[1]) S9 +
      (eat[3] gcr[1] gcl[2]) S11 +
      (eat[3] gcr[0] gcl[1]) S12

S3 == eat [3] S11 +
      eat[1] S18 +
      (eat[3] eat [1]) S17
```

Here we see that if chopsticks 3 and 4 are taken, which are on either side of philosopher 3, then we evolve to state `S1`. Similarly, any other single adjacent pair of chopsticks may be taken, causing evolutions to states `S2, S4, S7` and `S10`. The last five choices correspond to all the pairs of philosophers separated by at least one philosopher (e.g. philosopher 3 and 1) taking up chopsticks.

Once at state `S1` philosopher 3 may eat; prior to that, or simultaneous with that, philosophers 1 or 0 may pick up their chopsticks.

7.5. MODELLING LOGIC GATES

Level-based Modelling

In this section we present the first of two approaches to modelling the behaviour of digital hardware in XCircal.

A *delayless* inverter, as shown in Fig. 7.20 on page 166, can be modelled as:

```
Bool a, x
Process INV1

INV1 <- (a.0 x.1)INV1 +
        (a.1 x.0)INV1
```

The data type `Bool` is simply the aggregation of two atomic actions, and is predefined as:

```
struct Bool {
  Event v0
  Event v1
}
```

In the level-based style, we model a Boolean signal with a pair of Circal actions, stating that the signal is at level 0, the other stating that the signal is at level 1. The notation `a.0` is provided as a shorthand for `a.v0`, and similarly `a.1` is equivalent to `a.v1`.

The two summands of `INV1` represent each of the relationships between input, represented by the `a` actions, and the output, represented by the `x` actions. The behaviour describes a process which *simultaneously* accepts one of the alternative pairs of input/output actions and evolves back to itself. Given this as our method of modelling, it is very simple to construct the other standard logic functions in this truth-table style, e.g. a two-input AND gate, shown in Fig. 7.21, is described by the Circal term:

```
Bool a, b, x

Process AND

AND <- (a.0 b.0 x.0)AND +
       (a.1 b.0 x.0)AND +
       (a.0 b.1 x.0)AND +
       (a.1 b.1 x.1)AND
```

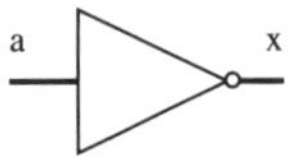

Figure 7.20

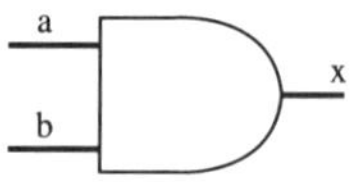

Figure 7.21 Circal description of a two-input AND gate.

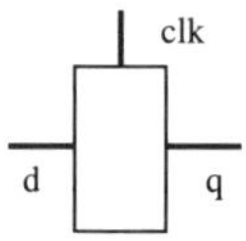

Figure 7.22 A D-type flip-flop storage device.

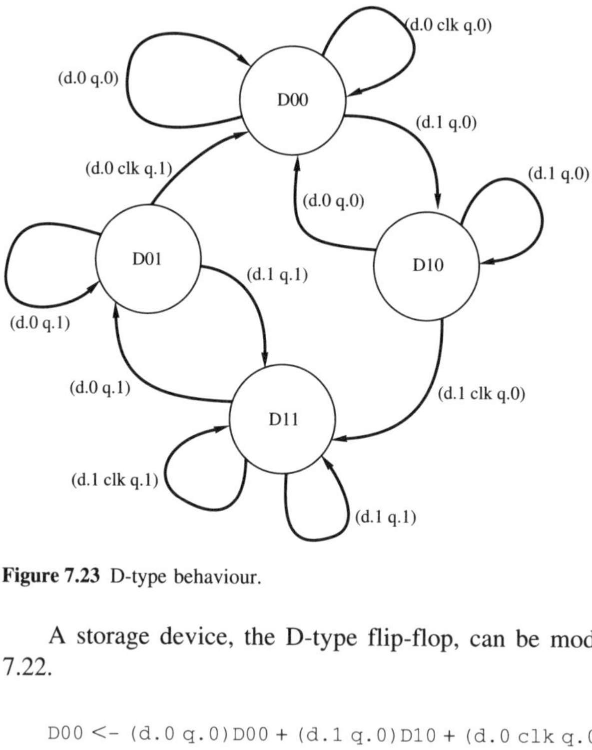

Figure 7.23 D-type behaviour.

A storage device, the D-type flip-flop, can be modelled as shown in Fig. 7.22.

```
D00 <- (d.0 q.0)D00 + (d.1 q.0)D10 + (d.0 clk q.0)D00
D10 <- (d.0 q.0)D00 + (d.1 q.0)D10 + (d.1 clk q.0)D11
D01 <- (d.1 q.1)D11 + (d.0 q.1)D01 + (d.0 clk q.1)D00
D11 <- (d.1 q.1)D11 + (d.0 q.1)D01 + (d.1 clk q.1)D11
```

This behaviour corresponds to the state diagram pictured in Fig. 7.23.

`D00` is a mnemonic name for the state where input `d` and the output `q` both have the value 0. The definition `D00` contains a choice of three guarded

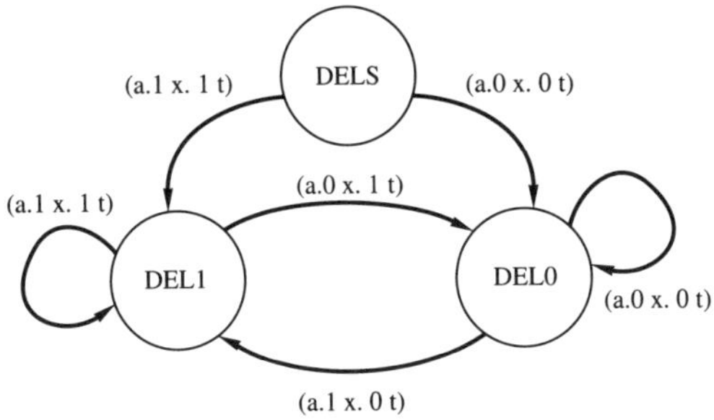

Figure 7.24 Delay behaviour.

expressions; the first merely maintains the current values, the second is where the input has changed to 1, and the third is where the device has been clocked whilst d and q are still 0. Note that in this state it is not possible to clock the device and change the current input value at the same time. This imposes the *constraint* that inputs must be stable before they are clocked, i.e. that we allow a setup time. The other states have a similar structure.

Timing information can be introduced by the composition of additional processes which model delays with respect to a global clock. A process adding a single unit, t, of transport delay, has the following behaviour:

```
Event t                    // global clock
Bool a, x                  // input a, output x
Process DELS, DEL0, DEL1

DELS <- (a.0 x.0 t)DEL0 + (a.1 x.1 t)DEL1
DEL0 <- (a.1 x.0 t)DEL1 + (a.0 x.0 t)DEL0
DEL1 <- (a.0 x.1 t)DEL0 + (a.1 x.1 t)DEL1
```

In this process we use the action t to represent time, whilst the a actions represent the input and the x actions the output. DELS represents the initialisation of the delay to a stable configuration, i.e. input is equal to output with no value propagating through. The state diagram corresponding to the process DELS is pictured in Fig. 7.24.

To construct a unit delay inverter we can compose this process with the inverter model, INV, given above. This composed circuit, pictured in Fig. 7.25, is denoted by the Circal expression shown:

```
INV1[p/x]*DELS[p/a] - p
```

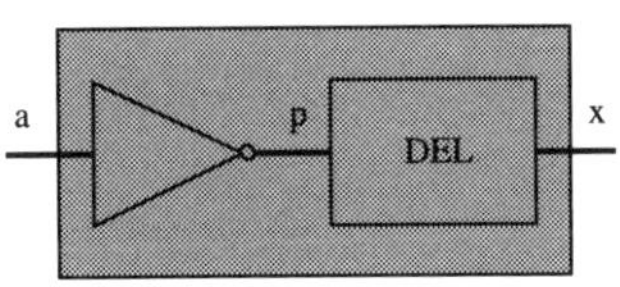

Figure 7.25 A unit delay inverter.

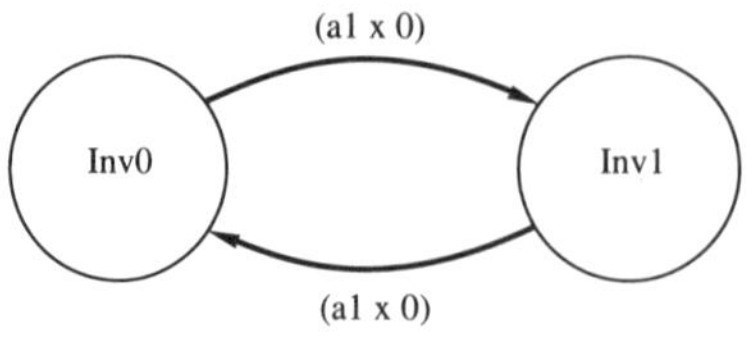


```
Bool a, x
Process Inv0, Inv1

Inv0 <- (a.1 x.0) Inv1
Inv1 <- (a.0 x.1) Inv0
```

Figure 7.26 Inverter behaviour.

Transition-based Modelling

An alternative to maintaining the level of a signal within a model is to represent only *changes* of signal level in the model, i.e. the events of interest are *transitions*.

In transition-based modelling, actions are used to represent changes in logic level rather than the actual level itself, i.e. `a0` represents a change from 1 to 0 on port `a` and `a1` a change from 0 to 1. This leads to the XCircal definition of an inverter shown above, and its corresponding state diagram, Fig. 7.26.

Unlike the level-based model of the previous section, this model has state (`Inv0` corresponds to the output being at level 0, `Inv1` being at level 1), and the actions take us between the states.

To allow flexible use of gate models, we must *package* the behaviour in an instantiation function. It is even more important that we do this for transition based models, because we now have more than one possible start state, i.e. do we start the process in state 0 or 1? Program 7.8 shows how to encapsulate a transition-based model.

Program 7.8

```
1     enum i1_states {S0,S1}
2
3     Process INV(Bool ia,ix, i1_states start_state){
4       static Bool a,x
5       static Process Inv[i1_states]{
6
7         Inv[S0] <- (a.0 x.1)Inv[S1]
8         Inv[S1] <- (a.1 x.0)Inv[S0]
9
10      }
11      return Inv[start_state][ia/a, ix/x]
12    }
```

Line 1 of Program 7.8 defines an enumerated type, `i1_states`, containing two elements. The formal parameters of the function now include `start_state` of type `i1_states` which is used to select the appropriate start state. In the definition of the behaviour, the process identifiers have now been replaced by a single identifier which is an array indexed by the type `i1_states`. In the return statement the `start_state` parameter is used to select which of the states to return. This function may be used to generate inverters that can be connected

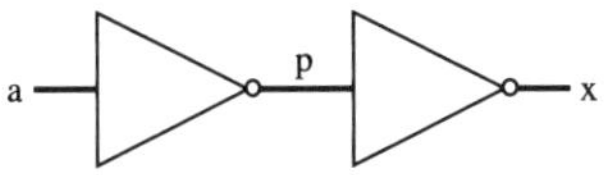

Figure 7.27 Two inverters in series.

```
Bool a, x, p
Process Buf

Buf <- INV(a, p, S0)*
       INV(p, x, S1) - p
```

together to faithfully model cascaded inverters, as pictured in Fig. 7.27. This constructed process `Buf` is shown above. Here the first cascaded inverter is started in state 0, and the other in state 1. Unlike level-based modelling, it is not immediately obvious here how other logic functions are modelled. Consider the model of an AND gate shown in Program 7.9.

Program 7.9

```
1     enum i2_states {S00,S01,S10,S11}
2
3     Process AND2(Bool ia,ib,ix, i2_states start_state){
4       static Bool a,b,x
5       static Process AND[i2_states]{
6
7             AND[S00] <- a.1 AND[S10] + b.1 AND[S01] +
8                        (a.1 b.1 x.1)AND[S11]
9
10            AND[S10] <- a.0 AND[S00] + (b.1 x.1)AND[S11] +
11                       (a.0 b.1)AND[S01]
12
13            AND[S01] <- (a.1 x.1)AND[S11] + b.0 AND[S00] +
14                        (a.1 b.0)AND[S10]
15
16            AND[S11] <- (a.0 x.0)AND[S01] + (b.0 x.0)AND[S10] +
17                        (a.0 b.0 x.0)AND[S00]
18
19            }
20      return AND[start_state][ia/a,ib/b,ix/x]
21    }
```

Line 1 of Program 7.9 introduces an enumerated type for indexing four states. The behaviour for two input gates requires four definitions and corresponds to the state diagram of Fig. 7.28. Since actions represent transitions, the behaviour need only respond when a change of value on a port occurs. This may be one or other or both for a two-input gate. In each case the current value on the port is represented by the state and the elements of `i2_states` have mnemonic names to represent this. Since the output is an instantaneous function of the inputs, only four such states are needed. This AND process has behaviour corresponding to that pictured in Fig. 7.28.

7.6 MODELLING CIRCUIT STRUCTURE

In this section we give examples of the composition of individual gate models into combinatorial and sequential digital circuits.

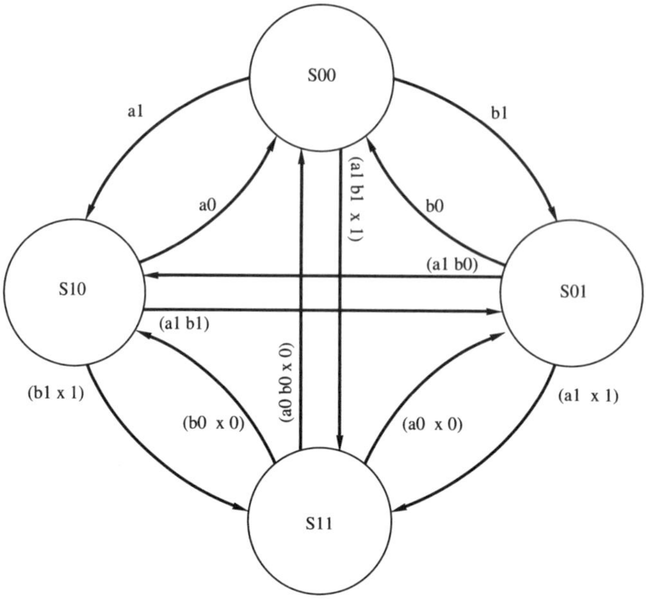

Figure 7.28 State transition diagram for transition-based AND gate model.

A Ripple-carry Adder

Program 7.10 gives an XCircal description of the parametrized ripple-carry adder, as shown in Figure 7.29. The adder has three obvious levels of hierarchy; an XOR and AND gate are combined to make a half-adder. A full-adder is constructed out of two half-adders and an OR gate. Finally, a ripple-carry adder, parametrized by length, joins together `n` full-adders.

- Line 3 of Program 7.10 uses XCircal's file inclusion facility to load in a library of level-based models of common gates, as discussed in the last section, such as `AND2`, `OR2`, and `XOR2`.

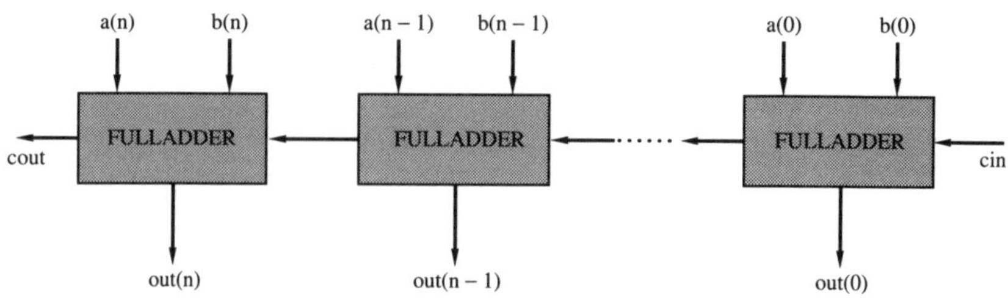

Figure 7.29 Ripple-carry adder.

Program 7.10

```
1     // Ripple Carry Adder
2
3     #include "level-gate-models"
4
5     Process HALF-ADDER(Bool X, Y, Sum, Cout) {
6       return XOR2(X, Y, Sum)*
7              AND2(X, Y, Cout)
8     }
9
10    Process Full-Adder(Bool X, Y, Cin, Cout, Sum) {
11      Bool s1, s2, s3
12
13      return Half-Adder(X, Y, s1, s2)*
14             Half-Adder(Cin, s1, Sum, s3)*
15             OR2(s2, s3, Cout)-(s1 s2 s3)
16    }
17
18    Process RippleCarry(Bool Cin, A[], B[], Sum[], Cout) {
19      n = sizeof A; m = sizeof B; o = sizeof Sum
20
21      if (n<1 || n != m || n!=o) {
22        Error "Bad Arguments to RippleCarry\n"
23      } else if (n==1) {
24
25        return Full-Adder(A[0], B[0], Cin, Cout, Sum[0])
26
27      } else {
28        Bool C[n-1]
29
30        p = Full-Adder(A[0], B[0], Cin, C[0], Sum[0])
31
32        for (i=1;i<n-1;i++)
33          p = p*Full-Adder(A[i], B[i], C[i-1], C[i], Sum[i])
34
35        p = p*Full-Adder(A[n-1], B[n-1], C[n-2], Cout, Sum[n-1])
36
37        return p-(*C)      // abstract away internal signals in C
38      }
39    }
40
41    n=2    // choose value for number of input pairs
42
43    Bool A[n],B[n],Sum[n],Cin, Cout
44    Process Adder
45
46    // Instantiate an Adder
47
48    Adder <- RippleCarry(Cin, A, B, Sum, Cout)
49
50    display ~Adder      // generate and then display the behaviour
```

- Line 5 starts the definition of a `HALF-ADDER` submodule, which is used in the definition of the `FULL-ADDER` at lines 13 and 14.
- `RippleCarry`, at line 18, is implicitly parametrized by the length of the `Bool` arrays `A`, `B` and `Sum`. The length of these arrays is determined at line 19, and consistency checks are made at line 21; the arrays must be non empty and all the same size. `Error` is a procedure provided by the Circal system to enable the user to generate error messages.
- Lines 28–38 deal with the case where there is more than one full-adder to be instantiated. In this case we need an array of internal signals, `C` at line 28, for the internal carries. Line 30 deals with the first full-adder, which must

have `Cin` connected, lines 32–33 deal with the middle adders, and line 35 deals with the last adder, which must pass out `Cout`.
- Line 41 controls the number of input pairs we will build.
- Line 50 generates the following output:

```
SO ==
  (Cout.0 Cin.0 B[1].0 B[0].0 A[1].0 A[0].0 Sum[1].0 Sum[0].0) SO +
  (Cout.0 Cin.0 B[1].0 B[0].0 A[1].1 A[0].0 Sum[1].1 Sum[0].0) SO +
  (Cout.0 Cin.0 B[1].1 B[0].0 A[1].0 A[0].0 Sum[1].1 Sum[0].0) SO +
  (Cout.1 Cin.0 B[1].1 B[0].0 A[1].1 A[0].0 Sum[1].0 Sum[0].0) SO +
  (Cout.0 Cin.1 B[1].0 B[0].0 A[1].0 A[0].0 Sum[1].0 Sum[0].1) SO +
  (Cout.0 Cin.1 B[1].0 B[0].0 A[1].1 A[0].0 Sum[1].1 Sum[0].1) SO +
  (Cout.0 Cin.1 B[1].1 B[0].0 A[1].0 A[0].0 Sum[1].1 Sum[0].1) SO +
  (Cout.1 Cin.1 B[1].1 B[0].0 A[1].1 A[0].0 Sum[1].0 Sum[0].1) SO +
  (Cout.0 Cin.0 B[1].0 B[0].0 A[1].0 A[0].1 Sum[1].0 Sum[0].1) SO +
  (Cout.0 Cin.0 B[1].0 B[0].0 A[1].1 A[0].1 Sum[1].1 Sum[0].1) SO +
  (Cout.0 Cin.0 B[1].1 B[0].0 A[1].0 A[0].1 Sum[1].1 Sum[0].1) SO +
  (Cout.1 Cin.0 B[1].1 B[0].0 A[1].1 A[0].1 Sum[1].0 Sum[0].1) SO +
  (Cout.0 Cin.1 B[1].0 B[0].0 A[1].0 A[0].1 Sum[1].1 Sum[0].0) SO +
  (Cout.1 Cin.1 B[1].0 B[0].0 A[1].1 A[0].1 Sum[1].0 Sum[0].0) SO +
  (Cout.1 Cin.1 B[1].1 B[0].0 A[1].0 A[0].1 Sum[1].0 Sum[0].0) SO +
  (Cout.1 Cin.1 B[1].1 B[0].0 A[1].1 A[0].1 Sum[1].1 Sum[0].0) SO +
  (Cout.0 Cin.0 B[1].0 B[0].1 A[1].0 A[0].0 Sum[1].0 Sum[0].1) SO +
  (Cout.0 Cin.0 B[1].0 B[0].1 A[1].1 A[0].0 Sum[1].1 Sum[0].1) SO +
  (Cout.0 Cin.0 B[1].1 B[0].1 A[1].0 A[0].0 Sum[1].1 Sum[0].1) SO +
  (Cout.1 Cin.0 B[1].1 B[0].1 A[1].1 A[0].0 Sum[1].0 Sum[0].1) SO +
  (Cout.0 Cin.1 B[1].0 B[0].1 A[1].0 A[0].0 Sum[1].1 Sum[0].0) SO +
  (Cout.1 Cin.1 B[1].0 B[0].1 A[1].1 A[0].0 Sum[1].0 Sum[0].0) SO +
  (Cout.1 Cin.1 B[1].1 B[0].1 A[1].0 A[0].0 Sum[1].0 Sum[0].0) SO +
  (Cout.1 Cin.1 B[1].1 B[0].1 A[1].1 A[0].0 Sum[1].1 Sum[0].0) SO +
  (Cout.0 Cin.0 B[1].0 B[0].1 A[1].0 A[0].1 Sum[1].1 Sum[0].0) SO +
  (Cout.1 Cin.0 B[1].0 B[0].1 A[1].1 A[0].1 Sum[1].0 Sum[0].0) SO +
  (Cout.1 Cin.0 B[1].1 B[0].1 A[1].0 A[0].1 Sum[1].0 Sum[0].0) SO +
  (Cout.1 Cin.0 B[1].1 B[0].1 A[1].1 A[0].1 Sum[1].1 Sum[0].0) SO +
  (Cout.0 Cin.1 B[1].0 B[0].1 A[1].0 A[0].1 Sum[1].1 Sum[0].1) SO +
  (Cout.1 Cin.1 B[1].0 B[0].1 A[1].1 A[0].1 Sum[1].0 Sum[0].1) SO +
  (Cout.1 Cin.1 B[1].1 B[0].1 A[1].0 A[0].1 Sum[1].0 Sum[0].1) SO +
  (Cout.1 Cin.1 B[1].1 B[0].1 A[1].1 A[0].1 Sum[1].1 Sum[0].1) SO
```

The displayed material, corresponding to the complete behaviour of a 2-bit ripple-carry adder, enumerates all possible combinations of input and output events.

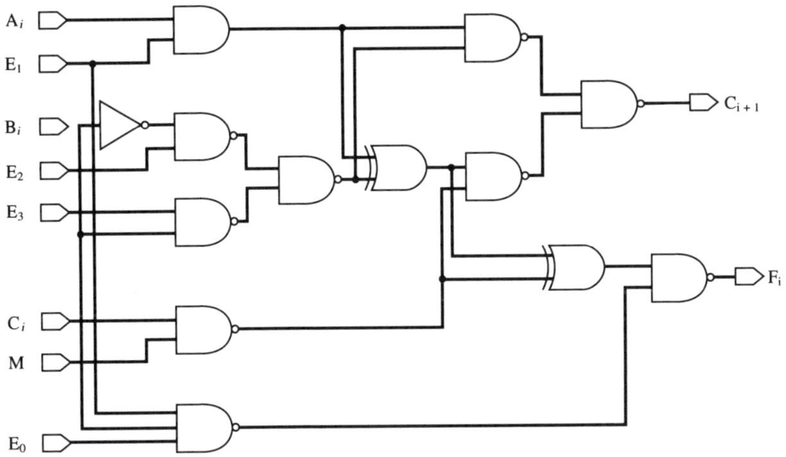

Figure 7.30 Single-bit stage of the 74181 ALU.

An ALU Implementation

Program 7.11 is a model of a single-bit slice of an ALU (Hutchison, 1981) whose schematic is given in Fig. 7.30:

Program 7.11

```
// ALU Implementation

#include "level-gate_models"

Process ALUImp(Bool A, B, E0, E1, E2, E3, M, Cin, Cout, F) {
    static Bool iA, iB, iE0, iE1, iE2, iE3, iM, iCin, iCout, iF
    static Process IMP {
        Bool o1, o2, 'B, o3 ,o4, o5, o6, o7, o8, o9, 'o9,
             o10, iCin', iCout'

        IMP <- ~(AND2(iA, iE1, o1)*
                 NAND2(iB, iE2, o2)*
                 INV(iB, 'B)*
                 NAND2(iE3, 'B, o3)*
                 NAND2(o2, o3, o4)*
                 AND2(iCin', iM, o5)*
                 XOR2(o1, o4, o6)*
                 NAND2(o1, o4, o7)*
                 NAND2(o6, o5, o8)*
                 NAND2(o7, o8, iCout')*
                 XOR2(o6, o5, o9)*
                 INV(o9, 'o9)*
                 NAND3(iA, iB, iE0, o10)*
                 NAND2('o9, o10, iF)*
                 AND2(iCout', iM, iCout)*
                 AND2(iCin, iM, iCin') - o1 o2 'B o3 o4 o5 //
                                          o6 o7 o8 o9 'o9 o10 iCin' iCout')
    }

    return IMP[A/iA, B/iB, E0/iE0, E1/iE1, E2/iE2,
               E3/iE3, M/iM, Cin/iCin, Cout/iCout, F/iF]
}
```

Line 5 is the start of the function that will build a single-bit stage of an ALU. Lines 6 and 7 declare the `Bool` and `Process` names of the master copy of the ALU implementation, which are then relabelled at line 30. We use the instantiation style since this will be more efficient than returning multiple fresh copies of the ALU bit-slice. At line 11 we construct the process `IMP` by composing together 16 calls of gate instantiation functions, using the $*$ operator, and then we abstract away the internal signals, using the – operator.

By comparing Program 7.11 with the schematic in Fig. 7.30 you may notice that the XCircal version has two extra AND gates. They are added to handle the 'don't care' values on the carry signals when performing logic operations. The comment at the end of line 26 enables the concatenation operator to continue over a line boundary.

A 4-bit circuit can be constructed as shown in Program 7.12.

Program 7.12

```
1     int n=4     // number of bit slices
2
3     Bool A[n],B[n],Cout[n],F[n],        // inputs, carry-out, function
4          Cin0,                          // carry in
5          E0, E1, E2, E3, M              // mode selectors
6
7     Process CON                         // Constrain to legal opcodes only
8     CON <- (M.1 E0.0 E1.1 E2.1 E3.0 Cin0.0) CON +
9            (M.1 E0.0 E1.1 E2.0 E3.1 Cin0.1) CON +
10           (M.1 E0.0 E1.1 E2.0 E3.0 Cin0.1) CON +
11           (M.1 E0.0 E1.0 E2.1 E3.0 Cin0.1) CON +
12           (M.0 E0.0 E1.1 E2.1 E3.0 Cin0.0) CON +
13           (M.0 E0.1 E1.0 E2.0 E3.0 Cin0.0) CON +
14           (M.0 E0.1 E1.1 E2.1 E3.0 Cin0.0) CON
15
16    Process Combine(Bool A[], B[], E0, E1, E2, E3, M, Cin0, Cout[], F[],
17                    Process Unit(Bool,Bool,Bool,Bool,Bool,
18                                 Bool,Bool,Bool,Bool,Bool)) {
19
20        p = CON * Unit(A[0], B[0], E0, E1, E2, E3, M, Cin0, Cout[0], F[0])
21        n = sizeof A
22
23        for (i=1;i<n;i++)
24          p = p * Unit(A[i], B[i], E0, E1, E2, E3, M, Cout[i-1], Cout[i], F[i])
25
26        for (i=0;i<n-1;i++)
27          p = p - Cout[i]    // abstract the inner carry signals
28
29        return ~p  // return the expanded behaviour
30    }
31
32    Process IMP  // Build an Implementation
33
34    IMP <- Combine(A, B, E0, E1, E2, E3, M, Cin0, Cout, F, ALUImp)
```

Line 1 of Program 7.12 allows us to specify how many slices we wish to use. The process definition on line 8 is a constraint which forces only legal operations to be considered (i.e. legal combinations of `M`, `E0`, `E1`, `E2`, `E3` and `Cin0`). It is important to model the constraints under which a circuit will operate in order to reduce the size of behaviour that is manipulated.

The function `Combine` at line 16 has a function parameter `Unit`. We pass `Combine` the function `ALUImp` at line 34. `Combine` calls the passed function using the passed signals the same number of times as the size of the `A` bus. The loop at line 26 causes the inner carry signals to be abstracted.

7.7. SIMULATION IN CIRCAL

The level-based and transition-based gate models we have introduced are very similar to the low-level case analysis code one would find in a gate-level simulator. This is not surprising, since both are models of circuit behaviour at that level. We can emulate the operation of a simulator quite simply in XCircal; given a description such as the 4-bit ALU, we can simply compose it with an XCircal process which models a test pattern, as in Program 7.13.

Program 7.13

```
1     #include "alu"
2
3     Event Add  = (M.1 E0.0 E1.1 E2.1 E3.0 Cin0.0) // Opcodes
4     Event Sub  = (M.1 E0.0 E1.1 E2.0 E3.1 Cin0.0)
5     Event IncA = (M.1 E0.0 E1.1 E2.0 E3.0 Cin0.0)
6     Event IncB = (M.1 E0.0 E1.0 E2.1 E3.0 Cin0.0)
7     Event Eor  = (M.0 E0.0 E1.1 E2.1 E3.0 Cin0.0)
8     Event And  = (M.0 E0.1 E1.0 E2.0 E3.0 Cin0.0)
9     Event Or   = (M.0 E0.1 E1.1 E2.1 E3.0 Cin0.0)
10
11    // Define Number Generator
12
13    Event Number(Bool N[], int num) {
14        e = NullE
15        j=1
16        for (i=0;i<sizeof N;i++) {
17          e = e (num&j ? N[i].1 : N[i].0)
18          j = j<<1
19        }
20        return e
21    }
22
23    // Do an Exhaustive Simulation of the Add Opcode
24
25    Process /\(M E0 E1 E2 E3 Cin0 (*A) (*B))  // define deadlock
26
27    for (i=0;i<=2^^(n-1);i++)
28      for (j=0;j<=2^^(n-1);j++) {
29        print i "+" j " = "
30        trace ~((Add (Number(A, i)) (Number(B, j))) /\ *
31                IMP-Add-(*A)-(*B))  // abstract away inputs
32      }
33
```

- Line 1 of Program 7.13 includes the ALU definitions of the last section.
- Lines 3–9 define opcodes for the ALU as combinations of the function selectors.
- Lines 13–21 define a function that, given an array of `Bools N`, will return the simultaneous set of events from that array that correspond to the number `num`, e.g. `Number(x,9) == (x[3].1 x[2].0 x[1].0 x[0].1)`, where `x` is declared `Bool x[4]`.

- Line 25 defines a deadlock process which will terminate the test pattern.
- Lines 27–28 loop through all possible values which we can apply to `A` and `B` input vectors (`^^` is integer exponentiation).
- Line 30 uses the function `trace` which displays the sequence of events associated with a process (which must not contain a choice term which is usually the case with simulation results).

The output of Program 7.13 begins:

```
0+0 =
(Cout[3].0 F[3].0 F[2].0 F[1].0 F[0].0)
0+1 =
(Cout[3].0 F[3].0 F[2].0 F[1].0 F[0].1)
0+2 =
(Cout[3].0 F[3].0 F[2].0 F[1].1 F[0].0)
0+3 =
(Cout[3].0 F[3].0 F[2].0 F[1].1 F[0].1)
0+4 =
(Cout[3].0 F[3].0 F[2].1 F[1].0 F[0].0)
0+5 =
(Cout[3].0 F[3].0 F[2].1 F[1].0 F[0].1)
0+6 =
(Cout[3].0 F[3].0 F[2].1 F[1].1 F[0].0)
0+7 =
(Cout[3].0 F[3].0 F[2].1 F[1].1 F[0].1)
0+8 =
(Cout[3].0 F[3].1 F[2].0 F[1].0 F[0].0)
1+0 =
(Cout[3].0 F[3].0 F[2].0 F[1].0 F[0].1)
1+1 =
(Cout[3].0 F[3].0 F[2].0 F[1].1 F[0].0)
```

. . . and so on.

Circal makes no distinction between 'input' and 'output' events, any distinction is in the mind of the modeller, not in the calculus itself. A powerful consequence of treating all events as equal is that we can simulate a system using a test pattern containing 'output' events mixed in with 'input' events.

As an analogy, think of a conventional hand-held electronic calculator. We can enter `7 - 3 =` and get the answer `4`, but we cannot enter `3 + X = 7` and expect to be told `X = 4`; the only way to solve such equations is to re-structure until the unknown is on the right-hand side. A Circal model of addition need not have this limitation, in fact, it can even answer questions like `X + Y = 7`, i.e. what are the possible combinations of `X` and `Y` such that they add up to `7`.

To illustrate this, we make use of the ripple-carry circuit, Program 7.10, and build a test pattern for it in Program 7.14:

Program 7.14

```
1    #include "RippleCarry"
2
3    n=3    // choose value for number of input pairs
4
5    Bool A[n],B[n],Sum[n],Cin, Cout
6    Process Adder
7
8    // Instantiate an Adder
9
10   Adder <- RippleCarry(Cin, A, B, Sum, Cout)
11
12   // Test Patterns
13
14   s = ((*Sum) Cin Cout)        // sort for test pattern
15
16   Process Test(s), /\(s)
17
18   Test <- (Cin.0 Sum[0].1 Sum[1].1 Sum[2].1 Cout.0) /\
19
20   display ~(Test*Adder-s)
```

- Line 1 of Program 14 includes the ripple-carry definition.
- Line 3 sets a precision of 3 bits.
- Line 14 calculates the sort we will use in the test pattern states `Test` and / \). It is important that for any `Bool`, say `X`, used in the test pattern, the `Events` `X.0` and `X.1` are included in the sort of the pattern. For this reason, we explicitly assign the correct sorts of line 16; if we did not, automatic sort determination would be evoked for `Test` at line 18, and the events `Cin.1`, `Sum[0].0`, `Sum[1].0`, `Sum[2].0` and `Cout.1` would not be found in the sort. Omitting these events prevents the test pattern from restricting these, untested, events from occurring in transitions, i.e. they would not be excluded from the resulting composed behaviour but would appear in unwanted choice terms, due to the independent action summations of the composition law. The correct choice of deadlock sort is very crucial in designing XCircal simulations.

  The test pattern of line 18 stipulates that we wish to set `Cin` to be 0, a familiar 'input' type 'variable', and that we are only interested in the behaviour when the `Sum` outputs represent 7 and `Cout` is 0.
- Line 20 generates the following output:

```
  S0 == (B[2].1 B[1].1 B[0].1 A[2].0 A[1].0 A[0].0) S1 +
        (B[2].0 B[1].1 B[0].1 A[2].1 A[1].0 A[0].0) S1 +
        (B[2].1 B[1].0 B[0].1 A[2].0 A[1].1 A[0].0) S1 +
        (B[2].0 B[1].0 B[0].1 A[2].1 A[1].1 A[0].0) S1 +
        (B[2].1 B[1].1 B[0].0 A[2].0 A[1].0 A[0].1) S1 +
        (B[2].0 B[1].1 B[0].0 A[2].1 A[1].0 A[0].1) S1 +
        (B[2].1 B[1].0 B[0].0 A[2].0 A[1].1 A[0].1) S1 +
        (B[2].0 B[1].0 B[0].0 A[2].1 A[1].1 A[0].1) S1
S1 == /\
```

Here all possible values of the `A` and `B` bit-vectors are generated such that they add up to 7.

7.8 SPECIFYING CIRCUIT BEHAVIOUR

In this section we give examples of models, which are more abstract than the gate-level models introduced so far, and which can be used to give the *specification* of the desired behaviour of a circuit.

Combinational Circuits

Combinational circuits are those which compute an output as a Boolean function of its inputs. The previous or current state of the circuit does not have any influence on the value, or values, produced. These circuits may be readily specified as truth tables, and as the composition of truth tables. We have seen in the low-level gate models how truth tables suggest a straightforward encoding in XCircal. The truth table for the ALU presented in Sec. 7.6 is given in Table 7.1. This is encoded in XCircal as illustrated by Program 7.15.

Lines 1–15 define a function which will build a truth table for an array of `Bool`s `a` and a personalization array `v`. Here we make the highest array-bound correspond to the most significant bit. The event concatenation on line 9 builds a simultaneous guard corresponding to the truth values of the current row; the variable `j` is the index for the current column and `k` corresponds to current bit of the current row value `v[i]`.

Table 7.1

Mode M	Function Selectors E_0	E_1	E_2	E_3	Function
1	0	1	1	0	ADD A to B (with carry in and out) ($C_0 = 0$)
1	0	1	0	1	SUBtract B from A (with borrow in and out) ($C_0 = 1$)
1	0	1	0	0	INCrement A ($C_0 = 1$)
1	0	0	1	0	INCrement B ($C_0 = 1$)
0	0	1	1	0	EOR of A_i and B_i
0	1	0	0	0	AND of A_i and B_i
0	1	1	1	0	OR of A_i and B_i

Program 7.15

```
Process TruthTable(Bool a[], int v[], Process P) {
  m = sizeof a
  n = sizeof v
  p = NullP
  for (i=0;i<n;i++) {
    e = NullE
    k = 1                            // start with lowest order bit
    for (j=0;j<m;j++) {
      e = e ((v[i]&k==k) ? a[j].1 : a[j].0)
      k = k<<1
    }
    p = p + e P
  }
  return p
}

Process ALUSpec(Bool A, B, E0, E1, E2, E3, M, Cin, Cout, F) {
    static Bool a[10]
    static int v[44]
    static Process ALU_SPEC {
      v[ 0]=0b1011000000; v[ 1]=0b1011001010; v[ 2]=0b1011010010
      v[ 3]=0b1011011001; v[ 4]=0b1011000110; v[ 5]=0b1011001101
      v[ 6]=0b1011010101; v[ 7]=0b1011011111; v[ 8]=0b1010100101
      v[ 9]=0b1010101110; v[10]=0b1010110111; v[11]=0b1010111101
      v[12]=0b1010100010; v[13]=0b1010101000; v[14]=0b1010110001
      v[15]=0b1010111010; v[16]=0b1010000000; v[17]=0b1010001000
      v[18]=0b1010010010; v[19]=0b1010011010; v[20]=0b1010000110
      v[21]=0b1010001110; v[22]=0b1010010101; v[23]=0b1010011101
      v[24]=0b1001000110; v[25]=0b1001010110; v[26]=0b1001001101
      v[27]=0b1001011101; v[28]=0b1001000000; v[29]=0b1001010000
      v[30]=0b1001001010; v[31]=0b1001011010; v[32]=0b0011000000
      v[33]=0b0011001010; v[34]=0b0011010010; v[35]=0b0011011000
      v[36]=0b0100000000; v[37]=0b0100001000; v[38]=0b0100010000
      v[39]=0b0100011010; v[30]=0b0111000000; v[41]=0b0111001010
      v[42]=0b0111010010; v[43]=0b0111011010;

      ALU_SPEC <- TruthTable(a, v, ALU_SPEC)
    }
    return ALU_SPEC[M/a[9], E0/a[8], E1/a[7], E2/a[6], E3/a[5],
                    A/a[4], B/a[3], Cin/a[2], F/a[1], Cout/a[0]]
}
```

This approach to constructing XCircal specifications from truth tables can be explained clearly with a smaller example:

```
Process Table
Bool a[3]
int v[4]
v[0] = 0b111
v[1] = 0b001
v[2] = 0b010
v[3] = 0b110
Table <- TruthTable(a,v,Table)
print Table
```

gives

```
Table <- (a[2].1 a[1].1 a[0].1) Table +
         (a[2].0 a[1].0 a[0].1) Table +
         (a[2].0 a[1].1 a[0].0) Table +
         (a[2].1 a[1].1 a[0].0) Table
```

The size of the `Bool` array determines the width of the table, and the length of the `int` array determines the height.

The original specification of the ALU does not say what the carry signals should do during logical operations. To simplify the expansion of the circuit, it proves more convenient to specify that these 'don't care' values should be zero, although this is not the actual behaviour of the circuit presented in Fig. 7.30, hence the presence of the extra gates added to the implementation to conform to this added constraint.

It would not be feasible to specify a 32-bit data path as a single truth table, because it would have 2^{31} rows; however, we can specify it in terms of the hierarchical composition of smaller bit/function slices. In fact, we can call the `Combine` function defined at line 16 of Program 7.12 with the specification instead of the implementation:

```
SPEC <- Combine(A, B, E0, E1, E2, E3, M, Cin0, Cout, F, ALUSpec)
```

thus building a specification, `SPEC`, parametrized on the length of the input vectors `A` and `B`.

Sequential Circuits

A binary coded decimal recognizer is a circuit which detects valid sequences of bits that constitute a BCD code (i.e. represents a number between 0 and 9). The sequence has the most significant bit leading, and after the end of the sequence the output will either be 1 for a valid sequence or 0 for an invalid sequence.

A formal specification of the BCD recogniser in predicate logic is given by the following:

$\forall t_n \forall k > 0$, if $n = 4k - 1$
    then
        if $X \in \{0---, 100-\}$
        then $O(t_n) = 1$
        else $O(t_n) = 0$
        else $O(t_n) = 0$

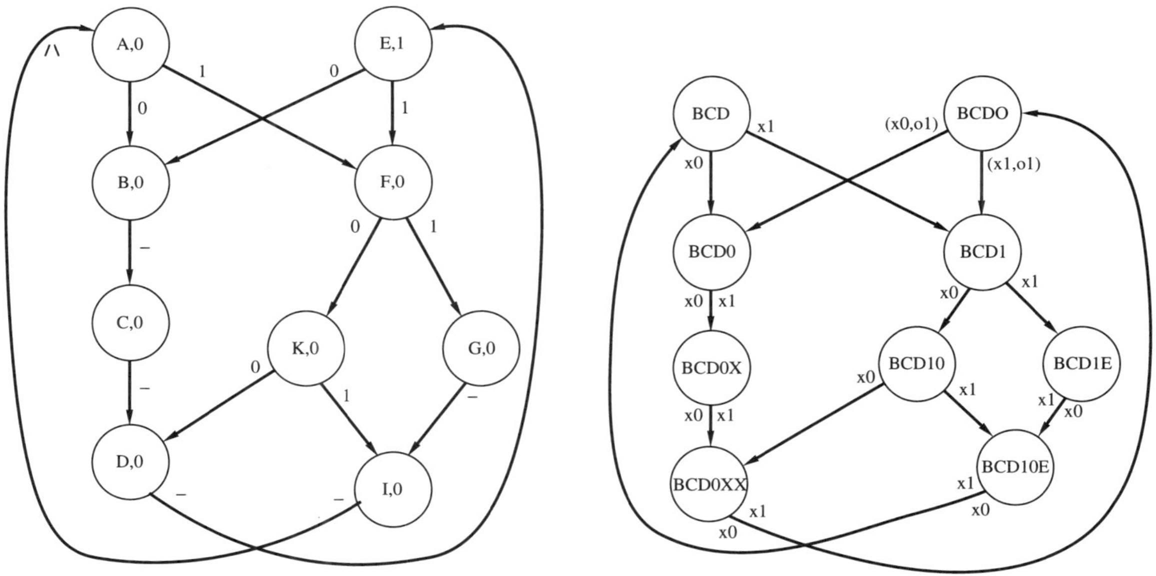

Figure 7.31 BCD Moore machine state graph and Circal transition graph.

This form of specification does not map into XCircal, owing to the assertional nature of predicate logic compared to the operational nature of XCircal, although a direct mapping could be established to HOL, following the specification techniques given in Chapter 5. However, the first step in designing the recognizer involves constructing a Moore state machine description of the system as shown in Fig. 7.31. It could be argued that for this particular class of problem a finite-state machine (FSM) type of description is more comprehensible. We find that FSMs map very readily into a corresponding XCircal description, giving us a specification which can then be used to verify the correctness of an implementation.

The XCircal specification of the BCD recognizer is given by the BCD process in Program 7.16.

Program 7.16

```
enum bcd_states {start, sO, sOX, sOXX, s0, s1, s10, s1E, s10E}

Process BCD(x o.1)[bcd_states]

BCD[start] <- x.0 BCD[sO]       + x.1 BCD[s1]
BCD[sO]    <- x.0 BCD[sOX]      + x.1 BCD[sOX]
BCD[sOX]   <- x.0 BCD[sOXX]     + x.1 BCD[sOXX]
BCD[sOXX]  <- x.0 BCD[s0]       + x.1 BCD[s0]
BCD[s0]    <- (x.0 o.1) BCD[sO] + (x.1 o.1) BCD[s1] // nb. s0 != sO
BCD[s1]    <- x.0 BCD[s10]      + x.1 BCD[s1E]
BCD[s10]   <- x.0 BCD[sOXX]     + x.1 BCD[s10E]
BCD[s1E]   <- x.0 BCD[s10E]     + x.1 BCD[s10E]
BCD[s10E]  <- x.0 BCD[start]    + x.1 BCD[start]
```

In Program 7.16, `BCD[start]` is the initial term for the specification and this corresponds to state `A` of the Moore machine description of Fig. 7.31. Notice that XCircal arrays may be indexed by elements of an enumerated type. `BCD[s0]` is the term that denotes successful recognition and corresponds to state `E`. These correspondences can be seen by comparing the Moore machine diagram and the XCircal transition graph of Fig. 7.31. Note that success is represented by the action `o.1`; no action occurs if the sequence is invalid, the states ending in `E`, and the term merely evolves to `BCD[sO]` or `BCD[s1]` depending on the first value of the next sequence.

CHAPTER

EIGHT

DESIGN VERIFICATION USING XCIRCAL

In the previous chapters we have shown how the Circal process algebra, and the XCircal description language, are used to describe structural and behavioural properties of hardware. In this chapter we discuss how the laws of Circal and equivalence checking algorithms, based on its *operational semantics*, can be used to construct verification proofs of the form

$$\text{specification} \equiv \text{implementation}$$

8.1. VERIFICATION IN PROCESS ALGEBRAS

We may reasonably assume that a digital system has been correctly designed if its specification and implementation have the same behaviour. The behaviour of two processes, one describing the specification and the other the implementation, may be shown to be *equivalent* using an *operational semantics* which gives meaning to the syntax of the XCircal language. The semantics actually gives a meaning to the operators of the Circal process algebra, from which the XCircal language is then derived.

The equivalence property is formulated as a relation which exists between certain pairs of processes. These processes may be syntactically different but the important thing is that they may be considered to have equivalent behaviour, regardless of their internal structure, as long as no experiment conducted from 'outside' the processes can distinguish them. Many different theories exist for providing the rules for distinguishing processes, with some equivalences being *stronger*, i.e. equating fewer pairs of processes, than others. A rich variety of equivalences have been defined for the various process algebras, such as CCS (Milner, 1989), CSP (Hoare, 1985), and Circal.

In Chapter 7 we presented a transition rule semantics, also known as structured operational semantics (SOS) (Plotkin, 1981), for assigning meaning to Circal processes. An associated testing equivalence (De Nicola and Hennessy, 1984) has been given to Circal by Moller (1989) and Mao (1992). The testing equivalence is based on the intuitively appealing concept that two processes are equivalent if they have the same responses to a collection of tests. The testing equivalence is relatively *weak*, i.e. it *usefully* equates a large number of processes. For these reasons, together with the existence of an efficient checking algorithm, testing equivalence is adopted as the automatic verification technique employed by the Circal system. The reader is referred to the work of Wenbo Mao (1992) for a detailed presentation of the semantic concepts which underpin the XCircal language and the Circal system.

An important property of behavioural equivalence is one of *substitutivity*. This can best be explained by the following example.

Assume that in a system `A`, a component has a specification `Spec`. The implementation of the component is called `Imp`. If the `Spec` and the `Imp` have equivalent behaviour (i.e. the `Imp` is a correct implementation of the `Spec`), then by replacing `Spec` in system `A` with `Imp`, we expect to obtain a new system, `B`, which should have the same behaviour as that of `A`. This is pictured in Fig. 8.1. Thus, from an intuitive point of view, a behavioural equivalence relation such as ~ should always consistently relate one behavioural description to another, where the other is obtained by replacing a component in the former by an equivalent description; replacing `Spec` by `Imp` in the above example. While this property is intuitively attractive, it is also necessary to enable processes to be manipulated as mathematical objects by applying algebraic techniques, such as the use of *axioms* for rewriting the syntax of a process, while retaining its meaning.

Formulating a Proof Using Axioms

Transition rules are used to explain the underlying meaning of the operators which constitute the Circal process algebra. These transition rules have been

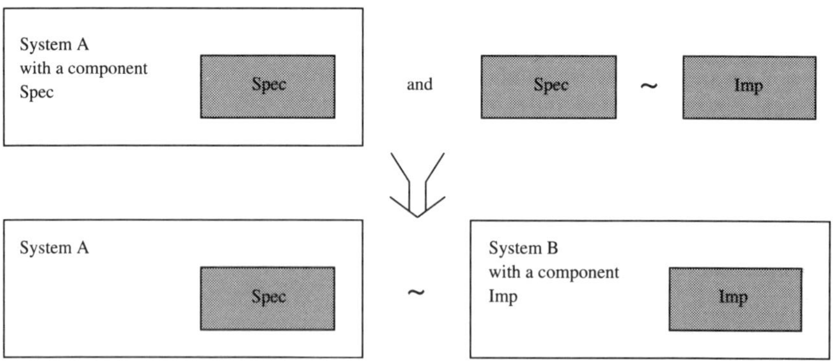

Figure 8.1 Property of substitutivity of an equivalence relation.

used to formally define the operational semantics of Circal, and then to define an intuitively realistic definition of equivalence between terms in the Circal syntax. Both Mao (1992) and Moller (1989) have shown that a collection of axioms capturing properties of Circal is sound. That is, each of these axioms, which can be written as an equation of the form P = Q, has been shown to be correct in that P and Q are equivalent.

For example, the choice operator should be both commutative and associative as the order of making choice should be immaterial, hence the following equations should hold:

$$X + Y = Y + X$$

$$X + (Y + Z) = (X + Y) + Z \ \forall X, Y, Z$$

This is in fact done by constructing equivalence proofs to show that

$$X + Y \equiv Y + X$$

$$X + (Y + Z) \equiv (X + Y) + Z \ \forall X, Y, Z$$

The transition rules used to define the composition and abstraction operators may also be formulated as axioms. These axioms, (+∗) and (+−) of Fig. 7.15, form the basis of an *expansion law* which applies the composition and abstraction operators, repeatedly replacing them by the simple behavioural operators.

The finite set of equations which form an axiomatic system can be used to construct proofs of the correctness of statements of the form

$$\text{specification} = \text{implementation}$$

This is achieved by manipulating the syntactic structure of the Circal terms which make up either side of the above equation. The reason for using this axiomatic approach is that the manipulation of equations using the axioms is more understandable than reasoning about the underlying semantics using the transition rules.

Example Consider two inverters connected in series as pictured in Fig. 7.27. If each inverter has unit propagation delay then we would expect that this two-component system would have the same behaviour as a two-delay buffer. As the XCircal language is an extension of the Circal process algebra, the Circal axioms may also be used to manipulate XCircal expressions. We will take two one-unit delay inverters, specify a two-delay buffer and use the axioms to show that the constructed system has the same behaviour as the specification.

The one-unit delay inverter can be defined in XCircal as:

```
Event t
Bool a, x
Process INS,IN0, IN1
```

```
INS <- (a.0 x.1 t) IN0 + (a.1 x.0 t)IN1
IN0 <- (a.0 x.1 t) IN0 + (a.1 x.1 t)IN1
IN1 <- (a.0 x.0 t) IN0 + (a.1 x.0 t)IN1

Process IN(Bool ia, ix) {
  return INS[ia/a,ix/x]
}
```

A two-delay buffer has the following XCircal definition:

```
Event t
Bool b, y

Process DELS, DEL00, DEL01, DEL10, DEL11

DELS  <- (b.0 y.0 t) DEL00 + (b.1 y.1 t) DEL11
DEL00 <- (b.0 y.0 t) DEL00 + (b.1 y.0 t) DEL10
DEL01 <- (b.0 y.1 t) DEL00 + (b.1 y.1 t) DEL10
DEL10 <- (b.0 y.0 t) DEL01 + (b.1 y.0 t) DEL11
DEL11 <- (b.0 y.1 t) DEL01 + (b.1 y.t t) DEL11

Process DEL2(Bool ib, iy) {
  return DELS[ib/b,iy/y]
}
```

The constructed system is described by the expression:

`IN(p,q)*IN(q,r)-q`

We now wish to show that this constructed process has the same behaviour as that of `DEL2(p,r)` using the axioms, in particular the expansion axioms for composition and abstraction. That is, we wish to prove that

`IN(p,q)*IN(q,r)-q = DEL2(p,r)`

- Step 1 Replace the inverter identifiers in the left-hand side of the above equation by their initial process states, with port relabelling being made explicit. The left-hand side then becomes

  `INS[p/a,q/x]* INS[q/a,r/x]-q`

- Step 2 Use the relabelling axiom to replace label `a` by label `p`, and label `x` by label `q`, in the definition of process `IN` in state `INS`. Similarly for the second instantiation of the one delay inverter component. The above expression then becomes:

```
(p.0 q.1 t)IN0[p/a.q/x]+(p.1 q.0 t)IN1[p/a,q/x]*

(q.0 r.1 t)IN0[q/a.r/x]+(q.1 r.0 t)IN1[q/a.r/x]-q
```

- Step 3 We now repeatedly use the relabelling axiom to create the appropriately relabelled process in state `INS`. We also rename each of the relabelled states, such that

```
IN0′ <- IN0[p/a,q/x]

IN1′ <- IN1[p/a,q/x]

IN0″ <- IN0[q/a,r/x]

IN1″ <- IN1[q/a,r/x]
```

  This results in the expression

```
(p.0 q.1 t) IN0′+ (p.1 q.0 t) IN1′*

(q.0 r.1 t) IN0″+ (q.1 r.0 t) IN1″-q
```

  Notice that reference to the relabelling operator `[-/-]` has been removed thanks to repeated use of the relabelling axiom, up to recursion, coupled with the introduction of the new identifiers.
- Step 4 We may now use the composition axiom (+∗), a constituent of the expansion law mentioned previously. This has the effect of applying the ∗ composition operator, resulting in the following expression:

```
((p.0 q.1 r.0 t)IN0′*IN1″+ (p.1 q.0 r.1 t) IN1′* IN0″)-q
```

  Note that the first summand of the left side of ∗, namely `(p.0 q.1 t)IN0′`, synchronizes with the second summand of the right side of ∗, the `(q.1 r.0t) IN1″`. Similarly, `(p.1 q.0 t)IN1′` synchronizes with `(q.0 r.1 t)IN0″`. These are the only synchronizations which the composition operator permits.
- Step 5 The composition axiom may now be used to expand `IN0′* IN1″`, `IN1′* IN0″` and the states which follow from them. This gives

```
IN0′* IN1″= (p.0 q.1 r.0 t)IN0′* IN1″+

            (p.1 q.1 r.0 t)IN1′* IN1″

IN1′* IN1″= (p.0 q.0 r.0 t)IN0′* IN0″+

            p.1 q.0 r.0 t)IN1′* IN0″

IN0′* IN0″= (p.0 q.1 r.1 t)IN0′* IN1″+

            (p.1 q.1 r.1 t)IN1′* IN1″

IN1′* IN0″= (p.0 q.0 r.1 t) IN0′* IN0″+

            (p.1 q.0 r.1 t)IN1′* IN0″
```

- Step 6 Axiom (+−) which encapsulates the definition of the abstraction operator, `-q`, may now be used on the expression given in Step 4, with the state expansion given in Step 5. This has the effect of removing all guards labelled by `q` and results in the following expression:

```
(p.0 r.0 t)IN0'* IN1"-q + (p.1 r.1 t)IN1'* IN0"-q
```

where

```
IN0'* IN1"-q = (p.0 r.0 t)IN0'* IN1"-q +
               (p.1 r.0 t)IN1'* IN16"-q
IN1'* IN1"-q = (p.0 r.0 t)IN0'* IN0"-q +
               (p.1 r.0 t)IN1'* IN0"-q
IN0'* IN0"-q = (p.0 r.1 t)IN0'* IN1"-q +
               (p.1 r.1 t)IN1'*IN1"-q
IN1'* IN0"-q = (p.0 r.1 t) IN0'* IN0"-q +
               (p.1 r.1 t) IN1'* IN0"-q
```

- Step 7 We may now rename the processes in a consistent fashion. This does not change the behaviour that has resulted from the use of the axioms. Let

```
SYS00 <- IN0'* IN1"-q
SYS11 <- IN1'* IN0"-q
SYS10 <- IN1'* IN1"-q
SYS01 <- IN0'* IN0"-q
```

The expression produced in Step 6 now becomes:

```
(p.0 r.0 t) SYS00 + (p.1 r.1 t) SYS11
```

where

```
SYS00 = (p.0 r.0 t) SYS00 + (p.1 r.0 t) SYS10
SYS10 = (p.0 r.0 t) SYS01 + (p.1 r.0 t) SYS11
SYS01 = (p.0 r.1 t) SYS00 + (p.1 r.1 t) SYS10
SYS11 = (p.0 r.1 t) SYS01 + (p.1 r.1 t) SYS11
```

This expression has the same behaviour as the initial expression `IN(p.q)* IN(q,r)-q`, remember. This is because we have only used the Circal axioms to rewrite one expression into another, and have simplified the resulting expanded expressions by using simplifying identifiers. Notice that `SYS00` is shorthand for

```
IN0'* IN1"-q
```

which is in turn shorthand for

```
IN0[p/a,q/x]* IN1[q/a.r/x]-q
```

- Step 8 We may now use our definition of the two-delay buffer and relabel it to have ports `p` and `r`. This produces the equation

```
DEL2(p,r) = DELS[p/b,r/y]
```

Using the relabelling axiom we obtain the identity

```
DEL2(p,r) = (p.0 r.0 t) DELL00[p/b,r/y]
          + (p.1 r.1 t) DELL11[p/b,r/y]
```

where

```
DELL00[p/b,r/y] = (p.0 r.0 t) DEL00[p/b,r/y]
                + (p.1 r.0 t) DEL10[p/b,r/y]
DELL01[p/b,r/y] = (p.0 r.0 t) DEL00 [p/b,r/y]
                + (p.1 r.1 t) DEL10[p/b,r/y]
DELL10[p/b,r/y] = (p.0 r.0 t) DEL01[p/b,r/y]
                + (p.1 y.0 t) DEL11[p/b,r/y]
DELL11[p/b,r/y] = (p.0 r.1 t) DEL01[p/b,r/y]
                + (p.1 r.1 t) DEL11[p/b,r/y]
```

- Step 9 We can now see that if we replace `DELL00[p/b,r/y]` by identifier `SYS00`, `DELL01[p/b,r/y]` by `SYS01`, `DELL10[p/b,r/y]` by `SYS10` and `DEL11[p/b,r/y]` by `SYS11`, then `DEL2(p,r)` is identical to the expression given in Step 7. Hence

```
DEL2(p,r) = (p.0 r.0 t) SYS00 + (p.1 R.1 t) SYS11
```

where `SYS00`, `SYS01`, `SYS10` and `SYS11` are defined in Step 7. The right-hand side of the equality was derived from `IN(p,q)*IN(q,r)-q` by Steps 1–7, and is thus equal to it. The following equation then holds:

```
DEL2(p,r) = IN(p,q)*IN(q,r)-q
```

This series of nine steps has illustrated how two XCircal descriptions may be shown to have equivalent behaviour by rewriting the descriptions into behaviourally equivalent descriptions using the axioms.

This manipulation of the syntax and of the descriptions continued until two syntactically identical expressions resulted; one obtained from `IN(p,q)*IN(q,r)-q` and the other from `DEL2(p,r)`. The outcome is a proof of the equivalence of the two descriptions, that is:

```
IN(p,q)*IN(q,r)-q ≡ DEL2(p,r)
```

as required.

Axiomatic Proof Versus Proof Using Semantics

Term rewriting systems, of which our axiomatic proof system is just a particular example, are difficult to automate fully. Think of how any axiomatic proof is performed, such as the Boolean algebra proof given in Sec. 1.7. At every step an axiom has to be selected, from an axiom scheme describing a related *family* of axioms, and used. The question then arises as to which axiom to be used next. For example, the simple axiom of commutativity states that `A + B = B + A`. This axiom could be applied repeatedly with example `X + Y` being replaced by `Y + X` using the schema once, then being used again to give `X + Y` and so on. This rewriting of terms will never cease, and more significantly, will not bring the description of an implementation 'closer' to that of the specification.

In term rewriting systems both the specification and implementation can be rewritten, but the descriptions need to be rewritten with a particular goal in mind. While this goal is to show the syntactic equality of the two terms they usually need to be first placed into a normal, or canonical, form. This is a standard way of rewriting a term so that the infinite use of axioms, such as the use of commutativity illustrated above, is avoided by having a canonical form for all terms. This form could involve ordering process identifiers alphabetically, for example. Term rewriting systems for process calculi, however, cannot be readily automated. They may be semi-automatic, but due to their semi-decidable nature when dealing with infinite processes, i.e. recursively defined processes, some form of user intervention is usually needed to guide the proof. Such a system is known as a *proof assistant*, and is a semi-automatic mechanical aid to help a user perform the proof. This is the approach taken by the HOL system (Gordon, 1986) which we discussed in Sec. 6.7.

An alternative approach to establishing the relationship between a specification and an implementation is to use the operational semantics directly and show them to be equivalent (or not, as the case may be). Using the underlying idea that the semantics of Circal is given by a *labelled transition system*, different approaches to mechanically realizing the equivalence relation may be taken. The various semantics, equivalences and mechanical realizations are discussed in detail by Mao (1992). Circal uses a *testing semantics* (De Nicola and Hennessy, 1984) to give meaning to its operators and the Circal system uses the *state space partitioning* method of Kanellakis and Smolka (1990) to establish testing equivalence (or inequivalence) in a fully automatic fashion. To the user of the Circal system, determining whether two processes, `P` and `Q`, are the same is as simple as writing `print (Spec==Imp)`.

Should the answer be `false`, diagnostic tools can then be used to locate the cause of the inequality.

In the remainder of this chapter we illustrate how proofs are 'set up' using the Circal system. As they are fully automatic, details of the proofs are invisible to the user. In fact the raw proof steps would be undecipherable, anyway, due to the equivalence technique used. This is perhaps the most serious deficiency of this approach; no understandable series of proof steps is available to help a user understand how the proof is performed. This contrasts with the axiomatic approach illustrated above, where the axioms are used in a particular order by a series of understandable proof steps.

Digital hardware design is an iterative procedure, with many incorrect designs occurring; errors are being discovered and then rectified throughout the design process. However, on its own, the result that an implementation *does not* satisfy a specification is not really of much use. What the designer also requires are diagnostics which say why the two descriptions, the specification and the implementation, differ. Such techniques, as mentioned above, are available in the Circal system and they help the designer in the necessary redesign of an incorrect implementation.

8.2 AUTOMATIC VERIFICATION USING THE CIRCAL SYSTEM

Finite-state Machine Equivalence

The Circal system may be used to prove that two finite-state machines (FSMs) which have distinct specifications, are in fact behaviourally equivalent. This example is taken from a textbook by Krishnamurthy (1985).

The FSMs have state diagrams as pictured in Fig. 8.2. They can be described in XCircal as follows:

```
Process FSMA_0, FSMA_1, FSMA_2
Bool i

FSMA_0 <- i.v0 FSMA_0 + i.v1 FSMA_1
FSMA_1 <- i.v0 FSMA_2 + i.v1 FSMA_1
FSMA_2 <- i.v0 FSMA_0 + i.v1 FSMA_1
```

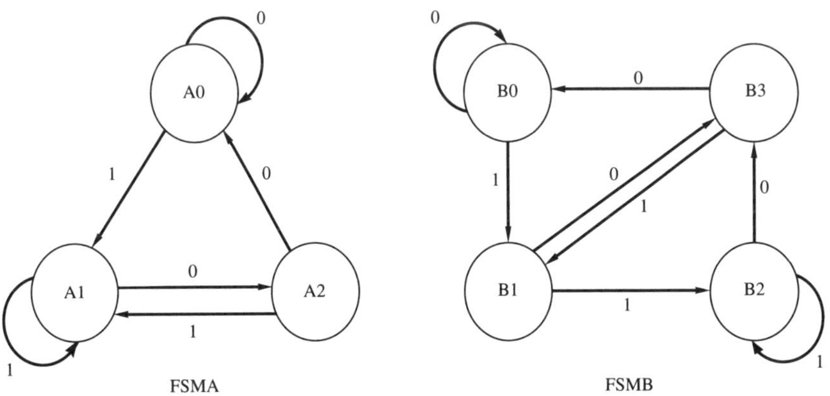

Figure 8.2 Two finite-state machines.

```
Process FSMB_0, FSMB_1, FSMB_2, FSMB_3

FSMB_0 <- i.v0 FSMB_0 + i.v1 FSMB_1
FSMB_1 <- i.v0 FSMB_3 + i.v1 FSMB_2
FSMB_2 <- i.v0 FSMB_3 + i.v1 FSMB_2
FSMB_3 <- i.v0 FSMB_0 + i.v1 FSMB_1
```

The final step is to show that the FSMs are testing equivalent. This is again achieved in the Circal system by using the == command to invoke the equivalence algorithm, as follows:

```
print (FSMA_0 == FSMB_0)
```

And indeed, the answer `true` is printed.

A Moore Machine

The XCircal specification and implementation described here are taken from an example given in a VHDL tutorial produced by Synopsys, a company producing circuit synthesis tools (Carlson, 1991). This document gives VHDL descriptions of desired circuit behaviour, in this case a simple Moore machine, and the corresponding gate level implementation generated by the Synopsys synthesis tool.

Here we demonstrate how XCircal can be used to show that the high-level specification and the synthesized gate-level implementation are equivalent.

Specification

We specify the Moore machine by means of a state table as in Fig. 8.3.

Implementation

Figure 8.4 gives a gate-level implementation which is produced by the Synopsys synthesis tool (Carlson, 1991).

XCircal descriptions

We can now use the Circal system to test for the equivalence of the specification and implementation. To do this we first describe both in XCircal, starting with the specification:

Present state	Next State $x = 0$	Next State $x = 1$	Output (z)
S0	S0	S2	0
S1	S0	S2	1
S2	S2	S3	1
S3	S3	S1	0

Figure 8.3 Moore machine state table.

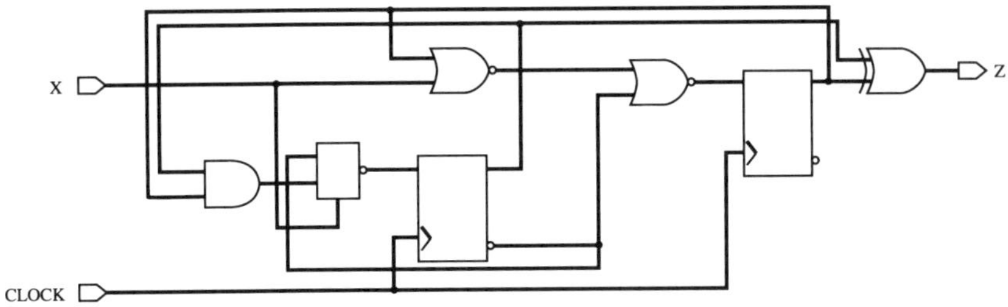

Figure 8.4 Moore machine schematic.

```
Process S0,S1,S2,S3
Bool x, z

S0 <- x.0 z.0 S0 + x.1 z.0 S2
S1 <- x.0 z.1 S0 + x.1 z.1 S2
S2 <- x.0 z.1 S2 + x.1 z.1 S3
S3 <- x.0 z.0 S3 + x.1 z.0 S1
```

The implementation uses two additional inverters, one for the inverted multiplexer output and one to produce a second inverted output for the lower D-type. This implementation is described as:

```
Proccess Moore(Bool x, z, Event clk) {

    Bool y, o1, f, 'f, o2, o3, o4, 'o4

    return NOR2(y,x,o1)*
           NOR2(o1,'f,o2)*
           DFF(o2,clk,y)*XOR2(f,y,z)*
           AND2(y,f,o3)*MUX2('f,o3,x,o4)*
           INV(o4,'o4)*DFF('o4,clk,f)*
           INV(f,'f) -(y o1 f 'f o2 o3 o4 'o4)
}
```

We constrain the model to ensure that the input is set before the clock tick and the output remains unset until after the clock tick. However, the model is level-based so we have to repeat the input with the clock tick (similar for output). This causes the model of the implementation to have repeated input and output events. To remove this duplication the input and output are buffered by internal events and these internal events are then abstracted away.

```
Process INCON, OUTCON
Event clk
Bool x, i, z, g

INCON <- (x.0 i.0) (i.0 clk) INCON +
```

```
          (x.1 i.1) (i.1 clk) INCON
OUTCON <- (g.0 clk) z.0 OUTCON + (g.1 clk) z.1 OUTCON +
          g.0 OUTCON + g.s1 OUTCON

Process IMP
IMP <- ~(INCON*OUTCON*Moore(i,g,clk)-(i g clk))
```

The behaviour produced by the Circal system for the implementation above is given below. Note that this is not an XCircal expression, but is simply output from the Circal system display function.

```
S0 = (x.v1 S1 + x.v0 S2)
S1 = S3
S2 = S4
S3 = z.v0 S5
S4 = z.v0 S0
S5 = (x.v1 S6 + x.v0 S7)
S6 = S8
S7 = S9
S8 = z.v1 S10
S9 = z.v1 S5
S10 = (x.v1 S11 + x.v0 S12)
S11 = S13
S12 = S14
S13 = z.v0 S15
S14 = z.v0 S10
S15 = (x.v1 S16 + x.v0 S17)
S16 = S9
S17 = S18
S18 = z.v1 S0
```

The final step is to show that the specification and implementation are testing equivalent:

```
print (IMP == S0) // invoke testing equivalence and print result
```

And indeed, once again the answer `true` is printed.

A Mealy Machine

The XCircal specification and implementation are again taken from Carlson (1991).

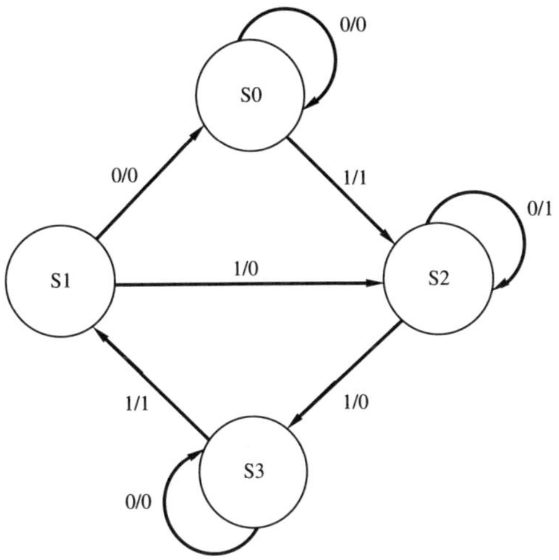

Present state	Next State		Output (z)	
	x = 0	x = 1	x = 0	x = 1
S0	S0	S2	0	1
S1	S0	S2	0	0
S2	S2	S3	1	0
S3	S3	S1	0	1

Figure 8.5 Mealy machine states.

Specification

A Mealy machine is specified in the same way as a Moore machine using a state diagram and table, as in Fig. 8.5.

Implementation

Figure 8.6 gives an implementation for the above specification.

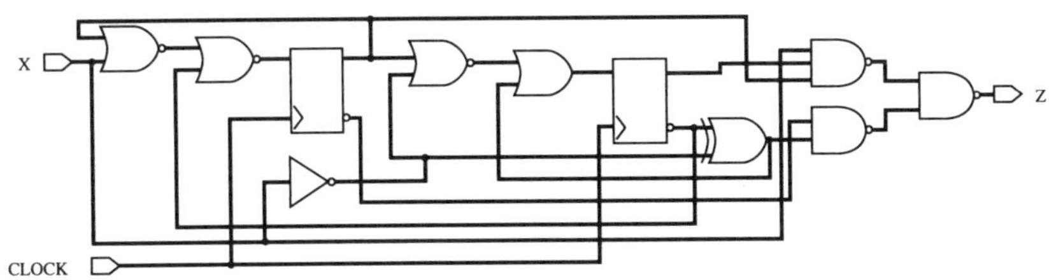

Figure 8.6 Mealy machine schematic.

XCircal descriptions

The Circal system is used to determine whether the specification and implementation are equivalent.

The XCircal specification is:

```
Process S0,S1,S2,S3
Bool x, z

S0 <- x.0 z.0 S0 + x.1 z.1 S2
S1 <- x.0 z.0 S0 + x.1 z.0 S2
S2 <- x.0 z.1 S2 + x.1 z.0 S3
S3 <- x.0 z.0 S3 + x.1 z.1 S1
```

The implementation is described by:

```
Process Mealy(Bool x,z, Event clk) {
    Bool d1,'d1,o1,o2,d2,'d2,o3,'x,o4,o5,o6,o7

    return NOR2(d1,x,o1)*NOR2(o1,'d2,o2)*
           DFF(o2,clk,d1)*INV(d1,'d1)*
           NOR2(d1,'x,o3)*
           INV(x,'x)*OR2(o3,o5,o4)*
           DFF(o4,clk,d2)*INV(d2,'d2)*
           XOR2('d2,'x,o5)*NAND2('d1,o5,o6)*
           NAND3(x,d2,d1,o7)*
           NAND2(o7,o6,z)-(d1 'd1 o1 o2 d2 'd2 o3 'x o4 o5 o6 o7)
}
```

The same timing constraints are used for the implementation as for the Moore machine example. The implementation results from the composition of the process Mealy with the two constraints as follows:

```
Process INCON, OUTCON
Event clk
Bool x,i,z,g

INCON <- (x.0 i.0)(i.0 clk) INCON +
         (x.1 i.1) (i.1 clk) INCON
OUTCON <- (g.0 clk) z.0 OUTCON + (g.1 clk) z.1 OUTCON +
          g.0 OUTCON + g.1 OUTCON

Process IMP

IMP <- ~(INCON*OUTCON*Mealy(i,g,clk) - (i g clk))
```

The behaviour produced by the Circal system for this implementation is:

```
S0 = (x.v1 S1 + x.v0 S2)
S1 = S3
S2 = S4
S3 = z.v1 S5
S4 = z.v0 S0
S5 = (x.v1 S6 + x.v0 S7)
S6 = S8
S7 = S3
S8 = z.v0 S9
S9 = (x.v1 S10 + x.v0 S11)
S10 = S12
S11 = S8
S12 = z.v1 S13
S13 = (x.v1 S14 + x.v0 S15)
S14 = S16
S15 = S4
S16 = z.v0 S5
```

Notice again that this is not an XCircal description; it is simply the output from the Circal system display function.

The final step is to show that specification and implementation are testing equivalent:

```
print (IMP == S0) //invoke testing equivalence and print result
```

They are, and the answer `true` is printed.

A Simple Language Recognizer

This example involves creating the XCircal specification and implementation of a finite-state machine for recognizing binary numbers that are divisible by 3.

The high level specification of the recognizer is in terms of a Moore machine. A gate-level implementation is then suggested for the recognizer, and we demonstrate how the Circal system is used to verify that the implementation meets the specification.

Specification

The DIV3 recognizer is specified informally as:

```
When E = 0,
    IN accepts binary sequences in {0,1}* and OUT = 0.
```

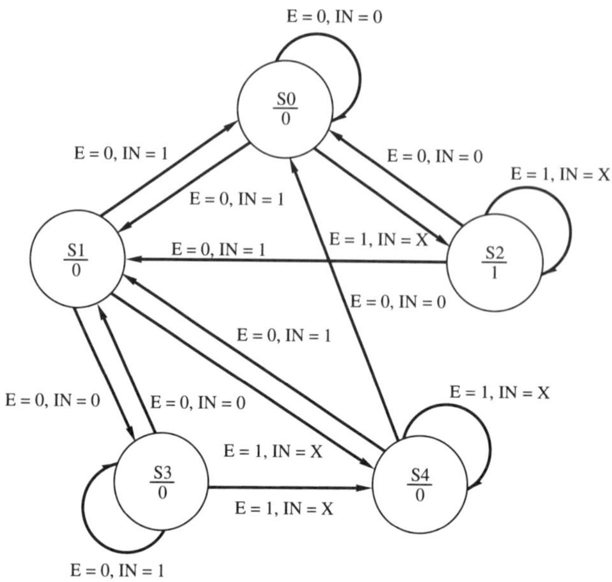

Figure 8.7 DIV3 state diagram.

```
When E = 1,
     IN is ignored,
     OUT = 1 if during the time when E = 0,
     IN has accepted a number that is divisible by 3.
     OUT = 0 otherwise.
```

This specification is depicted by the Moore machine in Fig. 8.7:

Implementation

The circuit given in Fig. 8.8 was designed by Andrew Bailey to implement the recognizer specified above.

We can now use the Circal system to verify the equivalence of the specification and implementation. To do this we again create two XCircal descriptions, starting with the specification:

```
Process DIV3_SPEC0, DIV3_SPEC1,
        DIV3_SPEC2, DIV3_SPEC3, DIV3_SPEC4
        Bool in, e
        Event out

        DIV3_SPEC0 <- (in.0 e.0) DIV3_SPEC0 +
             (in.1 e.0) DIV3_SPEC1 +
             (in.0 e.1) DIV3_SPEC2 +
             (in.1 e.1) DIV3_SPEC2
```

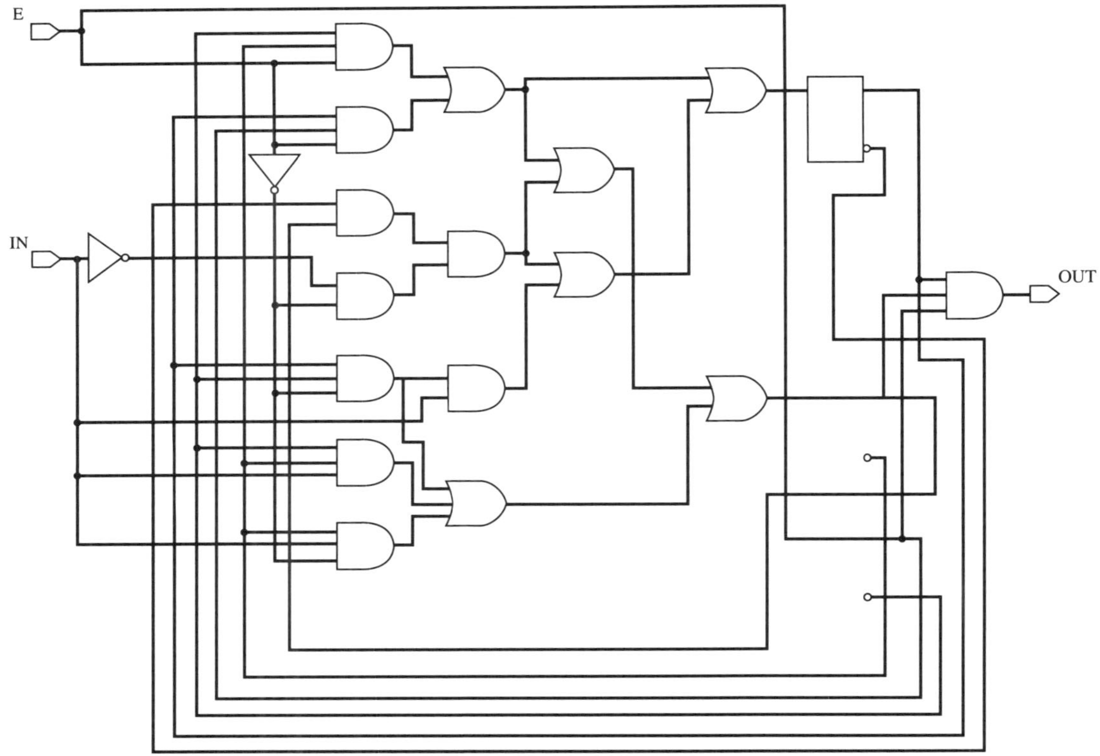

Figure 8.8 DIV3 schematic.

```
DIV3_SPEC1 <- (in.0 e.0) DIV3_SPEC3 +
     (in.1 e.0) DIV3_SPEC0 +
     (in.0 e.1) DIV3_SPEC4 +
     (in.1 e.1) DIV3_SPEC4

DIV3_SPEC2 <- (in.0 e.0 out) DIV3_SPEC0 +
     (in.1 e.0 out) DIV3_SPEC1 +
     (in.0 e.1 out) DIV3_SPEC2 +
     (in.1 e.1 out) DIV3_SPEC2

DIV3_SPEC3 <- (in.0 e.0) DIV3_SPEC1 +
     (in.1 e.0) DIV3_SPEC3 +
     (in.0 e.1) DIV3_SPEC4 +
     (in.1 e.1) DIV3_SPEC4

DIV3_SPEC4 <- (in.0 e.0) DIV3_SPEC0 +
     (in.1 e.0) DIV3_SPEC1 +
     (in.0 e.1) DIV3_SPEC4 +
     (in.1 e.1) DIV3_SPEC4
```

The implementation is described as follows:

```
Process ABS
Bool outbuff
ABS <- outbuff.v0 ABS + (outbuff.v1, out) ABS

Process DIV3(Bool IN, E, OUT) {

    Bool y0, y1, y2, 'y0, 'y1, 'y2, 'y3, y0', y2', o1, o2,
         o3, o4, o5, o6, o7, o8, o9, 010, o11, o12, o13, 'IN, 'E

         return AND3('y1, 'y2, E, o1)*AND3(y0, y1, E, o2)*
                AND2('y0, y2, o3)*AND2('IN, 'E, o4)*
                AND3(y0, 'y1, 'E, o5)*AND3(y1, IN, 'E, o6)*
                AND3('y1, 'y2, IN, o13)*
                OR2(o1, 02, o7)*AND2(o3, o4, o8)*
                AND2(o5,IN,o9)*OR3(o5, o6, o13, o10)*
                OR2(o7, o8, o11)*OR2(o8, o9, o12)*
                OR2(o7, o12, y0')*OR2(o11, o10, y2')*
                UDFF(E, y1)*INV(y1, 'y1)*
                UDFF(y0', y0)*INV(y0, 'y0)*
                UDFF(y2', y2)*INV(y2, 'y2)*
                AND3(y0,y1,y2,OUT)*INV(IN,'IN)*
                INV(E,'E) - ('y0, 'y1, 'y2, 'y3, y0 y1 y2 y0' y2', o1 o2//
                                 o3 o4 o5 o6 o7 o8 o9 o10 o11 o12 o13 'IN 'E)
}
```

```
Process IMP
IMP <- ~(DIV3(in,e,outbuff)*ABS - outbuff)
```

An abstraction is performed on the output so that an output event only occurs for a recognized string.

The behaviour produced by the Circal system for the implementation above is given by the following output from the Circal system `display` function:

```
S0 = ((((e.v1 in.v1)S1 + (e.v1 in.v0)S1) +
     (e.v0 in.v1)S2) + (e.v0 in.v0)S0)
S1 = ((((out e.v1 in.v1)S1 + (out e.v1 in.v0)S1) +
     (out e.v0 in.v1)S2) + (out e.v0 in.v0)S0)
S2 = ((((e.v1 in.v1)S3 + (e.v1 in.v0)S3) +
     (e.v0 in.v1)S0) + (e.v0 in.v0)S4)
S3 = ((((e.v1 in.v1)S3 + (e.v1 in.v0)S3) +
     (e.v0 in.v1)S2) + (e.v0 in.v0)S0)
S4 = ((((e.v1 in.v1)S3 + (e.v1 in.v0)S3) +
     (e.v0 in.v1)S4) + (e.v0 in.v0)S2)
```

The next step is to show that the specification and implementation are testing equivalent:

```
print (IMP == DIV3_SPEC0)
```

And indeed, the answer `true` is printed. The result `true` occurs, showing them to be equivalent as required.

A Binary-coded Decimal Recognizer

We return to the BCD circuit specified in Program 7.16, whose state diagram is given in Fig. 7.31.

Implementation

The implementation of the BCD recognizer is a minimal one based on D-type flip-flops, see Fig. 8.9. The Boolean algebra equations for this recognizer are as follows:

```
D0 = y2.y1.'y3.'y0 + 'y2.y1.y0 + x.'y2.'y1
D1 = 'y1 + y2.y0 + x.'y0
D2 = 'y2.y1 + y2.'y1 + y2.y0
D3 = y2.y1.y0 + y2.y0.x
0 = 'y3.'y2.'y1.y0
(where 'y1 means not(y1))
```

In Figure 8.9, each subcircuit `Tn` implements `Dn` for each of the terms above.

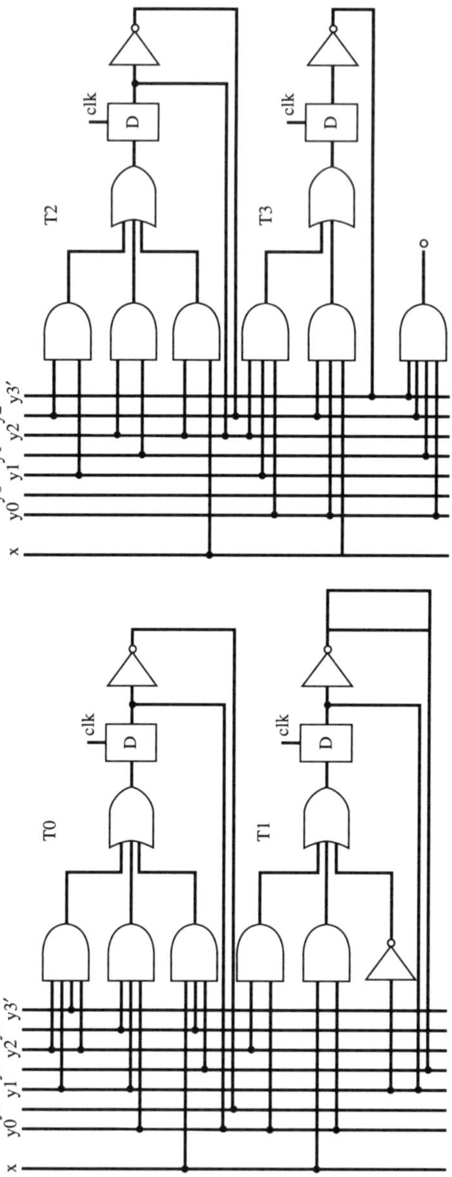

Figure 8.9 BCD implementation.

XCircal models

We can now use the Circal system to prove the equivalence of the specification and implementation.

The implementation is formulated by the interconnection of XCircal models of low-level gates. This can be constructed hierarchically in that we can model circuit `T0` by the following:

```
Process T0(Bool a, b, c, d, e, f, Event clk, Bool o, 'o) {
    Bool p,q,r,s

    return AND4(a,b,c,'o,p)*
           AND3(d,b,o,q)*
           AND3(d,e,f,r)*
           OR3(p,q,r,s)*
           DFF(s,clk,o)*
           INV(o,'o) - (p q r s)
}
```

In this description we compose together six gate models and then abstract away the internal signals `p, q, r` and `s.` XCircal descriptions for the other three `Dn` equations can be defined similarly.

The four `Tn` processes and the final `AND4` can be instantiated with appropriate connections between them as follows:

```
Process Imp(Bool x, Event clk, Bool o) {
    Bool y0, 'y0, y1, 'y1, y2, 'y2, 'y3

    return T0(y2,y1,'y3,'y2,x,'y1,clk,y0,'y0)*
           T1(y2,y0,x,clk,y1,'y1)*
           T2(y1,'y1,y0,clk,y2,'y2)*
           T3(y2,y1,y0,x,clk,'y3)*
           AND4(y0,'y1,'y2,'y3,o) - (y0 'y0 y1 y2 'y2 'y3)
}
```

Verification

In order to verify our implementation of the BCD recognizer, additional design information is required. We need to formalize how we intend to use the above circuit in order to show that it is correct. In this case we compose the implementation with an additional process that describes how the data is input into the circuit. We need to supply the value of the binary digit and then clock the D-types. To do this, we convert the specification's `x` input into an internal signal `i,` which is repeated immediately with the D-types `clk` input. This is formulated as the following XCircal process:

```
// Input Constraint Process
CON <- (x.0)(clk)CON + (x.1)(clk)CON
```

Also recall from our specification that we are only interested in the situation where the output of the system becomes 1. In order to detect this we compose on the following process that will output the specification's `o.1` action any time the circuit's output action `g.1` occurs, but otherwise merely absorbs `g.0` actions:

```
// Output Constraint Process
ABS <- (g.0)ABS + (g.1, o.1)ABS
```

Given these constraints we can now formulate an XCircal expression that denotes the circuit composed with the input and output constraints and, using the expansion laws which are evoked with the ~ operator, construct its behaviour:

```
Bool i, g, o
Process IMP_ABS

IMP_ABS <- ~ (CON*Imp(i,clk,g)*ABS-(g i clk))

display IMP_ABS
```

The `display` command causes the following representation of the behaviour of `IMP_ABS` to be printed:

```
S0 = (x.v1 S1 + x.v0 S2)
S1 = S3
S2 = S4
S3 = (x.V1 S5 + x.v0 S6)
S4 = (x.v1 S7 + x.v0 S8)
S5 = S9
S6 = S10
S7 = S11
S8 = S11
S9 = (x.v1 S12 + x.v0 S13)
S10 = (x.v1 S14 + x.v0 S15)
S11 = (x.v1 S16 + x.v0 S17)
S12 = S18
S13 = S18
S14 = S18
S15 = S19
S16 = S19
S17 = S19
S18 = (x.v1 S20 + x.v0 S21)
S19 = (x.v1 S22 + x.v0 S23)
S20 = S24
S21 = S24
S22 = S25
```

```
S23 = S25
S24 = (x.v1 S1 + x.v0 S2)
S25 = ((o.v1 x.v1)S26 + (o.v1 x.v0)S27)
S26 = S28
S27 = S29
S28 = (x.v1 S5 + x.v0 S6)
S29 = (x.v1 S7 + x.v0 S8)
```

The next question to ask is whether this behaviour is equivalent to our specification

```
print "Spec = Implementation ? "
print (BCD == IMP_ABS) // apply testing equivalence
```

The answer `true` is printed, indicating that the implementation has been verified correct.

8.3 VERIFYING ASYNCHRONOUS DESIGNS

Because of the clock distribution problems encountered in large synchronous designs, and the resulting restrictions on the performance of a system, asynchronous design methodologies have always been an active area of research. However, producing correct designs where there is no synchronization of data with a clock is a difficult task. The reason for this is that whereas exhaustive simulation of a synchronous design is feasible in certain situations, this is rarely the case in asynchronous design. Here the timing of inputs and outputs may take on many values, all of which must be considered if we are to have a high degree of confidence in the correctness of the design.

In recent years there has been an upsurge of research into the design of asynchronous circuits, exemplified by Ivan Sutherland's ACM Turing Award lecture on micropipelines (Sutherland, 1989). Brzozowski and Seger (1990, 1991) give a comprehensive coverage of the recent advances in asynchronous circuit theory, while Gopalakrishnan and Jain (1990) discuss various design methods.

Significant in this area is the work of Martin (Martin *et al.*, 1989), who has generated an asynchronous microprocessor, while van Berkel *et al.* (1991) at Philips Research have designed a system for synthesizing VLSI circuits from the language Tangram (van Berkel *et al.*, 1991) which is based around CSP (Hoare, 1985). In this section we show how the Circal system can be used to verify the direct hardware implementation of some of the Tangram operators. We show how the components are modelled in XCircal, show how to verify the operator implementation using constraints, and then illustrate how the system diagnostics can be used to discover where a fault exists in a circuit.

Basic Components and Their Models

The Philips asynchronous design method produces a class of interconnected handshake elements from a CSP-like language called Tangram. These handshake elements are constructed from a small set of primitive components; logical operators, a Muller-C element, and a variety of fork components. The behaviour of these components is given by a set of production rules. The form of a rule is that the left-hand side contains a logical expression and the right a transition. The logical expression specifies the condition which cause the transition on the right to occur. For example, the production rules for the NOT component are:

$$a \mapsto x\downarrow$$

$$\neg a \mapsto x\uparrow$$

The variable `a` is the component input, and when it has the value `true` the output of the operator will make a transition to `false`. When `a` is `false` the left-hand side expression of the second production rule becomes `true` and so the output makes a transition to `true`.

The Muller–C component is used frequently in sequential asynchronous circuits. Its production rules are

$$a \wedge b \mapsto x\uparrow$$

$$\neg a \wedge \neg b \mapsto x\downarrow$$

and the corresponding XCircal description is given in Program 8.1:

Program 8.1

```
Process C2(Bool ia,ib,ix, i3_states start_state){
    static Bool a,b,x
    static Process C[i3_states]{

        C[S000] <- (a.1)C[S100] + (b.1)C[S010] + (a.1 b.1 x.1)C[S111]
        C[S100] <- (a.0)C[S000] + (b.1 x.1)C[S111] + (a.0 b.1)C[S010]
        C[S010] <- (a.1 x.1)C[S111] + (b.0)C[S000] + (a.1 b.0)C[S100]
        C[S011] <- (a.1)C[S111] + (b.0 x.0)C[S000] + (a.1 b.0)C[S101]
        C[S101] <- (a.0 x.0)C[S000] + (b.1)C[S111] + (a.0 b.1)C[S011]
        C[S111] <- (a.0)C[S011] + (b.0)C[S101] + (a.0 b.0 x.0)C[S000]

    }
    return (C[start_state][ia/a,ib/b,ix/x])
}
```

When modelling the asynchronous components in XCircal we adopt the transition modelling technique introduced in Sec. 7.5, and use actions to represent changes in logic value. The models introduced in Sec. 7.5 are essentially functional in nature; we must, however, model the delay inherent in such gates, and the timing constraints this imposes on the use of the gates. For this purpose we introduce the process instantiation function CDELAY of Program 8.2:

CDELAY is used to add a causal delay to the output of transition models. As

Program 8.2

```
Process CDELAY(Bool ia, ix, i2_states start_state) {
        static Bool a,x
        static Process CD[i2_states], /\error(a x) {
            CD[S00] <- a.1 CD[S10]
            CD[S10] <- x.1 CD[S11] + a.0 /\error + (a.0 x.1)CD[S01]
            CD[S01] <- x.0 CD[S00] + a.1 /\error + (a.1 x.0)CD[S10]
            CD[S11] <- a.0 CD[S01]
        }
        return CD[start_state][ia/a,ix/x]
}
```

an illustration, Fig. 8.10 shows the state diagram for the inverter `INV` process with an added causal delay:

$$\texttt{INV(a,x}',\texttt{S0)}*\texttt{CDELAY(x}',\texttt{x, S11)} - \texttt{x}'$$

Figure 8.10 shows that `CDELAY` has two main effects: it causes the output `x` of the inverter to always happen *after* a change in input, and it evolves to deadlock if the input changes before the output has propagated through. The model will therefore only correctly operate in an environment which guarantees that inputs do not change before outputs have been allowed to occur. A violation of this constraint will cause an easily diagnosed deadlock. The separation of the issues of delay and function increases the modularity of our descriptions, and reduces the risk of error in what are otherwise quite complex transition systems.

The other class of components used in these designs are forks and wires. An isochronic fork is used to fan out a line to two components with the value arriving at each component at the same time, hence the name. In XCircal this is modelled by simply sharing the same transition event amongst multiple input ports, a property of the multi-way Circal composition operator.

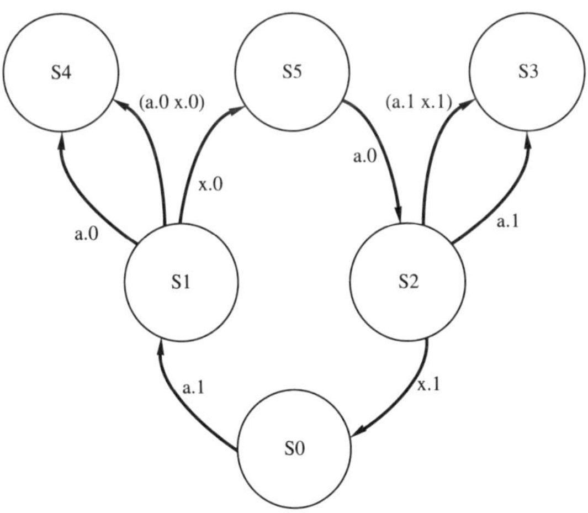

Figure 8.10 Inverter with causal delay.

The other variety of fork is the asymmetric isochronic fork. This is designed to have one branch deliver its value faster than the other, as coded in Program 8.3.

Program 8.3

```
Process ASY_FORK(Bool ia, ix, iy, i1_states start_state){
    static Bool a,x,y
    static Process AF[i1_states],/\w(a x y){

      AF[SO] <- (a.1)((x.1)((y.1)AF[S1] + (a.0)/\w) + (a.0)/\w)
      AF[S1] <- (a.0)((x.0)((y.0)AF[SO] + (a.1)/\w) + (a.1)/\w)
    }

    return AF[start_state][ia/a,ix/x,iy/y]
}
```

In Program 8.3 a is the input and x and y the outputs. x events always happen before y events. Like the CDELAY processes, the fork indicates an error (by evolving to deadlock) should the input change before both outputs.

Not included in the set of Tangram language operators is a general fork component which is necessary to model the implementations. This component fans-out an input with the outputs being able to occur either before, after or at the same time as each other. This component, which we call a wire fork, is given in Program 8.4.

Program 8.4

```
Process WIRE_FORK(Bool ia, iy, iz, i1_states start_state){
    static Bool a, y, z
    static Process W_FORK[i1_states], /\w(a y z){

       W_FORK[SO] <- (a.1)((y.1)((z.1)W_FORK[S1] + a.0 /\w) +
                           (z.1)((y.1)W_FORK[S1] + a.0 /\w) +
                           (y.1 z.1)W_FORK[S1] +
                           a.0 /\w)
       W_FORK[S1] <- (a.0)((y.0)((z.0)W_FORK[SO] + a.1 /\w) +
                           (z.0)((y.0)W_FORK[SO] + a.1 /\w) +
                           (y.0 z.0)W_FORK[SO] +
                           a.1 /\w)
    }
    return(W_FORK[start_state][ia/a,iy/y,iz/z])
}
```

Verifying the Implementation of Asynchronous Modules

In the verification of the Tangram asynchronous modules we use a constraint-based approach. The constraints capture the restricted behaviour of the particular environments that the modules are used in. In particular, the constraints capture the handshake rules which components both rely on and preserve.

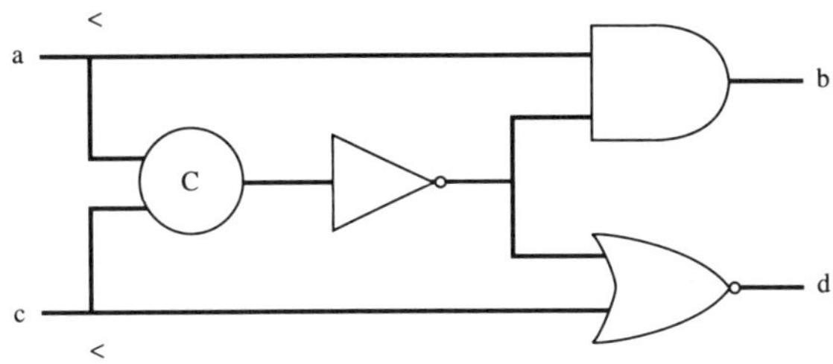

Figure 8.11 Implementation of S element.

An S Element

The S element is a component in the construction of the handshake operators. In the Philips' design method the behaviour of an operator is specified by a regular expression of rising and falling signals; for the S element this is:

```
(a↑; b↑; c↑; b↓; c↓; d↑; a↓; d↓)*
```

The semicolon is a sequencing operator, and the $*$ repetition. This maps into Circal in a straightforward manner:

```
SELEM <- a.1 b.1 c.1 b.0 c.0 d.1 a.0 d.0 SELEM
```

The implementation of the S element is shown in Fig. 8.11. The branches of the forks labelled with < indicate that this is the faster branch of an asymmetric fork. Thus, for example, the branch from c to the NOR gate is faster than that to the Muller-C. Given our library of models of components describing the implementation in XCircal is also straightforward, as shown in Program 8.5.

Program 8.5

```
S_IMP <- (ASY_FORK(a,p,q,S0)*
          ASY_FORK(c,s,r,S0)*
          C2NOT(q,r,x,S000))*
         (WIRE_FORK(x,y,z,S1)*
          (AND2(p,y,b',S01)*CDELAY(b', b, S00) - b')*
          (NOR2(z,s,d',S10)*CDELAY(d', d, S00) - d')) - (p q r s x y z)
```

The C2NOT function call of Program 8.5 instantiates a Muller-C element with an inverted output.

We need to show that this circuit implements the specification; however, there is not an equivalence between the two as they stand. Examining the specification, it can be seen that it can only accept inputs at certain points in its computation. Using the expansion law to apply the XCircal composition and abstraction operators to process S_IMP reveals that it can accept inputs at all points in its computation, as would be expected. What may not be expected is that such

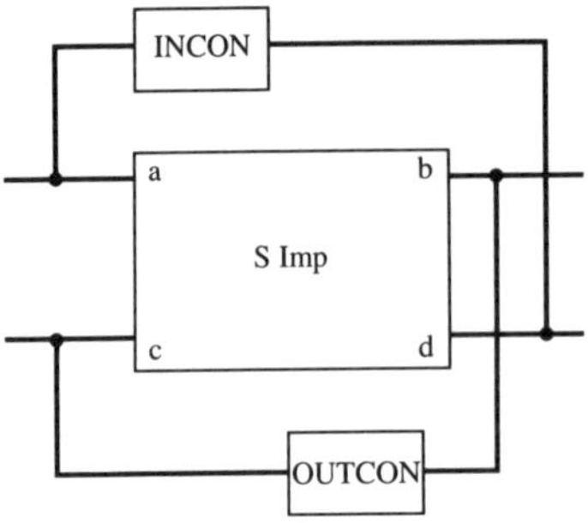

Figure 8.12 S element implementation with constraints.

a simple combination of components turns out to have a very rich behaviour with 9450 possible states, a huge difference from the much smaller specification. In order to verify the implementation we need to formalize the constraints under which the circuit will be operated. In examining the specification we deduce some relationships governing when the `SPEC` is receptive to inputs:

- changes to the value of `c` occur after changes of value on `b`
- after the initial `a1`, changes to the value of `a` occur after changes of value on `d`.

Figure 8.12 shows how the constraint processes are connected to the S implementation, with `OUTCON` capturing relationship 1, and `INCON` relationship 2. The reason for these names is that the constraints turn out to be the same as those needed for the four-phase handshake relation used in verifying the rest of the Tangram operators. The behaviour of `INCON` is given in Program 8.6.

Program 8.6

```
Process INCON(Bool req, ack) {
  static Bool a, b

  static Process CONS[4], /\c(a b) {
    CONS[0] <- a.1 CONS[1] + b.1 /\c
    CONS[1] <- b.1 CONS[2]
    CONS[2] <- a.0 CONS[3] + b.0 /\c
    CONS[3] <- b.0 CONS[0]
  }

  return CONS[0][req/a,ack/b]
}
```

In this program the `a` actions represent the request to send and the `b` the acknowledge. As this is a definition, not an instance, `a` actions correspond to `a` in Fig. 8.12, and similarly `b` to `d`. The first definition has a guarded term that accepts `a1`; this is the action we require to happen as part of this constraint. It also contains a set of guards which make transitions to `/\c` (deadlock of the appropriate sort) which are used to capture any unwanted activity on the `b` line thereby indicating a violation of the constraint. `CONS[1]` contains the required

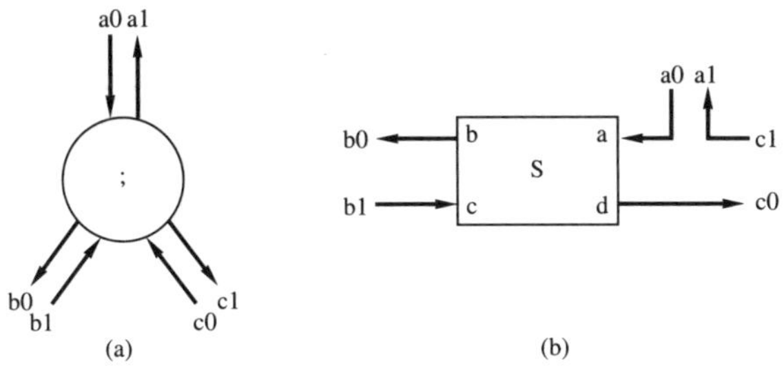

Figure 8.13 (a) Symbol for SEQ operator. (b) Implementation of SEQ operator.

activity of the output whilst CONS[2] and CONS[3] are similar to the first two but are for the negative-going transitions.

The behaviour of OUTCON, shown in Program 8.7, is very similar to INCON

Program 8.7

```
Process OUTCON(Bool req, ack) {
  static Bool a, b

  static Process CONS[4], /\c(a b) {
    CONS[0] <- a.1 CONS[1]
    CONS[1] <- b.1 CONS[2] + a.0 /\c
    CONS[2] <- a.0 CONS[3]
    CONS[3] <- b.0 CONS[0] + a.1 /\c
  }

  return CONS[0][req/a,ack/b]
}
```

but a in our definition is now an output from the circuit indicating a request to the next handshake circuit.

By composing these constraints on to the S element implementation, we find that the behaviour is equivalent to the supplied specification. This is achieved by having the system execute the following fragment of XCircal:

```
SELEM == S_IMP*INCON(a,d)*OUTCON(b,c)
```

The SEQ, PAR, and MIXER Operators

Following this technique of using constraints, the verification of the operators is straightforward. Wherever the request of a handshake is an input to a circuit then an INCON is used; when the request is an output an OUTCON is used.

The symbol for the SEQ operator is given in Fig. 8.13(a), and its specification by the following regular expression:

```
(a0 ↑; b0 ↑; b1 ↑; b0 ↓; b1 ↓; c0 ↑; c1 ↑; a1 ↑; a0 ↓; c0 ↓; c1 ↓; a1 ↓)*
```

This can be translated directly into a recursive XCircal definition:

```
SEQ <- a0.1 b0.1 b1.1 b0.0 b1.0 c0.1 c1.1 a1.1 a0.0 c0.0 c1.0 a1.0 SEQ
```

Figure 8.13(b) gives the implementation of `SEQ`. The verification prescription is to compose an `INCON` on to the `a` ports and `OUTCON`s on to the other two pairs, as shown below:

```
INCON(a0,a1)*
OUTCON(b0,b1)*
OUTCON(c0,c1)*
S(a0,c0,b0,b1)*
CDELAY(c1,a1,S00)
```

The Circal system shows that this term is equivalent to the specification.

The symbol for the `PAR` operator is shown in Fig. 8.14(a), and it is specified by the regular expression:

$$(a0\uparrow;\ ((b0\uparrow;\ b1\uparrow;\ b0\downarrow;\ b1\downarrow) \parallel (c0\uparrow;\ c1\uparrow;\ c0\downarrow;\ c1\downarrow));\ a1\uparrow;\ a0\downarrow;\ a1\downarrow)*$$

where the $\parallel$ symbol denotes that the two parenthesized sequences of actions are running in parallel. In XCircal we describe this by the use of two processes which are composed together to give the specification.

```
PAR1 <- a0.1 b0.1 b1.1 b0.0 b1.0 a1.1 a0.0 a1.0 PAR1
PAR2 <- a0.1 c0.1 c1.1 c0.0 c1.0 a1.1 a0.0 a1.0 PAR2

PAR <- ~(PAR1*PAR2)
```

`PAR1` models the `b` action sequence preceded and succeeded by the appropriate `a` actions, whilst `PAR2` models the `c` action sequence in a similar manner. The composition of these two yields our specification, which according to our procedure used above, is satisfied by the implementation shown in Fig. 8.14(b).

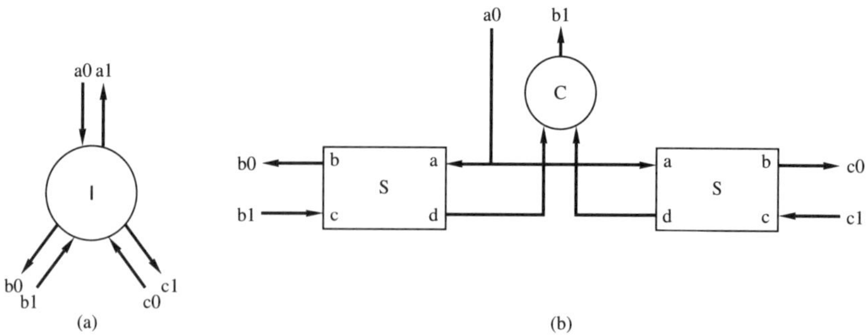

Figure 8.14 (a) Symbol for `PAR` operator. (b) Implementation of `PAR` operator.

The symbol for the MIXER operator is given in Fig. 8.15(a), and its regular expression specification is

```
((a0 ↑; c0 ↑; c1 ↑; a1 ↑; a0 ↓; c0 ↓; c1 ↓; a1 ↓) |
(b0 ↑; c0 ↑; c1 ↑; b1 ↑; b0 ↓; c0 ↓; c1 ↓; b1 ↓))*
```

Note that | is the CSP choice operator occurring between the left expression and the right expression. This maps directly into the following XCircal expression:

```
MIX <- a0.1 c0.1 c1.1 a1.1 a0.0 c0.0 c1.0 a1.0 MIX +
       b0.1 c0.1 c1.1 b1.1 b0.0 c0.0 c1.0 b1.0 MIX
```

When verifying this operator we need both the handshaking constraints and a mutual exclusion constraint. This expresses the fact that when this circuit is being operated, activity on the a and b channels (req and ack pairs) will never take place at the same time. This is captured in XCircal as

```
ME <- a0.1 a1.0 ME + b0.1 b1.0 ME
```

This means that if an a0.1 occurs then an a1.0 must occur before a b0.1 or b1.0 action. The constrained behaviour is generated from

```
MIXER_IMP*
INCON(a0,a1)*
INCON(b0,b1)*
OUTCON(c0,c1)*
ME_CON(a0.1,a1.0,b0.1,b1.0)
```

and is indeed equivalent to the specification of the MIXER.

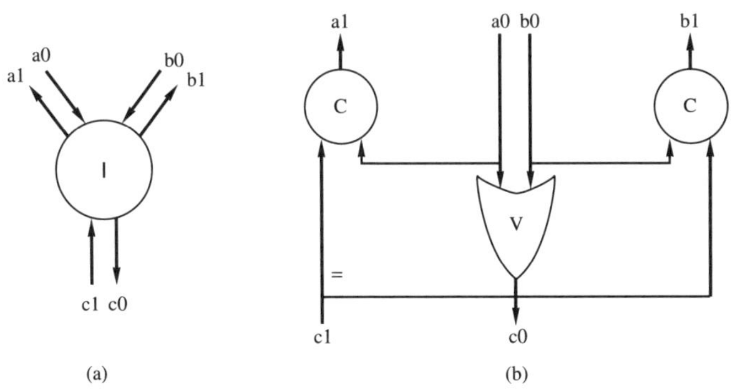

Figure 8.15 (a) Symbol for MIXER operator. (b) Implementation of MIXER operator.

XCircal as a Design Aid

Here we show how XCircal might be used to help in the design of the asynchronous operators introduced above. In a `MIXER` implementation such as Fig. 8.15(b) the `c1` input is fanned out to two Muller-Cs using an isochronic fork. However, a designer may initially have intended to use a wire fork. If we try to verify the `MIXER` circuit with a wire fork replacing the isochronic fork, we find that the Circal system will return `false`. However, the system can also be made to provide diagnostics that might help in explaining why it was unable to show equivalence with the specification. The relevant portion of the diagnostics for this example is:

```
Failed after following trace: a0.1 c0.1 c1.1 a1.1 a0.0 c0.0 c1.0
a1.0 b0.1
Reason: Language subset test failed.
IMP can do (c0.1 b1.1) or b1.1 or c0.1
SPEC can do c0.1
```

The failure is due to the mismatch between the actions that `SPEC` and the `IMP` can do after the given trace. By examining this trace, the specification and the circuit structure, it can be inferred that the preemptive `b1.1` is due to the fact that the `c1.0` from the previous activation (the `a` branch of the specification) has yet to reach the `b` channel Muller-C due to the uneven delay of the wire fork. We may then deduce that this should be replaced by an isochronic fork, as used in the correct design.

8.4. PROPERTY VERIFICATION

While the Circal system is generally used to verify design correctness by showing specification/implementation equivalence, particular properties of a design may also be shown to hold by use of a related verification technique.

The BCD verification of Sec. 8.2 was carried out using delayless gate models. When the verification is repeated using models with unit delays, the verification fails because of a race hazard which causes a spike in the output of the circuit. A full explanation of the race hazard is given in Bailey *et al.* (1991); in this section we present a technique for detecting the occurrences of such spikes.

Here we show how the Circal system can be used to detect ‘spikes’ in the outputs of circuits. We define a ‘spike’ to be a change in the output of a circuit where the new level is not sustained for a sufficient time to allow the environment being driven by the output to register the change. Using XCircal we can model a ‘spike detector’ to spot and report such outputs.

A Process for Spike Detection

Spike detection can be achieved using XCircal by composing on to the circuit model a process that checks for and reports spikes. The environment being driven by the circuit determines what outputs are to be considered valid and what outputs are to be considered spikes. For this example, where outputs should be stable for eight time units, we consider output values held for three time units or less to be spikes.

The model of the BCD recognizer we are using as an example has its output denoted by the Boolean `o`. The model is event-based, but the process shown below can be easily modified to detect spikes for level-based models:

```
Detect <- o.v0 Detect0 + o.v1 Detect1

Detect0 <- o.v0 Detect0_1 + (o.v1 S) Detect1
Detect0_1 <- o.v0 Detect0_2 + (o.v1 S) Detect1
Detect0_2 <- o.v0 Detect0_2 + o.v1 Detect1

Detect1 <- o.v1 Detect1_1 + (o.v0 S) Detect0
Detect1_1 <- o.v1 Detect 1_2 + (o.v0 S) Detect 0
Detect1_2 <- o.v1 Detect 1_2 + o.v0 Detect0
```

The detector works by signalling a spike, by an `S` event, if the output value changes again from the previous change after less than four time units.

We can now simulate the BCD recognizer with attached spike detector to demonstrate how such a spike is detected. The following pattern of actions results from this simulation:

```
(t x.v1 o.v0) // first bit of number is 1.
(t o.v0)      // the input propagates through circuit
(t o.v0)
(t o.v0)
(t o.v0)
(t o.v0)
(t o.v0)
(t x.v0 o.v0) // next bit is a 0.
(t o.v0)
(t o.v1)      // output goes to 1.
(S t o.v0)    // output goes to 0 - duration was one time unit - a
                 spike is denoted by event S.
```

When the output changes value to 1 the spike detector enters state `Detect1`. In this state the change in output value back to 0 in the next time interval causes a spike to be reported.

8.5. MODELLING CONCURRENT SYSTEMS

This section illustrates the applicability of XCircal and the Circal system beyond digital hardware. We give as examples a system of one-dimensional cellular automata and a communications protocol.

Cellular Automata

Program 8.8 illustrates some advanced XCircal modelling techniques. It can be used to generate any of the 256 one-dimensional cellular automata (Wolfram, 1986).

- Lines 14–20 of Program 8.8 contain a function which fills the array `c` with a bit representation of the current update rule.
- Line 12 attempts to explain the constants used as indexes into `c`.
- Lines 21–31 contain the instantiation function for a single cell. Its behaviour is parametrized according to the contents of the rule array `c`.
- Line 24 starts the definition of a dead cell `CELL[0]`. Each of the four deterministic choices corresponds to the current behaviour of the two neighbouring cells: either none are alive, the left one `l` is alive, the right one `r` is alive, or both are alive. The contents of `c` determine which state the current cell should evolve to, either alive `CELL[1]` or dead `CELL[0]`.
- Line 27 starts a similar definition for a live cell.
- Line 30 returns an appropriately relabelled cell, which is either dead or alive according to the Boolean `seed`.
- Lines 33–48 create an array of length `n`, rule number `rule` and seed function `f`.
- Line 34 declares an array of events p_i which correspond to cell `i` being alive (i.e. the p_i ultimately relabel the `fire` action of the `CELL` process).
- Line 38 calls `set` to fill `c` according to the current rule number.
- Line 50 starts the definition of a seed function that only returns `true` if it is passed the integer 40.
- Line 54 starts a definition of a seed function that returns randomly `true` or `false` (without reference to its parameter).

Figure 8.16 depicts the behaviours generated at lines 58 and 63; time proceeds down the page, each row represents which cells are alive (black) or dead (space). The first automaton has a cyclic behaviour; once it has had 55 generations, it returns to the eighth generation (i.e. 8 lines down from the top line). This automaton starts from a single live cell. The second automaton, which has a disordered start state, uses a deadlock terminated clock to limit the behaviour to the first 60 generations.

In the analysis of two-dimensional automata (such as the Game of Life), we have many combinations of neighbours' 'aliveness' to consider. The following

Program 8.8

```
// One dimensional cellular automata generator

Event t          // global clock

// Define constants for Rule array "c"

int D=0   // Dead Cell
int L=1   // Left neighbour
int A=2   // Alive Cell
int R=4   // Right neighbour

// e.g. c[D|L|R] holds the status for a dead cell with both neighbours alive

void Set(int c[], int Number) {    // fill rule array
  j=1
  for (i=0;i<sizeof c;i++) {
    c[i] = (Number&j==j) ? 1 : 0
    j = j<<1
  }
}

Process Cell(int c[], Event il, ic, ir, bool seed) {
    static Event l, r, fire
    static Process CELL[2] {
        CELL[0] <- t CELL[c[D]] + (t l)CELL[c[D|L]] + (t r)CELL[c[D|R]] +
                    (t l r)CELL[c[D|L|R]]

        CELL[1]  <- (t fire)CELL[c[A]] + (t fire l)CELL[c[A|L]] +
                    (t fire r)CELL[c[A|R]] + (t fire l r)CELL[c[A|L|R]]
    }
    return (seed ? CELL[1] : CELL[0])[il/l,ic/fire,ir/r]
}

Process MkArray(int n, rule, bool f(int)) {
    Event p[n]      // the cells "firing" events
    int c[8]        // Rule array
    Process Array

    Set(c, rule)

    Array = Cell(c, p[n-1], p[0], p[1], f(0))

    for (i=1; i<n-1; i++)
        Array = Array * Cell(c, p[i-1], p[i], p[i+1], f(i))

    Array = Array * Cell(c, p[n-2], p[n-1], p[0], f(n-1))

    return Array
}
bool Seed40(int i) {
  return i==40              // single site seed
}

bool Rand(int i) {
  return 1==random(2)       // randomly true or false
}

display ~(MkArray(80, 90, Seed40))

Process CLOCK(t),/\t(t)

CLOCK <- (t 60) /\t
display ~(MkArray(50, 150, Rand)*CLOCK)
```

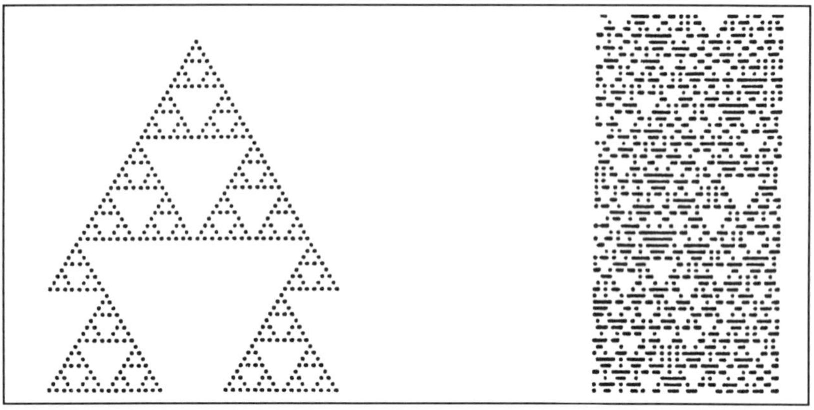

Figure 8.16 Two one-dimensional cellular automata.

function (Program 8.9) allows us to build a process corresponding to `k` selections of n events guarding the given process.

Program 8.9

```
// Generate C(n k) combinations (on set a[0]....a[n-1] : 1 < k <= n)
// algorithm from page 181, Combinatorial Algorithms, E.M. Reingold et. al.

Process C(int n, k, Event a[], t, Process P) {
  int c[k+1]
  c[0] = -1
  j=1
  s = NullP                          // null Process (P + NullP == P)
  for (i=1; i<=k; i++) c[i]=i;
  while (j != 0) {
    e = t                            // always include clock tick

    for (i=1; i<=k; i++) e = e a[c[i]-1]      // for C(n,k) selections
                                              // of events in "a"
    s = s + e P                      // accumulate deterministic choice term
    j = k;

    while (c[j]==n-k+j) j = j - 1
    c[j] = c[j] + 1
    for (i=j+1; i<=k; i++) c[i] = c[i-1] + 1
  }
  return s                           // return k selections from "a" guarding P
}

Process P
Event t, a[6]

print (C(6, 3, a, t, P))
```

This code generates the following output:

```
(a[2] a[1] a[0] t)P + (a[3] a[1] a[0] t)P +
(a[4] a[1] a[0] t)P + (a[5] a[1] a[0] t)P +
(a[3] a[2] a[0] t)P + (a[4] a[2] a[0] t)P +
(a[5] a[2] a[0] t)P + (a[4] a[3] a[0] t)P +
```

```
(a[5] a[3] a[0] t)P + (a[5] a[4] a[0] t)P +
(a[3] a[2] a[1] t)P + (a[4] a[2] a[1] t)P +
(a[5] a[2] a[1] t)P + (a[4] a[3] a[1] t)P +
(a[5] a[3] a[1] t)P + (a[5] a[4] a[1] t)P +
(a[4] a[3] a[2] t)P + (a[5] a[3] a[2] t)P +
(a[5] a[4] a[2] t)P + (a[5] a[4] a[3] t)P
```

A Simple Communications Protocol

As a further non-hardware example we use a simple communication protocol and prove it correct. The protocol described here was used in the TAV system 'Tools for Automatic Verification' produced by Godskesen *et al.* (1989). Here we demonstrate how the Circal system can also be used to show the equivalence of the protocol and its specification.

The specification

The protocol must provide a service that accepts a message from the external environment and then delivers that message to the external environment before being able to accept another message. Every message accepted must be delivered, and after every delivery the protocol must be able to accept a new message.

This specification is described easily in XCircal:

```
Spec <- acc del Spec
```

where event `acc` denotes the acceptance of a message and event `del` delivery of a message.

The protocol

The protocol is composed of a sender, a communication medium and a receiver.

The sender accepts a message from the external environment through an `acc` event. It passes this message to the medium via a `tran` event. It then waits for an acknowledge (`ack`) or an error message (`err`), indicating that the message was lost. If the sender receives an acknowledge it returns to its initial state, otherwise it tries to resend the message.

The medium receives a message via a `tran` event and passes it on to the receiver via a `rec` event or loses the message and reports this to the sender via an error message (`err`).

The receiver receives a message from the medium via a `rec` event, delivers it to the external environment by a `del` event and acknowledges delivery with an `ack` event.

The protocol can be described in XCircal:

```
Send <- acc Send1
Send1 <- tran (ack Send + err Send1)
```

```
Medium <- tran (err Medium + rec Medium)

Receiver <- rec del ack Receiver

Protocol <- ~(Send*Medium*Receiver) - (tran err ack rec))
```

The behaviour produced by the Circal system for the above protocol and output by the display function as:

```
S0 = acc S1
S1 = S2
S2 = (S1 & S3)
S3 = del S4
S4 = S0
```

The next step is to show that the specification and protocol are testing equivalent:

```
print (Spec == Protocol)
```

And indeed, the answer `true` is printed along with a message reporting that the protocol is *divergent*. The divergence in this case is caused by the possibility that each attempt to send a message may result in the message being lost. The protocol will then get stuck in the resend loop. This resend loop is shown in the behaviour as the recursive loop `S1` → `S2` → `S1`.

CHAPTER

NINE

THE CIRCAL SYSTEM

9.1. XCIRCAL DATA-TYPES

Events

An `Event` is a data-type corresponding to a Circal action set. When an `Event` is first declared, it causes the construction of the action set containing the atomic action labelled by the declaring identifier. An array of `Events` may be declared (e.g. `Event a[7]`) in which case an atomic action labelled by the declaring identifier concatenated with the bracketed index number is constructed for each array element. If the declaring identifier is contained within a block (e.g. in a function body), the atomic action is made unique by concatenating a number on to its label (this is only seen when printing behaviours):

Running the following program

```
Event a, b, c, s
Event array[4]

s = a b c

print a
print "\n"
print s
print "\n"
print (*array)
print "\n"
```

```
{
  Event a, array[4]
  print a
  print (*array)
}
print "\n"
```

gives

```
a
(c b a)
array[3] array[2] array[1] array[0]
a_1 array_0[3] array_0[2] array_0[1] array_0[0]
```

Given `Events a, b` and `array`, the following operations are supported:

- `a b` concatenation. The result is the `Event` containing the union of `a` and `b`.
- `a&b` intersection. The result is the `Event` containing the intersection of `a` and `b`.
- `a-b` difference. The result is the `Event` containing the set difference of `a` and `b`.
- `a==b` equality. The result is the Boolean corresponding to the set equality of `a` and `b`.
- `a/b` relabelling (see Sec. 9.1).
- `a=b` assignment `a` becomes a copy of `b`. (Warning: this is not relabelling.)
- `*array` return the `Event` which consists of the union of all elements of `Event` array `array`.
- `NullE` null event. Acts as identitfy for event concatenation: `a NullE` is equivalent to `a`.

Processes

A `Process` is a data-type corresponding to a Circal term. When a `Process` is declared, it causes the construction of a Circal term with the associated name given by the declaring identifier. This name will be made unique by the concatenation of a number, if the `Process` is defined within a block. An array of `Processes` may be declared; in this case the associated name has the bracketed array index concatenated on. A `Process` may be declared with an `Event` parameter corresponding to its sort. A `Process` declared with an identifier starting with the characters `/\` is constructed as a deadlock of the appropriate sort (the remainder of the name can be used mnemonically with respect to the sort). Note that `/\` must have its sort given at declaration (assuming it is non-empty); for other processes the Circal kernel can evoke its automatic sort determination procedure (Traub, 1987).

Running

```
Event a, b
Process P, Q(a b), /\a(a)
Process Array(a)[4]

print (*Array)
```

gives

```
Array[0] * Array[1] * Array[2] Array[3]
```

Given `Event a`, `Processes P, Q`, `Process` array `Parray`, and `int n`, the following operations are supported:

- `P <- Q` definition. `Process P` (which must be a `Process l`-value and not a general expression) is defined to have the behaviour of `Process Q`. This is not assignment, we are registering the association of the `l`-value `P` with the behaviour of `Q`. (`P` may be a simple `Process` variable or the element of an array, in both cases the declared name is associated with the term binding).
- `P==Q` equality. Returns a Boolean corresponding to the result of performing testing equivalence on `P` and `Q`.
- `P+Q` choice. Returns the `Process` corresponding to the deterministic choice of `P` and `Q`.
- `P&Q` non-deterministic choice. Returns the `Process` corresponding to the non-deterministic choice of `P` and `Q`.
- `P*Q` returns the `Process` corresponding to the composition of `P` and `Q`. Note that this implies no application of the Circal composition law.
- `*P` applies the Circal composition law once on `P` and returns the resulting `Process`.
- `*Parray` returns the `Process` which is the composition of all elements of the `Process` array `Parray`. The composition law is not applied to expand the behaviour.
- `normalize P` returns the `Process` which is `P` re-written into the normal form where all non-determinism in `P` (if any) is brought up to the top level, i.e. `normalize` constructs a non-deterministic sum of deterministic processes, e.g. `a+(b&c)` becomes `(a+b)&(a+c)`.
- `~P` applies the Circal composition and abstraction laws up to recursion, or applies `normalize` if `P` is neither a $*$ or $-$ term.
- `P-a` abstraction. Returns the Process corresponding to the abstraction of the action set `a` from `P`. The abstraction laws are not applied.
- `P>a` applies the Circal abstraction laws once to `P` and `a`.
- `P<<a` applies the Circal abstraction laws up to recursion on `P` and `a`.
- `!P` applies the Circal abstraction laws up to recursion.

- `P[a/b, c/d]` relabelling. Returns the `Process` corresponding to `P` such that `a` replaces `b` and `c` replaces `d`.
- `a P` guarding. Returns the `Process` corresponding to `P` guarded by `Event a`.
- `(a n) P` replication. Returns the `Process` corresponding to `n` consecutive `a` `Events` guarding `P`, e.g. `(a 4) P` is equivalent to `a a a a P`.
- `P=Q` assignment. `P` holds a copy of `Q`. This is not the same as `<-` since the identifier `P` is not associated with the term denoted by `Q`.
- `NullP` null process. Acts as an identity for any process operation, e.g. `P * NullP` is equivalent to `P`.

Bools

The data type `Bool` is the pre-declared aggregation of two `Events`:

```
struct Bool {
  Event v0
  Event v1
}
```

Arrays of `Bools` may be constructed. The `Event` components of a `Bool b` may be referenced by `b.0` and `b.1`, as well as `b.v0` and `b.v1`.

Given `Bools a` and `b`, `Event e` and `Process P`, the following operations are defined:

- `a b` concatenation. Returns an `Event` corresponding to `(a.0 a.1 b.0. b.1)`.
- `a e` concatenation. Returns an `Event`.
- `P[a/b]` relabelling. Equivalent to `P[a.0/b.0,a.1/b.1]`.
- `P - a` abstraction. Equivalent to `P–a.0 - a.1`.
- `a=b` assignment.

9.2 PREORDERS ON PROCESSES

As well as checking testing equivalence, the Circal system can check the various preorder relations as described by De Nicola and Hennessy (1984). The entry-points all return `Bool` and are as follows (given `P` and `Q` of type `Process`):

- `P == Q` testing equivalence, the conjunction of must and may equivalence. (Repeated from Sec. 9.1 for completeness).
- `test_eq(P,Q)` function entrypoint, same as ==.
- `P << Q` testing preorder, `P` *less than or equal to* `Q`.
- `test_lt(P,Q)` function entrypoint, same as <<.
- `P >> Q` testing preorder, `P` *greater than or equal to* `Q`.
- `test_gt(P,Q)` Function entrypoint, same as >>.

- `must_eq(P,Q)` Must equivalence.
- `P <= Q` Must preorder.
- `must_lt(P,Q)` Function entrypoint, same as <=.
- `P >=Q` Must preorder.
- `must_gt(P,Q)` Function entrypoint, same as >=.
- `may_eq(P,Q)` May equivalence.
- `P < Q` May preorder.
- `may_lt(P,Q)` Function entrypoint, same as <.
- `P > Q` May preorder.
- `may_gt(P,Q)` Function entrypoint, same as >.

Diagnostics can be obtained by appending `_d` to any of the function entrypoints, e.g. `test_eq_d(P,Q)`. Alternatively, the command line option `-INFO DIAG` can be used.

The diagnostics will describe why each relation being checked failed and will provide a trace to the point of failure. If a `must` relation check fails, then the acceptance sets at the point of failure are printed for both processes along with the processes used to generate the acceptance sets. If a `may` relation check fails, then the language accepted at the point of failure is printed for each process.

9.3. DISPLAY COMMANDS

- `print e` print an `Event e`.
- `print b` print a `Bool b`.
- `print P` print the term denoted by `Process P`.
- `display P` print a display of `Process P` (a terser version of `print`, with numbered state names).
- `trace P` print a 'trace' of `Process P`, where `P` denotes a process without choice terms. The trace consists of the sequence of guards associated with the process.
- `view P` evoke an X-window display of `Process P` (not available in all versions). The viewer uses standard (and self-explanatory) widgets.

Saving Behaviours

- `save P` save `Process P` in the file `P.xtc`. The saved file does not contain declarations of the events; this avoids duplicated declarations when many saved processes are `#included` within the same file. The `save` command can be used to save time and memory by pre-computing parts of large behaviours.

XTC

This section summarizes some of the XTC language features used in the program examples of Chapters 7 and 8; the XTC reference manual (McCaskill, 1991) gives further details.

- `random` Takes an integer parameter `n` and returns a random number $0 \leqslant$ `x` $<$ `n`.
- `sizeof` Returns the number of elements in an array.
- `print` Works for strings, integers and `bools`.
- `Error` Takes a string parameter, which is printed as an error message. Causes the program to terminate.

Most arithmetic expressions of the C language are implemented in XTC, except for assignment variants such as +=. Pointer arithmetic is not supported.

9.4. RECENT SYSTEM DEVELOPMENTS

Binary decision diagram (BDD) representation techniques (Bryant, 1986; Enders *et al.*, 1991) have been applied to a new implementation of the Circal system. BDDs greatly increase the number of circuit elements that can be modelled at a single level in the hierarchy, and they permit the use of more detailed models with respect to timing issues, if required. The BDD version of the Circal system has already enabled us to perform a detailed analysis of a 20-input synchronous arbiter (which uses 40 flip-flops), and large blocks of combinatorial logic can now be easily handled. The combination of BDD 'raw power' and automatic verification based on process algebra verification makes feasible the verification of larger and more commercially significant designs than those presented in earlier chapters.

9.5. RUNNING THE CIRCAL SYSTEM

The Circal system is provided in four versions:

- `circ` Default SUN4 version.
- `ngcirc` Non-garbage-collecting version. The default version uses a garbage collector which may cause problems on some SUN hardware configurations (indicated by run-time error messages). In this case, `ngcirc` (which is a little less memory efficient) can be used.
- `circ3, ngcirc3` SUN3 versions of `circ` and `ngcirc`.

All versions of the installed system are run by typing their name followed by the name of a file containing XCircal code (example XCircal files can be found in the directory `demo`), eg.

```
circ mealy.xtc
```

All files to be processed must have the `.xtc` extension, but the extension can be omitted when running the command, so

```
circ mealy
```

is also valid.

The input and output of the system commands may also be provided on standard input and standard output, allowing the system to be placed in pipelines, or the output to be saved in files, so

```
circ ⟨mealy.xtc⟩saveout
```

is also valid.

All system messages go to standard error.

Messages from the Circal System

The Circal system announces information such as errors and diagnostics using messages with the following format:

```
-W- circ: ⟨alu.xtc:98⟩ "{" nested re-declaration of "A" hides previous
```

Such messages contain the following parts:

- `-W-` 'warning' message. Such reports do not affect the execution of the XCircal code.
- `-E-` 'error' message relating to the XCircal file being processed. Such errors prevent the XCircal code from being executed.
- `-F-` 'fatal' error message. Causes immediate termination of the Circal system.
- `-I-` information message. No effect on execution.
- `circ:` the name of the program being executed.
- `⟨alu.xtc:98⟩` file and line number relating to error.
- `"{"` character near error.
- `nested...` actual message.

Some messages may ask you to submit a bug report, e.g. let `div.xtc` contain the single line:

```
2/0
```

dividing 2 by 0 should cause an arithmetic exception:

```
circ div
```

results in:

```
-I- circ: Product HardLab Circal Tools v1.1; Component CIRC v3.1.1
-W- circ: ⟨div.xtc:1⟩ statement returns a value of type int
-I- circ: all done, with 0 errors
"what is truth?" Release
-F- circ: internal error, please submit a bug report
Aborting circ
```

More information about such fatal errors can be obtained using the `-DEBUG` qualifier.

```
circ div -DEBUG
```

causes

```
-I- circ: (xtc) Product HardLab Circal Tools v1.1; Component v3.1.1
-W- circ: (xtc) ⟨div.xtc:1⟩ statement returns a value of type int
-I- circ: (xtc) all done, with 0 errors
"what is truth?" Release
-F- circ: (err) [error.c:75] caught signal Arithmetic exception
Aborting circ
```

In some cases the user may understand why the program aborted (as above), and avoid the need to submit a bug report.

System Diagnostics

Extra diagnostic information from the Circal system can be produced using the `-INFO` command line option (which must come after the name of the `.xtc` file being processed). Six flags are available:

- `MEMORY` calls to the functions `print` and `display` will append statistics concerning memory and CPU usage of the system (since invocation). The statistics consist of:

number of processes in the process memory, i.e. the number of processes created and stored by the system;
number of hits in the process memory, i.e. the number of processes not built because copies already exist;
total heap space used;
total heap space explicitly freed (this does not include heap freed by the garbage collector);
CPU time elapsed since invocation.

- `COMPACT` calls to `print` and `display` will not leave a blank line between lines of output.
- `PRINTNONL` calls to `print` will not take a new line after the + and & operators.
- `DISPLAYNL` calls to `display` will take a new line after the + and & operators.
- `DIAG` the equivalence and preorder operators (see next section) will display diagnostics if the processes are inequivalent or not in the preorder.
- `CLOBB` the save function will clobber an existing file (in the UNIX sense). If this command is not chosen and a file already exists then the system will request confirmation before overwriting.

These commands can be combined using +, e.g.

```
circ mealy -INFO MEMORY+DIAG
```

APPENDIX

THE HOL AND CIRCAL SYSTEMS

A.1 OBTAINING THE HOL SYSTEM

The HOL system can either be obtained on tape from:

HOL Support — `hol-support%cam.sri.com`
University of Cambridge — `hol-support@cl.cam.ac.uk`
Computer Laboratory
New Museums Site
Pembroke Street
Cambridge CB2 3QG, UK

or on tape or by anonymous FTP from:

Phil Windley — `windley@cs.uidaho.edu`
Department of Computer Science
University of Idaho
Moscow, ID 83843, USA

To obtain HOL sources on tape, send a 450-foot Sun cassette or a 600-foot standard magnetic tape to one of the above contacts, *together with sufficient funds to pay the cost of return postage*. HOL is available via anonymous FTP at `ted.cs.uidaho.edu (129.101.100.20)` in the directory `~ftp/pub/hol`. Instructions for installing HOL are supplied with the system.

A.2 OBTAINING THE CIRCAL SYSTEM

The Circal system can be obtained on tape from:

Circal System
School of Computer and Information Science
University of South Australia
The Levels
Adelaide
S.A. 5095
Australia

The Circal system can be obtained by anonymous FTP. We have set up an FTP service on

```
circal-ftp.cs.strath.ac.uk (130.159.136.126)
```

and on

```
lux.levels.unisa.edu.au (130.220.16.65)
```

use 'anonymous', password ⟨your email address⟩. Take a copy of

```
/pub/CircSys.4.1.1.tar.Z (for U.K. site).
/pub/circal/CircSys.4.1.1.tar.Z (for Australia site)
```

Please set 'bin' mode.
The command:

```
zcat CircSys.4.1.1.tar.Z | tar xvf -
```

will generate a `CircSys` directory structure (3 megabytes). Installation notes are in the `doc` directory.

REFERENCES

F. Anceau. *The Architecture of Microprocessors*. Addison-Wesley, Wokingham, 1986.

A. Bailey, G.A. McCaskill, J. McIntosh, and G.J. Milne. The description and automatic verification of digital circuits in CIRCAL. In P. Camurati and P. Prinetto, (eds) *Advanced Research Workshop on Correct Hardware Design Methodologies*, Turin, 255–271. Elsevier/North-Holland, Amsterdam, 1991.

M.R. Barbacci and D.P. Siewiorek. *The Design and Analysis of Instruction Set Processors*. McGraw-Hill, London, 1982.

H.G. Barrow. Proving the correctness of digital hardware designs. *VLSI Design,* **5**(7): 64–77, 1984.

D. Borrione, L. Pierre, and A. Salem. PREVAIL: A proof environment for VHDL descriptions. In P. Camurati and P. Prinetto (eds), *Advanced Research Workshop on Correct Hardware Design Methodologies*, Turin. Elsevier/North-Holland, Amsterdam, 1991.

R.S. Boyer and J.S. Moore. *A Computational Logic Handbook*. Academic Press, Boston, 1988.

M. Breuer. *Design Automation of Digital Systems*, volume 1. Prentice-Hall, Englewood Cliffs, NJ, 1972.

M.C. Browne, E.M. Clarke, D.L. Dill, and B. Mishra. Automatic verification of sequential circuits using temporal logic. *IEEE Transactions on Computers,* **35**(12): 1035–1044, 1986.

Randal E. Bryant. A switch-level model and simulator for MOS digital systems. *IEEE Transactions on Computers,* **33**(2): 160–177, 1984.

Randal E. Bryant. Graph based algorithms for Boolean function manipulation. *IEEE Transactions on Computers,* **35**(8): 677–691, 1986.

J.A. Brzozowski and C.-J. Seger. Advances in asynchronous circuit theory, part i. *Bulletin of the European Association of Theoretical Computer Science*, 1990.

J.A. Brzozowski and C.-J. Seger. Advances in asynchronous circuit theory, part ii. *Bulletin of the European Association of Theoretical Computer Science*, 1991.

Cambridge SRI International. *HOL System Documentation*. SRI International, Cambridge, UK, 1989.

Steve Carlson. *Introduction to HDL Based Design using VHDL*. Synopsis Inc., Mountain View, CA., 1991.

Ed Clarke, D. Dill, and J. Burch *et al.* Symbolic model checking: 10**20 states and beyond. In P.A. Subramanyam (ed.), *ACM 1991 Int. Workshop on Formal Methods in VLSI Design*, Miami, 1991.

R. De Nicola and M. Hennessy. Testing equivalence for processes. *Theoretical Computer Science,* **34**(1/2): 83–133, 1984.

M.M. Denneau. The Yorktown simulation engine. In *Nineteenth Design Automation Conference*, 55–69, IEEE Computer Society Press, 1982.

E.W. Dijkstra. Hierarchical ordering of sequential processes. *Operating Systems Techniques*, 1972.

R. Enders, T. Filkhorn, and D. Taubner. Generating BDDs for symbolic model checking in CCS. *Third International Workshop on Computer Aided Verification*, Aalborg, 1991. In K.G. Larson and A. Skon (eds), Vol. 575, *Lecture Notes in Computer Science*. Springer-Verlag, New York, 1992.

European Silicon Structures, ES2 Publications Unit, Mount Lane, Bracknell, UK, *Solo 1400 Reference Manual*, 1990.

Gateway Design Automation Corporation. *Verilog-XL: Product Description*, 1989.

Jens C. Godskesen, Kim G. Larsen, and Zeeberg Michael. *TAV (Tools for Automatic Verification) Users Manual*. Department of Mathematics and Computer Science, Institute for Electronic Systems, Aalborg, Denmark, 1989.

Ganesh Gopalakrishnan and Prabhat Jain. Some recent asynchronous system design methodologies. Technical Report UU-CS-TR-90-016, Department of Computer Science, University of Utah, 1990.

G.C. Gopalnakrishnan. Specification and verification of pipelined hardward in HOP. In John A. Darringer and Franz J. Rammig (eds), *IFIP Ninth International Symposium on Computer Hardware Description Languages and their Applications*, Washington DC, 117–131. Elsevier, Amsterdam, 1989.

M. Gordon. Proving a computer correct using the lcf_lsm hardware verification system. Technical Report No. 42, Computing Laboratory, Cambridge University, 1985.

M. Gordon. Why higher-order logic is a good formalism for specifying and verifying hardware. In G.J. Milne and P.A. Subrahmanyam (eds), *Formal Aspects of VLSI Design*, 153–177. Edinburgh Workshop on VLSI, North-Holland, Amsterdam, 1986.

M. Gordon. A proof generating system for higher-order logic. In G. Birtwistle and P. Subrahmanyam (eds), *VLSI Specification, Verification and Synthesis*, 73–128. Kluwer Academic Publishers, Boston, 1988.

M. Gordon and T.F. Melham. *Introduction to HOL*. Cambridge University Press, 1993.

M. Gordon, R. Milner, and C. Wadsworth. *Edinburgh LCF*, vol. 78, *Lecture Notes in Computer Science*. Springer-Verlag, New York, 1979.

J. Halpern. A hardware semantics based on temporal intervals. Technical Report STAN-CS-83-963, Dept. of Computer Science, Stanford University, Stanford, CA, 1983.

F.K. Hanna and N. Daeche. Computer hardware description languages and their applications. In C.J. Koomen and T. Moto-oka (eds), *IFIP Seventh International Conference, Tokyo*, 418–433. North-Holland, 1985.

W. Hatcher. *The Logical Foundations of Mathematics*. Pergamon Press, Oxford, 1982.

John P. Hayes. A unified switching theory with applications to VLSI design. *Proceedings of the IEEE*, **70**: 1140–1151, 1982.

J.P. Hayes. Digital simulation with multiple logic values. In *IEEE Trans. Computer Aided Design, CAD-5*, 274–283, 1986.

M. Hennessy. *Algebraic Theory of Processes*. MIT Press, Boston, MA, 1988.

R.B. Hitchcock. Timing verification and the timing analysis problem. In *19th Design Automation Conference*, IEEE Computer Society Press, 1982.

C.A.R. Hoare. *Communicating Sequential Processes*. International Series in Computer Science. Prentice-Hall, Englewood Cliffs, NJ, 1985.

John E. Hopcroft and Jeffrey D. Ullman. *Introduction to Automata Theory, Languages and Computation*. Addison-Wesley, Reading, MA, 1979.

John E. Hopcroft and Jeffrey D. Ullman. *Formal Languages and their Relation to Automata*. Addison-Wesley, Reading, MA, 1969.

W.M. Hunt. The mechanical verification of a microprocessor design. In D. Borrione (ed.), *IFIP WG 10.2 International Working Confernece on From HDL Descriptions to Guaranteed Correct Circuit Designs, Grenoble*, 89–125. Elsevier, Amsterdam, 1986.

D. Hutchison. *Fundamentals of Computer Logic*. Ellis Horwood, Chichester, 1981.

IEEE. *Standard VHDL Reference Manual*. IEEE Computer Society Press, 1988.

P.C. Kanellakis and S.A. Smolka. CCS expressions, finite state processes, and three problems of equivalence. *Information and Computation,* **86**(1): 43–68, 1990.

B.W. Kernighan and D.M. Ritchie. *The C Programming Language*. Prentice-Hall, Englewood Cliffs, NJ, 1978.

E.V. Krishnamurthy. *Introductory Theory of Computer Science*. Macmillan, 1985.

Tony Larsson. Hardware verification based on algebraic manipulation and partial evaluation. In G.J. Milne (ed.), *IFIP WG 10.2 Working Conference on The Fusion of Hardware Design and Verification, Glasgow, Scotland*, 231–252. Elsevier, Amsterdam, 1988.

Wenbo Mao. *Verification of Concurrent Finite State Systems*. PhD thesis, Department of Computer Science, University of Strathclyde, Glasgow, Scotland, 1992.

Alain J. Martin, Steven M. Burns, T.K. Lee, Drazen Borkovic, and Pieter J. Hazewindus. The design of an asynchronous microprocessor. In C.L. Seitz, (ed.), *Decennial Caltech Conference on VLSI*, 351–373. MIT Press, Boston, MA, 1989.

G.A. McCaskill. The XTC language reference manual. Technical Report HDV-14-91, Department of Computer Science, University of Strathclyde, Glasgow, Scotland, 1991.

M.C. McFarland, A.C. Parker, and R. Camposano. The high-level synthesis of digital systems. *Proceedings of the IEEE,* **78**(2): 301–318, 1990.

G.J. Milne. Circal and the representation of communication, concurrency and time. *ACM Trans. on Programming Languages and Systems,* **7**(2): 270–298, 1985.

G.J. Milne. The formal description and verification of hardware timing. *IEEE Transactions on Computers,* **40**(7): 811–826, 1991.

R. Milner. *Communications and Concurrency*. Prentice-Hall, Englewood Cliffs, NJ, 1989.

F. Moller. The semantics of Circal. Technical Report HDV-3-89, Department of Computer Science, University of Strathclyde, Glasgow, Scotland, 1989.

J.D. Morison, N.E. Peeling, and T.L. Thorp. The design rationale of ELLA, a hardware design and description language. In C.J. Koomen and T. Moto-oka (eds), *Computer Hardware Description Languages and their Applications*, 303–320. IFIP, North-Holland, Amsterdam, 1985.

B. Moszkowski. A temporal logic for reasoning about hardware. In T. Uehara and M. Barbacci (eds), *6th Int. Conf. Computer Hardware Description Languages, Pittsburgh*, 79–90. Elsevier, Amsterdam, 1983.

L.W. Nagel. A computer program to simulate semi-conductor circuits. Technical Report ERL-M250, Electrical Engineering and Computer Science Department, University of California, Berkeley, 1975.

L.C. Paulson. *Logic and Computation*. Cambridge University Press, 1987.

J.L. Peterson. *Petri Net Theory and the Modeling of Systems*. Prentice-Hall, Englewood Cliffs, NJ, 1981.

G.F. Pfister. The Yorktown simulation engine: Introduction. In *Nineteenth Design Automation Conference*, 51–54. IEEE Computer Society Press, 1982.

R. Piloty, M. Barbacci, D. Borrione, D. Dietmeyer, F. Hill and P. Skelly. *Conlan Report*, Vol. 151, *Lecture Notes in Computer Science*. Springer-Verlag, New York, 1983.

G.D. Plotkin. A structural approach to operational semantics. Technical Report DAIMI-FN-19, Computer Science Department, Aarhus University, Denmark, 1981.

C.E. Shannon. A symbolic analysis of relay and switching circuits. *Transactions of the AIEE,* **57**: 713–723, 1938.

P.A. Subrahmanyam. Synthesising VLSI circuits from behavioural specifications: A very high level silicon compiler and its theoretical basis. In F. Anceau and A.J. Aas (eds), *VLSI 83*. IFIP, North-Holland, Amsterdam, 1983.

I.E. Sutherland. Micropipelines. *CACM,* **6**: 720–738, 1989.

C. Terman. *Simulation Tools for Digital LSI Design*. PhD thesis, MIT, 1983.

D.E. Thomas and Philip Moorby. *The Verilog Hardware Description Language*. Kluwer Academic Publishers, Boston, MA, 1991.

N. Traub. *A Formal Approach to Hardware Analysis*. PhD thesis, University of Edinburgh, 1987.

Kees van Berkel, Joep Kessels, Marly Roncken, Ronald Saeijs, and Frits Schalij. The VLSI-programming language Tangram and its translation into handshake circuits. In *Proceedings of the European Conference on Design Automation*, Amsterdam, 384–389. IEEE Computer Society Press, 1991.

John P. Van Tassel. A formalisation of the VHDL simulation cycle. Technical Report 249, Computer Laboratory, University of Cambridge, 1992.

J.D. Williams. A graphical compiler for high level LSI design. In *AFIPS Conference Proceedings*, vol. 47, 289–295, 1978.

S. Wolfram. *Theory and Applications of Cellular Automata*. World Scientific, Singapore, 1986.

INDEX